RESOURCES, DEPRIVATION, AND POVERTY

RESOURCES, DEPRIVATION, AND POVERTY

BRIAN NOLAN
and
CHRISTOPHER T. WHELAN

CLARENDON PRESS · OXFORD

1996

Oxford University Press, Walton Street, Oxford OX2 6DP

Oxford New York
Athens Auckland Bangkok Bombay
Calcutta Cape Town Dar es Salaam Delhi
Florence Hong Kong Istanbul Karachi
Kuala Lumpur Madras Madrid Melbourne
Mexico City Nairobi Paris Singapore
Taipei Tokyo Toronto
and associated companies in
Berlin Ibadan

Oxford is a trade mark of Oxford University Press

Published in the United States
by Oxford University Press Inc., New York

British Library Cataloguing in Publication Data
Data available

Library of Congress Cataloging-in-Publication Data
Nolan, Brian, 1953–
Resources, deprivation, and poverty / Brian Nolan and Christopher
T. Whelan.
Includes bibliographical references and index.
1. Income distribution—Ireland. 2. Poverty—Ireland—Evaluation.
3. Economic assistance, Domestic—Ireland. I. Whelan,
Christopher T. II. Title.
HC260.5.Z9I5153 1996 339.2'09415—dc20 95–47230

ISBN 0–19–828785–2

Typeset by Best-set Typesetter Ltd., Hong Kong
Printed in Great Britain
on acid-free paper by
Bookcraft (Bath) Ltd., Midsomer Norton, Bath.

To the next generation
Eimear, Claire, and Daniel
Karl and Alan

ACKNOWLEDGEMENTS

We would like to express our gratitude to the many without whom we would have been unable to write this book. Our most important debt is to colleagues at the Economic and Social Research Institute, with whom we have worked on a programme of research on poverty, inequality, and related topics for what is now approaching a decade. Close collaboration with Tim Callan throughout that period has been invaluable as well as enjoyable, and we draw extensively on work co-authored with him. Brendan Whelan and Damian Hannan were prime movers of the 1987 household survey on which we rely: the body of research that the survey has spawned is a tribute to their vision and efforts. Brendan and the staff of the Survey Unit organized and carried out the survey in exemplary fashion. The research programme has received unfailing support and encouragement from the Director of the Institute, Kieran Kennedy. Patient and good-humoured back-up have been provided by Maura Rohan, Pat Hopkins, Mary Cleary, and other members of the administrative staff.

The European Commission, Eurostat, the Department of Social Welfare, and the Combat Poverty Agency provided financial support for the survey and/or important elements of the research.

Some of the material in Chapters 2, 4, 5, and 7 has appeared in the *Journal of Economic Surveys* ('Concepts of Poverty and the Poverty Line', by T. Callan and B. Nolan, 1991), the *Journal of Social Policy* ('Resources, Deprivation and the Measurement of Poverty', by T. Callan, B. Nolan, and C. T. Whelan, 1993) and the *European Sociological Review* ('Marginalization, Deprivation and Fatalism in the Republic of Ireland: Class and Underclass Perspectives', by C. T. Whelan, 1996). We have benefited from the comments of referees and others on those papers, as well as from comments from participants at conferences and seminars where material from the book has been presented—in particular, several organized by the European Consortium for Sociological Research. Tony Atkinson had an important input in providing advice as the research programme was getting under way, and his work has been an inspiration throughout.

Finally, we would like to thank Andrew Schuller and his colleagues at Oxford University Press for their work on the production of this book.

B.N. and C.T.W.

CONTENTS

LIST OF TABLES

1

Introduction

1.1 The Point of Departure

Poverty is a notoriously ill-defined term, both in common usage and in academic application. Empirical research on poverty has to deal first of all with the ambiguities and confusions associated with the term and concept: what is it that one is actually trying to measure? It then has to address the problem that the various approaches to measuring poverty that are used in practice may not adequately implement the underlying concept: they may not correctly identify those one would wish to call 'poor'. Despite the attention poverty statistics receive from policy-makers and the broader public, there is remarkably little consensus among social scientists on how best to measure the condition. In this book our aim is to identify and address key problems with the ways in which poverty has generally been conceptualized and measured in relatively rich countries. The core issue is how to define and measure poverty in such countries in a way that is valid, meaningful in the context, and valuable for policy-making.

The measurement of poverty can be seen as consisting of two distinct though interrelated exercises: the *identification* of the poor, and the subsequent *aggregation* of the statistics regarding those identified as poor to derive an overall index of poverty (Sen 1976). Much of the recent academic literature on the methodology of poverty measurement, notably by economists, has focused on the second element, with Sen's own proposal for a summary poverty measure generating a substantial sub-literature. This has been particularly valuable in drawing attention to the shortcomings of simply looking at the numbers in poverty without taking into account the depth and distribution of their poverty. However, the value of sophisticated summary measures is predicated on having a satisfactory approach to the identification of the poor in the first place, which has been relatively neglected. It is on how best to identify the poor, which we regard as the major challenge currently facing poverty research, that this book concentrates.

That does not mean that we are searching for a unique objective scientific measure of poverty on which everyone can agree. Such a search is not, in our view, likely to be fruitful and has certainly not been successful so far. No single satisfactory and convincing method of setting a poverty line that is 'objective' and appropriate for all purposes has emerged or is likely to emerge. Piachaud (1981) likened the search for an objective or scientific method of setting a poverty line that could command universal acceptance to the quest for the Holy Grail. Since the Grail was eventually found (though only by a select few), a more appropriate analogy might well be the search for the Philosopher's Stone which would turn base metal to gold. This is not a counsel of despair: research on poverty can be a great deal more productive if it does not focus on chasing a will-o'-the wisp. Instead, as Atkinson (1987) and Foster and Shorrocks (1988a) have advocated, the diversity of possible judgements should be acknowledged and taken into account in the measurement procedure. While this may permit less all-embracing conclusions, it does offer the prospect of unambiguous con-clusions in certain circumstances; equally importantly, results that do depend on the choices made in the course of measurement can be recognized as such.

Thus, we do not set out to show how the poor can be 'correctly' identified in a way with which everyone will agree. Less ambitiously, but more use-fully, our aim is to develop an approach to poverty measurement which is more consistent with the most commonly cited definition of poverty than conventional methods, which results in a more reliable identification of those who meet that definition and a greater understanding of the processes at work. Our starting-point is therefore the definition that is currently most commonly applied in economically advanced societies, which sees poverty as exclusion from the life of the society owing to a lack of resources. This definition, spelt out in Townsend's (1979) classic formulation, appears to be widely (though not universally) accepted, as evidenced by its incorporation into a variety of official formulations including that of the Council of the European Union. Most often, it is implemented empirically by attempting to identify an income line that distinguishes the poor from the non-poor—the income poverty line—and measuring how many households have in-comes below that line. Various procedures have been advanced for selecting a particular line as 'the' poverty line, all of which face problems which we will describe.

More fundamentally, reliance on income in the first place has been strin-gently criticized by Ringen (1987, 1988), on the grounds that low income is not a reliable measure of exclusion arising from lack of resources—which is what researchers or statisticians generally say they are trying to measure. He asserts that there is a clear inconsistency between the way poverty is being conceptualized and the way it is conventionally measured; the result-ing poverty estimates are invalid and misleading not only because of this inconsistency, but because low income and low consumption do not overlap to anything like the extent implicitly assumed.

This critique, though clearly touching a nerve among social scientists involved in mainstream poverty research, has not in our view been taken seriously enough, nor has it drawn the substantive response we believe it merits in terms of a programme of research. It raises fundamental questions about the relationship between income and deprivation which need to be addressed. Among the reasons for its limited impact may be the confusion Ringen himself generates in the way he seeks to support his argument empirically, and the sweeping and rather quarrelsome tone he adopted. What is perhaps more surprising is that greater interest in exploring the relationship between income and deprivation has not been sparked off by the results of the limited number of poverty studies which have included both income and direct measures of deprivation—notably, Townsend's (1979) pioneering British work, followed up by Mack and Lansley (1985) and Townsend and Gordon (1989), and that of Mayer and Jencks (1988) in the USA. While taking quite different stances on the way poverty should be measured, these all show an income–deprivation relationship that is rather looser than commonly supposed. So far, little attempt has been made to follow through on the implications of these results. Against this background, it is vital that the relationship between income and deprivation is examined and understood if poverty is to be measured with confidence.

1.2 The Present Study

In a response to Ringen's critique, Donnison (1988) proposes a research agenda that would set out to measure poverty on the basis of deprivation of things regarded in the society as necessities, taking income and other resources into account; this would entail drawing on but developing available research on deprivation indicators by Townsend and by Mack and Lansley. What we describe in this book can be seen, to a significant extent, as an implementation of such a research agenda. However, we feel that insufficient attention has been paid in that agenda to the need to respond to the challenge posed not so much by Ringen as by the empirical evidence on the limited overlap between low income and deprivation. Unless one can explain how this comes about, what it means, one cannot be comfortable about using income, deprivation, or both in measuring poverty. Our aim is therefore first of all to develop an approach to identifying the poor which implements Ringen's suggestion that both income and deprivation be incorporated into the measure, and to examine the implications of taking that approach rather than relying entirely on income. More fundamentally, though, we set this in the broader framework of an attempt to understand how the observed income–deprivation relationship comes about.

We do so using information on income and a range of non-monetary indicators of deprivation for a large representative sample of Irish households produced by a survey especially designed for this purpose and carried out by the Economic and Social Research Institute in 1987. This allows us first of all to assess empirically whether Ringen's central critique of reliance on income in measuring exclusion is well founded. We conclude that it is:

many of those currently on low incomes do not appear to be experiencing deprivation, so identifying those below an income poverty line as excluded because of a lack of resources is not satisfactory. (Since many of those experiencing deprivation are not on low incomes, focusing on a deprivation standard alone would be equally problematic.) We then pursue the logic of Ringen's conclusion that, if poverty is characterized by both a low standard of consumption and a low level of income, it is necessary to identify the poor by using both a deprivation and an income criterion. We show how such an approach could be implemented in practice, and how the results differ from those produced by conventional income poverty lines. In doing so we delve into the thorny and little researched topic of how best to select indicators of deprivation suitable for this purpose.

Implementing this approach serves to illuminate the processes at work in producing the income–deprivation relationship we observe, and the forces that lead to specific types of individual and household facing a high probability of experiencing exclusion because of a lack of resources. In particular, it highlights the importance of resources over and above current income, and the way income and labour force dynamics over a long period affect the accumulation and erosion of resources and thereby current living standards. Focusing on those who are seen to be currently experiencing deprivation because of a lack of resources, while consistent with the Townsend-type definition of poverty, also brings out some of the implications of adopting that definition which tend to be obscured or glossed over. The contrast with a conceptualization of poverty based on rights to resources associated with citizenship, rather than with an exclusive focus on standard of living, is brought out and linked with the discussion of social rights which has recently aroused a great deal of interest at both academic and political levels.

The research we describe has a number of features that are worth emphasizing at this point. Room (1994) has noted an emerging change in perspective in poverty research in the European Union, involving *inter alia* a shift from a focus on income or expenditure to one on multidimensional disadvantage, and from a static account of states of disadvantage to a dynamic analysis of processes. The approach set out in this volume focuses precisely on incorporating multidimensional measures of disadvantage into poverty measurement, and the results in effect force one to make the shift to a dynamic analysis of processes. In addition, Room notes the apparent ghettoization of research on poverty measurement in Europe, with few links to the broader concerns of economics, sociology or politics such as mainstream analyses of the labour market, class and social mobility, or the structuring of welfare state 'regimes'. In this book (written by an economist and a sociologist), the emphasis on dynamic processes of accumulation and erosion of resources provide links with those mainstream concerns, which we attempt to sketch out in particular in exploring the relevance of the notion of an 'underclass', which has generated more heat than light in the recent research literature across all three disciplines.

Although one would not overstate the connection, our focus on non-monetary indicators of deprivation together with income can also provide some links between conventional poverty research and the extensive philosophical literature on measuring inequality, poverty, and well-being arising from Sen's 'capability' approach to assessing living standards (see Sen 1980, 1983, 1987, 1992, 1993). That literature, although bearing directly on the measurement of poverty, has not so far had much impact on empirical practice in poverty measurement in developed countries. This is certainly attributable in part to the fact that capability, and 'functionings' which play a central part in the capability approach, are at a level of generality that makes empirical implementation difficult. *Functionings* Sen defines as the various things a person manages to do or be in leading a life. The *capability* of a person then reflects the alternative combinations of functionings that a person can achieve, and from which he or she can choose one collection (see e.g. Sen 1993: 31). For the most part, the implications of the capability perspective for poverty measurement have been discussed at a conceptual level rather than empirically investigated, certainly as far as developed countries are concerned. Sen sees Townsend's being able 'to participate in the life of the community' as a specific capability (see Sen 1992: 115); non-monetary indicators of deprivation such as those to be employed in this study can be seen as direct, if crude, measures of success or failure in achieving particular concrete aspects of the broader functionings it entails. Also taking income into account provides some, again limited, basis for distinguishing those whose failure to achieve is attributable to lack of resources, and therefore goes some way towards incorporating opportunity sets rather than simply achieved states. We discuss how our results, viewed in this light, help to bring to the fore the problems that would arise in actually implementing the capabilities approach, as well as some conceptual implications.

While based on Irish data, this is a book about measuring and understanding poverty in developed countries, not a book about poverty in Ireland. The results we present are intended to illustrate the implications of adopting different approaches to measuring poverty, and they highlight causal processes of general relevance, rather than inform about the position in Ireland. For that reason we do not provide a detailed description of the Irish institutional background, recent macroeconomic and demographic trends, and so on. Most readers will have some familiarity with the UK literature on poverty measurement, which has been influential internationally: for most purposes here it will be necessary to know little more than that the Irish labour market and tax and social security systems are very similar in structure to those of the UK, but the level of unemployment is considerably higher, agriculture is more important as a source of household income, and income per capita is about 70 per cent of the UK level. However, throughout the volume we will mention features peculiar to or particularly pronounced in Ireland which appear necessary to understanding specific aspects of the findings. Those interested in knowing what has been learnt about poverty in Ireland *per se* from the programme of research we have been engaged on with ESRI colleagues based on the 1987 survey may wish to read the edited volume, which brings together the main results (Nolan and Callan 1994) and also contains a full bibliography of the publications it has produced. Our concern in the present volume is rather to take advantage of the unusual potential of the data available to us, described in the following chapters, which provide the basis for an in-depth exploration of resources, deprivation, and the measurement of poverty.

1.3   Structure of the Volume

Having outlined in broad terms in this introductory chapter what the book sets out to achieve, we go on in Chapter 2 to spell out in more detail the point from which it departs in terms of current practice in measuring poverty. The conceptualization of poverty, the yardsticks used to assess poverty status, and the different ways in which poverty standards are derived are discussed in some detail, and approaches officially adopted in measuring poverty in the USA, the UK, and the European Union are also described. The failure to link what has been learnt from non-monetary indicators of poverty with mainstream poverty measurement based on income or expenditure data is identified as a major gap, with implications not only for how the poor are identified but also for how the processes at work are understood.

To provide a point of comparison for subsequent chapters, we set out in Chapter 3 the results of applying income poverty lines to the dataset on which this study is based. These poverty lines are constructed using the purely relative approach, which has a number of advantages for present purposes. A set of relative lines is used, representing 40, 50, and 60 per cent of average income, and the difference made by varying the equivalence scales which seek to take differences in household size and composition into account is also analysed. Trends over time from the early 1970s in relative income poverty are described and comparisons with other developed countries are made, to put into perspective the extent of income poverty in Ireland at the time of our survey.

Exploring the relationship between income and deprivation and assessing the reliability of low income as a 'marker' for exclusion are of central interest here, so Chapter 4 turns from income to the measurement of deprivation. The manner in which indicators of deprivation have been used in the limited number of previous poverty studies that have employed them is discussed, and a number of serious problems noted. The key issues at this stage are what criteria to apply in selecting suitable indicators, and how best to aggregate across indicators in order to provide a summary measure of deprivation. Our approach to these issues is governed by our objective, which is not to provide a comprehensive picture of deprivation in all its aspects, but rather to be able to identify households experiencing generalized deprivation enforced by lack of resources. The life-style items on which we have data, largely drawn from previous studies such as Townsend and Mack and Lansley, are described, and the way they relate (individually and in the form of a summary index) to income is set out. We then implement an approach which seeks to take into account the facts that deprivation may best be treated as multidimensional rather than unidimensional and that various dimensions may behave rather differently. This involves using factor analysis to see the extent to which the various items cluster together. Three different dimensions are identified, three sets of items which cluster together, which we term the basic, secondary, and housing dimensions. Separate indices for each are then constructed, the scores showing how many of the items in that set a household lacked and said this was because it could not afford them.

Chapter 5 then analyses in some depth the relationship between the extent of a household's deprivation on each of these dimensions, household income, broader measures of resources, and a wide range of household characteristics. It first examines the relationship between the different dimensions or clusters and household income. Since current income has serious limitations as a measure of the resources available to a household, a priority is then to broaden the measure of resources by making use of information about household savings and other assets, as well as variables likely to affect the longer-term or 'permanent' income of the household. In addition, households differ in the demands on their resources for a variety of reasons, which will affect their consumption patterns and observed life-styles. This chapter therefore explores the extent to which household scores on the summary indices for the different dimensions can be explained in terms of a wide range of variables relating to resources and needs. By demonstrating that deprivation scores are in fact strongly related to such variables, in a way that differs across the dimensions, a number of objectives are achieved. First, the indicators themselves can be taken with much greater confidence knowing that the counsel of despair—that they are primarily a product of tastes rather than resource constraints—is unfounded. Second, the value of distinguishing between the different dimensions is reinforced. Finally, the results underpin the use of a particular sub-set of indicators, together with income, in measuring poverty in Chapter 6.

Chapter 6 follows through on the argument that, if poverty is defined as exclusion owing to lack of resources, the poor must be identified by using both a consumption/deprivation and an income criterion. It first discusses how the deprivation indicators developed in previous chapters are best employed together with income information with this aim in view, arguing that the basic deprivation index is most appropriate for this purpose. It therefore focuses on households that are both below income thresholds and reporting enforced basic deprivation. The number and characteristics of these households are compared with those falling below the relative income poverty lines described in Chapter 3, showing the difference that the use of combined income-plus-deprivation criteria makes. Multivariate analysis is then employed to look at the factors distinguishing households that (1) have low incomes and are experiencing enforced basic deprivation, (2) report enforced deprivation but do not have low incomes, (3) have low incomes but do not report enforced deprivation, and (4) do not have low incomes and do not report basic deprivation. The validity of this categorization is assessed by reference to a number of other characteristics of the households, and the explanations for how households find themselves in the 'inconsistent' groups is considered. Finally, the levels of enforced deprivation of housing and secondary items being experienced by each of these groups is described, and the relationship between these items, resources, and generalised exclusion is discussed.

Data available on deprivation, labour market histories, and attitudes are then used in Chapter 7 to examine whether the much-discussed concept of an 'underclass' can be fruitfully applied in societies such as Ireland facing sustained high unemployment. The ambiguities surrounding the term are discussed, and an operationalization put forward in terms of labour market marginality, extreme deprivation, and a distinctive sub-culture as the crucial elements constituting an underclass. A marginalized working class in terms of labour market experience is identified, and the levels of deprivation and fatalism are compared with those found among those of the non-marginalized working class. This allows the value of distinguishing those who are marginalized to be demonstrated, without accepting the connotations of sub-cultural effects often carried by the term 'underclass'.

Chapter 8 then explores the implications of the analysis and results set out in previous chapters for the way poverty is conceptualized and measured, highlighting the extent to which they illuminate current debates. The key concepts of deprivation and poverty underpinning the analysis and the central message of the results are restated. These are then related to some preoccupations of the recent literature in this area: the influential capability approach put forward by Sen, debates about defining and measuring deprivation and the implications of its multidimensionality, the relationship between poverty and social exclusion, the rights approach to poverty and minimum income, and poverty and the underclass.

Chapter 9 turns to what the book's approach to poverty measurement and its findings mean for anti-poverty policy. It looks first at their relevance to assessment of the adequacy of the levels of support provided by the social security system, which is of central importance in effectively alleviating poverty. In the light of what have been shown to be the key processes that make and keep some people poor, it then teases out lessons for the role of social security versus other policies in combating poverty, and for the design of social security systems.

Finally, the concluding chapter sets out the central thrust of the argument advanced in this volume, reviews the key findings and their implications, and draws attention to some issues for the future.

2

The Meaning and Measurement
of Poverty

2.1 Introduction

This chapter outlines the ways in which poverty has generally been conceptualized and measured in relatively rich countries, in order to identify the
key problems that subsequent chapters seek to address. It begins with a
discussion of how poverty has been defined or viewed in such societies, and
an overview of the ways in which it has been measured. The different
approaches to deriving and applying a poverty standard are then examined
in more detail. This is followed by a description of current official practice
in the UK, the USA, and the European Union, to provide concrete illus-
trations of the way conventional approaches are applied. Given this point
of departure, the route to be taken by the current study is then outlined.

2.2 Concepts and Measures

What does it mean to be poor in the 'rich' countries of, for example, the
European Union or North America? Ensuring that everyone has a subsistence level of nutrition, clothing and housing—though still relevant—would
not generally be seen as sufficient to eradicate poverty. Poverty continues to
be a term widely applied in rich societies, but with enormous scope for
disagreement about what it means and how it is best applied. What does
appear to be common ground is the notion that poverty is a condition that
is unacceptable. Dasgupta (1993) notes that concepts like 'undernourish-
ment' or 'destitution' are not simply descriptive, but also contain an evaluative component. The same is true of poverty: indeed, that is precisely why
the use of the term is so hotly debated.

In everyday use, poverty in rich countries is often seen as inability to
attain a decent or adequate living standard. What is considered adequate,
what are generally perceived as needs, will change over time and differ
across societies: poverty is in that sense relative. This is not a new definition,
since poverty has always been defined in relation to the standards with
which people in a particular time and place are familiar. This was put with
admirable clarity by Adam Smith, in a much-quoted passage, when he

wrote that 'necessaries' included 'not only the commodities which are indis-
pensably necessary for the support of life, but what ever the custom of the
country renders it indecent for creditable people, even the lowest orders, to
be without'. The examples he gives are leather shoes and linen shirts:
neither essential for survival, but in late eighteenth-century England 'the
poorest creditable person would be ashamed to appear in public without
them'. What are seen as needs are thus inevitably socially determined. As
Sen (1983) emphasizes, it is in the notion of shame that the core of the
concept of poverty is to be found: the absence of resources puts people in a
situation where they cannot live with dignity in their society.

The most influential attempt to spell out a definition of poverty that has
general applicability is that of Peter Townsend:

Individuals, families and groups in the population can be said to be in poverty when
they lack the resources to obtain the type of diet, participate in the activities and
have the living conditions and amenities which are customary, or at least widely
encouraged, or approved, in the societies to which they belong. Their resources are
so seriously below those commanded by the average individual or family that they
are, in effect, excluded from ordinary living patterns, customs and activities.
(Townsend 1979: 31)

This emphasis on participation versus exclusion serves to make explicit
the relative nature of the concept and has been widely adopted in recent
discourse on poverty in developed countries. There are some dissenting
voices, who see poverty as primarily an absolute notion, but the dominant
view appears to be that expressed by Piachaud: 'Close to subsistence level
there is indeed some absolute minimum necessary for survival but apart
from this, any poverty standard must reflect prevailing social standards: it
must be a relative standard' (1987: 148). In practice, as we shall see, standards presented as aiming to measure 'absolute' poverty in developed countries have been heavily influenced by prevailing conditions and expenditure
patterns in the society in question. Their true distinguishing feature is not
the way the standard is set initially, but the way it is adjusted over time, in
line with prices. Standards constructed in this way to represent (at least in
principle) an unchanged standard of living do have value, but over any
prolonged period where real incomes are rising they will lose contact with
the reality of expectations and perceptions of needs, and therefore with
what people see as poverty.

How then are the poor to be distinguished from the non-poor? It is
necessary to be clear at the outset that this involves two distinct elements:
one is deciding on the indicator or yardstick on which to focus in measuring
poverty, and the other is deriving a poverty standard applying to that
yardstick. A brief reference to the literature on poverty measurement in
developing countries helps in developing this point. The most common
approach to measuring poverty in those countries involves specifying what

are regarded as 'minimally adequate' (or some such formulation) levels of consumption of items such as food, clothing, and shelter, and using information on prevailing prices to arrive at the minimum expenditure level that allows this basket of goods to be obtained (perhaps with some provision for waste or inefficient expenditure). Most often, household incomes are then compared with this minimum to judge whether the members of the household are in poverty. Alternatively, it is also quite common for household *expenditure* to be used for that purpose: households with expenditure rather than income below the minimum are considered poor. However, the 'basic needs' literature has focused instead on measurement of the extent to which minimal levels or standards are actually being attained by a household in terms of food, clothing, shelter, health care, and so on.[1] This multidimensional approach allows for the possibility that someone may be 'clothing-poor' but not 'food-poor', and requires direct observation of the consumption patterns and living conditions of individuals/households.

Sen (1979: 290–1) calls the last of these approaches, whereby one checks whether actual consumption baskets leave some minimum need unsatisfied, the 'direct' method of identifying the poor. He emphasizes the importance of the conceptual distinction between that approach and the 'income' method of comparing household income with the cost of the minimum consumption basket: the former identifies those whose actual consumption levels across a range of commodities fail to meet minimum accepted levels, while the latter identifies those who do not have the *ability* to attain those levels (within the behavioural constraints on expenditure patterns typical in their community). Atkinson (1985) makes the related distinction between a concern with the attainment of *minimum standard of living* and a concern with people's rights as citizens to a *minimum level of resources*, the disposal of which is a matter for them; entitlement to a minimum level of resources is seen both as a reward for citizenship and as a prerequisite for participation in society. In the same vein, Ringen makes a distinction between poverty as deprivation and poverty as lack of resources (1988: 35).

These distinctions are not as straightforward as they might appear, however, and there is a good deal of confusion in the literature surrounding them. This is illustrated by the fact that Atkinson mentions the official US poverty line, constructed by costing a basket of consumption 'needs' as described in detail below, in the context of concern with standard of living, whereas Ringen uses this same line as an example of a concern with resources rather than deprivation! The scope for confusion is partly but not entirely attributable to the point stressed by both Atkinson and Ringen, that it is common to define the poverty line in terms of living standards but then to use income in assessing whether a household falls below it (which is precisely what is done with the US official line). There has also been a good

---

[1] For an introduction to the extensive literature on basic needs, see ILO (1976), Streeten *et al.* (1981), Stewart (1985).

deal of confusion about the use of expenditure rather than income in assessing whether a household is below the line, which is sometimes justified in terms of a concern with standard of living rather than resources. In conceptual terms, comparing expenditure rather than income with the aggregate cost of meeting minimum needs actually represents something of a halfway house between a standard of living and a resources focus. It allows one to see whether total consumption suffices to reach the minimum specified standards, irrespective of how that is financed, but reaching that consumption level does not necessarily mean that expenditure has in fact been allocated in such a way as to reach the specified minima for the various elements in the basket. (An alternative justification sometimes advanced for using expenditure is that it may be more accurately measured in some instances than income; the fact that conceptual choices are also involved is not always made clear.)

Even if one is happy to derive a poverty standard by specifying minimum consumption levels across a range of commodities, therefore, clarity at the conceptual level about what one is trying to measure is needed before selecting the yardstick against which success or failure in meeting that standard is assessed. The early studies of poverty in developed economies, such as Rowntree's pioneering British ones, did follow the 'basket of goods' approach but were aware of the significance of these choices. Rowntree defined 'primary poverty' by specifying a diet required to meet minimum nutritional needs, pricing the components of this diet, and adding elements for housing and clothing and an allowance for other expenditure. However, he further included as experiencing 'secondary poverty' those who were living in 'obvious want and squalor', although not below the minimum income level produced by pricing the target basket. Thus he in effect employed both 'income' and 'direct' methods in identifying the poor.

Currently, income is the yardstick most often used in measuring poverty in developed countries, with expenditure sometimes employed as an alternative, while very few studies have sought to identify the poor directly in terms of possessions and activities. The other element in the poverty measurement exercise—deriving the poverty standard—is accomplished in a variety of ways. The basket of goods or budget standard approach underlies a number of poverty lines, the US official poverty line being the best known. An offshoot from the same stock is the use of the ratio of food expenditure to total expenditure to derive an income poverty line or to identify the poor directly. Other approaches now in common use derive a minimum standard, without the need to specify or cost a basket of necessities, from social security payment rates, perceptions of minimally adequate income, the average level of income in the society, or observed living standards at different income levels. Direct measures of deprivation have been neglected until recently in the poverty measurement literature in developed countries, but Townsend's (1979) pioneering British study used information on levels of deprivation to derive an income poverty line, while Mack and Lansley (1985) identified the poor directly using such information. In this book, building on those studies, we intend to demonstrate the importance and value of directly measuring deprivation and employing those measures as well as income in the analysis of poverty. To put this in context, it is necessary first to look in more detail at the advantages and shortcomings of current approaches to poverty measurement, beginning with the budget standard method.

2.3   Approaches to Measuring Poverty

The Budget Standard Approach

The budget standard method, as employed by Rowntree and in the construction of the US official line, is based initially on the specification and costing of a nutritionally adequate diet. Non-food expenditures can then be taken into account either by specifying and costing requirements for each commodity or group of commodities—such as clothing, housing, transport—or by simply multiplying the 'necessary' food expenditure by a factor, to reflect the relationship between food and non-food expenditure considered to be desirable. This method, on the face of it, has a number of appealing features. First, the required expenditures are apparently being calculated in an objective and scientific manner. Secondly, it allows a line to be specified which can be taken to represent a fixed basket of goods and services, which are believed to represent the bare necessities of life (as Sawhill 1988 puts it in discussing the US line). This can then be indexed to prices, and progress against this fixed poverty line over time can be monitored.

However, the extent and nature of the judgements being made need to be emphasized. Even for food, nutritional studies do not permit a precise estimate of what is 'needed'; as Atkinson (1983: 226) has stressed, there is 'rather a broad range where physical efficiency declines with falling intake of calories and proteins'. For other expenditures, and to some extent for food as well, needs as defined by experts will be based on what are in effect social rather than scientific criteria, and with a significant degree of arbitrariness. This will be true of both the selection of commodities deemed to be necessities and the minimum quantity required. In addition, most budget standards have in practice made allowances for items that are not considered necessities, and for the fact that consumers do not actually allocate their expenditure 'optimally'; again, the scope for judgement and arbitrariness is wide.

Budget standards have tended to deal with these issues by employing data on actual household expenditure patterns; in effect, the level of income needed to provide the 'required' consumption, given prevailing expenditure patterns, is used. This leads to what Townsend has identified as the weakest feature of the approach, the element of circularity. 'Needs' are, to a large extent, being determined by the actual expenditures of those at low incomes. The budget-standard poverty lines cannot therefore be seen as representing requirements that are in any sense 'absolute' or needed for subsistence: the terminology employed can give the quite misleading impression that an immutable set of 'needs' is being measured.

They can serve as the basis for a line which is then held fixed over time in real terms, as in the US example; however, there seems no reason why such a fixed standard should necessarily be based on the budget standard method. Much of the debate about absolute versus relative poverty measures hinges not on whether poverty should be assessed on the basis of a set of requirements absolutely necessary for subsistence, but rather on whether the poverty line should be held fixed in real terms over time or rise as the general standard of living in the society rises. Assessing change against a standard fixed in real terms clearly provides important information—as Lampman (1971) put it, in fighting a 'War on Poverty' one may want to monitor how well one is doing in meeting a fixed target rather than redefining the target as income changes. However, many argue that it fails to capture what is inherent in the everyday understanding of the notion of poverty, that the standards being applied will be socially determined and therefore will change over time as incomes rise and living patterns change.[2]

The Food Ratio Method

The food ratio method has the appeal of simplicity, in terms of its conceptual basis. It is based on the observation (first credited to Engel in 1895) that the proportion of income spent on necessities tends to fall as incomes rise. A threshold distinguishing the poor from the non-poor can be framed either in terms of the income level at which a specified proportion spent on necessities is just reached on average, or in terms of the target proportion itself. The former approach is employed by Statistics Canada to produce 'low-income cut-offs': the Engel Curve relationship (between the proportion spent on necessities and income, controlling for other relevant variables such as family size and location) is used to produce an income line

---

[2] Costing a specified consumption basket may still have a role to play in assessing the adequacy of social security support, while explicitly acknowledging that the 'needs' involved are socially defined and that there is a substantial element of judgement and arbitrariness involved. For example, Piachaud's (1979) analysis of the cost of a specified consumption bundle for children in Britain showed that support rates for teenagers were less generous than those for younger children relative to their needs, and Bradshaw and Morgan's (1987) costing of a basket of goods illustrated that those on social security could afford only 'an extremely restricted and dull lifestyle' (p. 14), with food consumption deficient in nutrition. We return to this topic of the assessment of the adequacy of social security support in Ch. 9: the point to be made here is that it is conceptually distinct from measurement of poverty.

at which a specified proportion of spending goes on necessities on average. The latter has been widely used in developing countries (see e.g. Rao 1981).

However, neither variant of this method provides a basis on which to select a particular proportion for the proportion of spending going on food or 'necessities'. In constructing the low-income cut-offs (LICOs)—which Statistics Canada repeatedly insists are not official poverty lines—the cut-off proportion is simply the overall average percentage of household expenditures going on necessities plus an arbitrary figure.[3] A number of other problems also arise in applying the method (see for example the review of the Canadian methodology by Wolfson and Evans 1989). The definition of 'necessities' raises many issues, since simply taking all expenditure on food, clothing, and housing includes luxury items such as caviar and fur coats, and excludes other types of expenditure which might be considered necessities. The proportion of expenditure going on necessities varies widely at any given income level—Engel's Law holds only approximately—so a significant number of those below the derived income threshold will not be spending less than the cut-off proportion on necessities, while some of those above the line will be spending more than that proportion. There is also the critical question of how the poverty lines are to be changed over time: are they to be indexed to consumer prices, or are they also to be revised as consumer expenditure patterns change, and if so how often? While they may serve a useful descriptive purpose, lines produced by the food ratio approach represent an uneasy mix of absolute and relative conceptions of poverty, and are unsatisfactory in a number of respects as poverty lines.

The 'Social Security' Poverty Line Approach

Much of the empirical work on measuring poverty in developed countries has taken as benchmark the rates of income support offered by the social security system's safety-net. At its most basic level, this may rest simply on the inference that the State must expect recipients to be able to subsist on this income level. More generally, the assumption—explicit or implicit— may be that these rates represent a consensus on the minimum level of income acceptable in the society, or an official expert view on that minimum.[4] This approach was adopted by Abel-Smith and Townsend (1965) in their pioneering work on poverty in post-war Britain, and by many academic and official studies since then.

While the levels of support may initially have borne some relation to the

[3] For example, if on average 35% of household expenditure goes on necessities, the cut-off proportion is 35% plus 20 percentage points, or 55%: the income level at which households spend 55% of their income on necessities—taking variations in family size, location, etc., into account—is then estimated and constitutes the low-income cut-off.

[4] In Britain, where this approach has been most prevalent, its origins may lie in the fact that the rates of social security support recommended in the Beveridge Report (1942) were influenced by the budget standard results produced by Rowntree—as we discuss in Ch. 9.

costs of what were thought to be subsistence standards of diet, clothing, and housing, both these levels and their adjustment over time are the product of a complex political process, influenced by many other factors. The subsistence concept involved is clearly relative, influenced by changing standards of living in society generally. Levels of support provided by the State may rise in line with, or more or less rapidly than, average income in the society, depending on a wide range of influences including the state of the economy, the demands on the social security system, and a variety of socio-political factors. It is, therefore, difficult to accept the status that either the consensus or the expert interpretation would accord these levels of support as 'poverty lines'.

Further, their use as a poverty line gives rise to obvious anomalies. One major conceptual problem is highlighted by the fact that, while raising the minimum level of social security payments tends to raise the incomes of the poorest groups in society, it will tend to lead to a rise in measured poverty on this definition. In a *reductio ad absurdum*, the numbers in poverty could be almost eliminated by reducing the minimum level of official income support towards zero. This conceptual flaw gives rise to problems not only in the measurement of poverty at a point in time, but also in measuring changes in poverty over time and comparisons across countries. Changes in the extent of poverty over time can be masked or exaggerated by changes in the generosity of the social security system (relative to average incomes), as can differences between countries. Thus, the basic measure is not one of poverty, but a combined measure of poverty and the generosity of the social security system's safety net. Sen (1983: 158) points to a further conceptual flaw in the 'policy definition' of poverty: 'the fact that elimination of some specific deprivation—even of starvation—might be seen, given particular circumstances, as infeasible, does not change the fact of that deprivation. Inescapable poverty is still poverty'.

Apart from these major conceptual difficulties, there are problems in the implementation of poverty lines based on official standards. There may, in many cases, be no legal minimum income for all guaranteed by the social security system, but rather a range of schemes catering for different contingencies. In either case, the minimum income provided by the scheme(s) may not be unambiguously defined. For example, various additions may be made to basic rates to cater for one-off items or special needs, which has been one reason for the widespread use of 120 per cent or 140 per cent of the basic rates as poverty lines, for example, in Britain. This in turn leads to the highly unsatisfactory result that many of those actually in receipt of all the safety-net transfers to which they are entitled are found to be below the 'official' poverty line.

The application of a 'social safety-net' line—leaving aside the practical problems of defining it—does have a clear and indeed essential function. It allows those who are falling below the social security safety net to be identified and the reasons why explored, so that the performance of the social security system in meeting its own minimum income objective can be assessed. As the basis for the measurement of poverty, however, it has many shortcomings.

Consensual Income Poverty Lines

Viewing the poverty line as deriving from prevailing social standards, one apparently straightforward approach is to try to measure views in the population about minimum income needs, and base an income poverty line on these views. Such consensual income poverty lines have been developed mainly in the Netherlands and the USA. Theoretical underpinnings have been provided primarily by researchers at Leyden and Tilburg. These have explored the way in which poverty lines may be based on respondents' evaluations of different income levels, and the relationship between these subjective evaluations and welfare.

A number of variants of the basic approach have been applied, with varying degrees of sophistication (see Bradbury 1989). Respondents may be asked:

1. how they would rate particular income levels for a list of hypothetical families of different composition (Dubnoff 1985), or what income hypothetical families would require to reach different levels of living (Rainwater 1974);
2. how they feel about their own current income level (Dubnoff *et al.* 1981);
3. what income they consider to be the minimum they themselves need to make ends meet (Goedhart *et al.* 1977);
4. what income levels they would consider, in their own circumstances, to be 'very bad', 'bad', on a scale up to 'very good' (van Praag *et al.* 1982).

There is a clear distinction between those approaches that obtain views about hypothetical families, and those that focus on respondents' views about their own situations or what a particular income would mean to them. The former has the advantage that each respondent's views about the needs of a range of household types can be obtained, and is also simple. However, people may have quite limited knowledge of the needs of those in families differing in size and composition from their own. Asking about their own situation or how they evaluate income for themselves gets over this problem, and also allows the full range of household types to be covered.

The most developed forms of this approach are the Leyden method, employed by van Praag and colleagues (see van Praag *et al.* 1982; Hagenaars 1986), and the related subjective poverty line method used by Kapteyn (see Kapteyn *et al.* 1985). The latter is based on responses to question 3 above (the 'minimum income question'), which are then related by regression to income and other relevant variables such as household size. For a particular household size, the poverty line is derived as the point where, on average, actual income is equal to the stated minimum income needed. The more complex Leyden method is based on responses to question 4 (the 'income evaluation question'), with income levels rated on a scale from 'very good' to 'very bad'. Individual 'welfare functions of income' are estimated, relating income and welfare evaluations. A critical welfare level must then be chosen (introducing an arbitrary element into the method) and the corresponding level of income derived for each individual. The overall poverty line is then estimated as before, i.e. analysing these derived incomes in the same way as the responses to the minimum income question.

A number of difficulties with the consensual approach can be raised, both at the conceptual level and in implementation. Clearly, critical assumptions are involved about the way in which responses to questions of this type can be interpreted. The relationship between 'making ends meet' and what the respondents, or most people in society, would regard as poverty is quite uncertain. It is also far from clear that different people will regard 'making ends meet' in the same light. Despite the claims sometimes put forward, the poverty lines produced do not represent a democratic consensus as to the minimum necessary level of income. The use of a fixed point from a regression of the perceived poverty line on actual income in both the subjective poverty line and Leyden methods implies a rather complex weighting structure: it is claimed that those with incomes well above or well below the poverty line are given less weight, apparently because they misperceive the poverty line. Further, as Piachaud (1987) emphasizes, there may not in fact be a social consensus on minimum needs. Finally, some important problems in the actual operationalization of the method have been pointed out by Walker (1987) and others, for example, it may matter who in the household is interviewed, and the concept of income they have in mind may not always be the same as the researcher's. More generally, Walker expresses the concern that relying on large-scale survey methods may not have done the approach justice, and that it may be difficult to tease out the intricacies of people's views in such a sensitive and complex area.

Purely Relative Poverty Lines

The view that poverty has to be seen in terms of the standard of living of the society in question has led some to frame poverty lines explicitly, and purely, in terms of relative income. Customarily, this involves setting the poverty line at a particular percentage of mean or median income, for example 50 per cent. The general rationale is that those falling more than a certain 'distance' below the average or normal income level in the society are unlikely to be able to participate fully in the life of the community. This method is not the same, it should be emphasized, as simply taking the bottom X per cent of the income distribution as 'the poor': the number in poverty can then neither rise nor fall, which it clearly can with the poverty line set at, say, 60 per cent of the median.

The relative poverty line approach has been adopted in a number of studies by the OECD (1976) and the EC Commission or Eurostat (see e.g. Commission of the European Communities 1981; O'Higgins and Jenkins 1990; ISSAS 1990; Hagenaars *et al.* 1994). Other cross-country analyses using this approach include Smeeding *et al.* (1988) and Buhman *et al.* (1988). Single-country studies applying relative income lines include Ringen (1987) for Sweden. This approach also provides the basis for the official British statistics on Households Below Average Income (HBAI), introduced in 1988, replacing a series that had used means-tested income support rates as the benchmark. (Both the Eurostat and British series are described in detail in the next section.)

Some of the problems with adopting a purely relative approach in this way have been highlighted by Sen (1983). Any improvement in living standards of low-income groups which are shared by the rest of the population are discounted. Likewise, a general decline in prosperity, even if it leads to a lot of additional people in misery, will not show up as an increase in poverty if the relative picture has not changed. There is a considerable diversity of views, among those who view poverty primarily in relative terms, about the precise nature of the relativity concerned and therefore the extent to which a purely relative income approach is satisfactory (see e.g. Sen 1983 and Ringen 1988 for an exploration of the issues). Most would presumably be much less happy with its application over a period of recession than growth. Even in a steadily growing economy, do socially perceived needs necessarily rise *pari passu* with average incomes? If they rise more slowly, then steady income growth from which everyone gained would be guaranteed to eliminate poverty at some future date even if relative positions remained unchanged, with that date depending on the arbitrary choice of base year. Clearly, considerable care needs to be exercised in applying the methodology to specific situations, and it may be more suitable for some than for others. It does have the considerable appeal of simplicity and transparency: it yields results that can be readily understood and can serve at least as a starting-point for the analysis of poverty, the relative position of low-income groups, and the composition of these groups. This may be a particularly useful point of departure for comparisons across countries or over time, for example.

Even if a purely relative conception of poverty were accepted, though, the method would not produce a unique poverty line because, quite simply, the choice of cut-off is arbitrary. Most applications have used 50 per cent of mean or median income, but there is no firm basis for the selection of any particular ratio to serve as 'the' poverty line. The application of a range of relative lines, allowing the sensitivity of the results to the precise location of the line to be assessed, has clear advantages. This is clearly in the spirit of the approach advocated by Atkinson (1985, 1987) and Foster and Shorrocks (1988a), who argue that the diversity of possible judgements about the specification of the poverty line should be explicitly taken into account in the measurement procedures adopted. Of course, this extends beyond the use of a range of purely relative lines to include lines produced by other approaches: none the less, the application of a set of relative lines appears a useful first step in making comparisons across countries or over time (see e.g. Buhman et al. 1988; Nolan and Callan 1989, 1990).

Style of Living and Deprivation

The impetus for focusing directly on patterns of living and deprivation in measuring poverty has come primarily from Townsend's research for Britain (1979). He aimed at analysing styles of living and at developing indicators of objective deprivation, where households lack an amenity or do not participate in an activity which a majority of the population have or participate in. In Townsend's own work, these deprivation indicators are employed in an attempt to validate an income poverty line, though many have been unconvinced by that exercise. Mack and Lansley (1985), by contrast, measure deprivation indicators as socially prescribed necessities and use them directly in identifying the poor. Subsequent work in this area includes Townsend and Gordon (1989) for Britain, Mayer and Jencks (1988) for the USA, and Muffels and Vrien (1991) for the Netherlands. Since the use of deprivation indicators is central to the present study, an in-depth discussion of this literature is necessary, and this is provided in Chapter 4 where it serves as a prelude to our own development and application of these indicators. The many problems that have to be faced in such an exercise will be outlined at that stage, including how to select and aggregate items whose enforced absence can be taken to represent deprivation, and how to take account of the role of tastes versus resource constraints in determining whether absence is in fact 'enforced'. We will argue that despite these problems the key questions posed by the results of these studies (though not always emphasized by their authors) have been largely ignored but must be addressed: that is, why is the relationship between income and deprivation not nearly as pronounced as often assumed, and what does this imply for reliance on income in measuring poverty?

Before reaching that stage, however, some more background on conventional methods of poverty measurement relying on income or expenditure is required. In the next section of this chapter we describe in more detail current institutional practice in measuring poverty via income or expenditure in three settings already mentioned briefly, namely in the USA, the UK, and the European Union. In Chapter 3 we then apply income poverty lines to our own dataset. At that stage we will also discuss a number of general issues that arise when measuring living standards through household income which we have not touched on so far, i.e. the choice of period over which income is measured, the way differences in household size and composition are taken into account, and the choice of income recipient unit.

2.4   Poverty Measurement in Practice

In order to illustrate conventional methods of setting poverty standards and measuring the extent of poverty in developed countries, so that the present study can be seen in context, we now describe the way in which this is approached in an official setting in the USA, the UK, and the European Union (EU). Of these three, only the USA has an official poverty line, but officially produced statistics in the UK are intended to inform about trends in poverty and living standards, and the Commission of the European Union has sponsored or carried out research on which it has drawn to make statements about the extent of poverty in member states. It is therefore particularly relevant to see the differences and similarities in the approaches adopted in these three rather different cultural and socio-economic settings. The issues that have dominated debate about these poverty measures, which in many instances will recur when we come to our own research, are also discussed (without of course seeking to review the entire *corpus* of research on poverty in the USA, UK, or EU).

The United States

As already mentioned, the United States is unusual among developed countries in having an official poverty line, and this line is based on the budget standard approach. In the mid-1960s, as the War on Poverty commenced, this methodology was used by Mollie Orshansky to construct poverty lines for households of given size and composition for the Social Security Administration (see Orshansky 1965). This was done by taking the Department of Agriculture's so-called economy food plan, setting out the cost of a nutritionally adequate diet, and multiplying this cost by a factor of three for families of three or more persons.[5] This multiplier was derived from a 1955 survey showing that, on average, such families spent 35 per cent of their disposable income on food. In 1969 a slightly modified version of the Orshansky scale was adopted as the standard poverty measure for the government statistical establishment. The poverty standards for different household types are up-rated from year to year by indexation to the Consumer Price Index. (Figures for earlier years were also produced by backward indexation to the CPI.) The 'headline' official series on the extent

---

[5] A higher multiplier was used for one- or two-person households.

of poverty is based on annual household incomes reported in the Current Population Survey (CPS), where persons in families with total money income before tax below the threshold are counted as poor. The main official series produced in this way shows the percentage of persons in poverty in the USA at 22 per cent in 1960, falling to 17 per cent in 1965 and 12 per cent in 1969, remaining at 11–13 per cent during the 1970s, rising in the early 1980s and subsequently fluctuating between about 13 and 15 per cent. Among the major trends since the 1960s in composition of those below the line are the increase in the percentage of children living in poor families, the declining risk of poverty for the elderly, and the increasing importance among the poor of female-headed families (frequently referred to as the 'feminization of poverty').

We have already made the point that poverty lines based on the budget standard approach cannot be said to be absolute, in the sense of relating to a minimum needed for subsistence or an immutable set of needs, and the degree of judgement and indeed arbitrariness involved in their construction has also been emphasized. This was pointed out by US critics at an early stage: Rein (1969), for example, argued that any subsistence-level definition was 'arbitrary, circular, and relative'. Indeed, Orshansky herself subsequently wrote that 'The link to nutritional economy and food–income consumption patterns endowed an arbitrary judgement with a quasi-scientific rationale it otherwise did not have' (1988: 23). The key characteristic is rather that the line is held fixed over time in real terms. This can lead to conclusions about trends in poverty over time which differ substantially from those shown by a purely relative line. For example, when the official poverty standard was introduced in 1965 it came to 46 per cent of the median (for a family of four), but by 1986 it had fallen to 32 per cent; while the number below the official line fell over the period, that below a line maintained at 46 per cent of the median would have risen (see Danziger et al. 1986).

The fact that the poverty standards were originally based on budget standards and observed consumption behaviour, but are adjusted over time only in line with prices, also gives rise to internal inconsistency within the logic of the method. Not only does the general level of prices (and relative incomes) change over time, so do price relativities, consumption patterns, and the goods and services available for consumption. An approach that relies on indexing alone will fail to take into account these changes, which may affect the income needed to provide for the basic necessities originally built into the standards. Thus, expenditure patterns observed in the mid-1950s—for example the share spent on food versus other items—have little relevance currently, when the share going on food is a good deal smaller. It would be possible to rebase the poverty standards every ten years or so to take such changes in spending patterns into account, but over any significant period the whole notion of an unchanging set of necessities itself becomes untenable. Ruggles (1990) therefore proposes instead that a comprehensive budget standard exercise, involving the selection by experts of a minimum basket of goods across the full range, be undertaken regularly about every ten years: 'if an absolute standard is to maintain any meaning over several decades it must be updated periodically' (p. 48). This of course illustrates how misleading the label 'absolute' is, but it also highlights the problems with the apparently straightforward and appealing procedure of indexation of the poverty line to prices over time.

A number of other issues of general relevance have been highlighted by studies of the sensitivity of the US official poverty estimates to variations in the measurement procedure. The relativities between the standards for families of different sizes have been questioned: being based on food requirements/expenditures, they incorporate smaller economies of scale than may be present for other items, such as housing, and show a somewhat irregular pattern as size increases (Sawhill 1988; Ruggles 1990). The way resources available to the family are measured has been widely criticized, in relating to before- rather than after-tax income, in failing to take assets into account, and in ignoring non-cash benefits such as health care. Income before tax has traditionally been used, because tax paid has not been asked in most household surveys, and has been justified on the assumption that the poor would not come into the tax net. This has not been valid for many years, and biases the official poverty rate downwards, but probably by only about 1 percentage point.[6] Some of those below the poverty line have assets, particularly the elderly, and a number of studies have looked at the impact of incorporating wealth as well as income into the measure of economic well-being. However, most of the non-elderly below the line have relatively little in financial assets which can be drawn on to smooth consumption; taking assets into account serves primarily to further reduce the currently already relatively low poverty rate for the elderly (see Moon 1977; Ruggles 1990).

The most lively debate on measurement has been about including non-cash benefits, particularly food stamps and health care, in the measure of resources. Smeeding's (1982) study for the Census Bureau looked at various procedures which differed in the valuation approach adopted and in breadth of coverage, and a number of these were incorporated in the official statistics, which as well as cash income now present variants of the poverty count including non-cash benefits. The most inclusive estimate adds the value of food, housing, and health care provided to money income, at either market cost or at what they are estimated to be worth to the recipients. The numbers below the poverty line are lower when non-cash benefits are included in this way, particularly again for the elderly for whom health care

---

[6] See Sawhill (1988: 1079), Ruggles (1990: 137). Gross income reporting itself in the CPS may also be less complete than in more intensive surveys, with a lower poverty rate found in e.g. the Survey of Income and Program Participation.

is most important, but the results vary substantially with the valuation procedure, while the trend in poverty is less affected.[7] Serious reservations have been expressed about including free health care in particular in this way, because it is not convertible into other types of consumption and because its value to the recipient is greatest for those who need most care—so the measure of resources would be highest for the sick. An alternative that has been suggested is that two separate poverty standards be used, one for cash and cashlike benefits such as food stamps, the other for those needs, principally medical care, that are often met out of non-fungible resources. Cash in excess of the cash standard could be converted to health care but not vice versa, and a person would have to meet both standards to be counted as non-poor.

US poverty research has also paid particular attention to the question of the appropriate accounting period in measuring resources. The CPS-based poverty estimates use annual income, but the availability of panel survey data tracking the incomes of individuals over time has opened up the whole issue of time and income dynamics. The Michigan Panel Study on Income Dynamics (PSID), running since 1968, also employs an annual accounting period for income but has allowed researchers to trace the way it changes from one year to another. On this basis, people who remain persistently poor over a number of years can be distinguished from those who are in poverty for only a year or two, though it is important to take into account the problem of sample censoring—that one does not know how long those *currently* in poverty will remain in that situation.[8] The use of an annual accounting period may not always be appropriate, however—someone may have an annual income above the poverty line and yet spend a substantial part of the year below it, because labour force or family circumstances changed during the year, and hardship may result. (Eligibility for public income support is thus based mostly on income over a much shorter period—in the USA, generally monthly income.) The Survey of Income and Programme Participation (SIPP), introduced in the early 1980s, measures income for a sample on a monthly basis repeatedly over a period, and has shown that substantial variation does take place from one month to another. Ruggles and Williams (1989) show, for example, that about half those in the sample with 1984 annual incomes below the official poverty line were below that line in every month of the year, but the number who were below the line in at least one month was more than twice the annual poverty

[7] For example, the poverty rate in 1987 was 13.5% using cash income only, 11% when food, housing, and medical benefits were included at estimated value to the recipient, and 8.5% when these were included at market value (Ruggles 1990: 142, table 7.2).

[8] Bane and Ellwood's (1986) estimates, which do take this into account, suggested that over half the non-elderly poverty population were in the midst of a spell lasting more than 8 years. Duncan *et al.* (1984) and Hill (1981), by contrast, simply looked at actual poverty status over a 10-year period and found about 20–25% of the annual poverty population in poverty for 8 out of 10 years. (Bane and Elwood also used a more generous poverty standard.)

rate. Studies using the SIPP have also shown that most of those entering poverty have quite short spells, though most of those observed as poor at any point in time will be on much longer spells (because those on longer spells have a higher probability of being sampled when unemployed), and overall poverty persistence also has to take into account repeat spells.

Related to persistence, probably the most contentious strand of poverty research in the USA has centred on the notion of a growing underclass trapped in poverty. This plays a central role in Murray (1984) and Hernstein and Murray (1994), for example, which have provoked an acrimonious debate extending well beyond the groves of academe. As Sawhill (1988) points out, research on this topic has generally foundered on the lack of consistent definitions of the subgroup in question, with some emphasizing location (in inner-city ghettoes), others the persistence of poverty, and still others dysfunctional behaviour. Location was emphasized in Wilson's (1987) influential work, but only a small proportion of those below the official poverty line (less than 10 per cent) live in urban areas with high poverty rates (Sawhill 1988; Ricketts and Sawhill 1988). However, the poor do seem to be becoming more concentrated in such areas over time. Studies seeing location as a key variable have generally suggested a link between the characteristics of neighbourhoods (such as poor housing and employment opportunities) and behavioural deviancy, for example out-of-wedlock births and dropping out of school. Those focusing on poverty persistence *per se*, on the other hand, emphasize individual and family characteristics which are associated with detachment from the labour market. Some of those writing on the underclass emphasize persistence not only over time for an individual or family but across generations, particularly the notion that being brought up in particular kinds of poor families and/or neighbourhoods can greatly increase the chances of being trapped in poverty. The evidence suggests that those born into poverty do have a substantially increased probability of being poor in adulthood, but—like the size of the underclass at a point in time—the scale of intergenerational transmission of poverty can be easily exaggerated (Sawhill 1988; Ruggles 1990). (The tangled literature on the underclass will be discussed in more depth when we come to our own work on that topic in Chapter 7.)

The United Kingdom

The United Kingdom does not have an official poverty standard, nor does the government statistical apparatus produce estimates of the extent of poverty. However, there are officially produced statistics relating to households on low incomes which are widely used in official and academic discussion of poverty. From 1974 up to 1988, the Department of Social Security (DSS, previously the DHSS), produced an annual series entitled Low Income Families (DSS 1988a). This used administrative statistics to show the numbers in receipt of safety-net supplementary benefit (SB) or housing benefit, and information on a random sample of households in the annual Family Expenditure Survey (FES) to show the numbers not in receipt but with incomes below the SB support level, as well as those below 110 per cent, 120 per cent, and 140 per cent of that level. In discussing these figures, people with incomes below SB level were often treated as being 'in poverty', and those below 140 per cent (which would be all those included in the tables) as being 'on the margins of poverty', though this interpretation was officially discouraged (Johnson and Webb 1989). The series was open to a number of criticisms (see Nolan 1989; DSS 1988b), the most fundamental of which was that use of social security rates as the (implicit poverty) standard gave rise to the anomalies already mentioned: raising support levels could increase measured poverty, and comparisons over time conflated changes in the generosity of the safety-net with those in low incomes.

In 1988 this series was discontinued and replaced by Households Below Average Income (HBAI—see DSS 1988c), which no longer relies on official social security rates as standards or draws on administrative statistics on recipients as source. Instead, the FES is employed to show the numbers and types of households falling below a range of income thresholds, with one set of thresholds calculated as proportions of average equivalent income and another derived in that way for the base year but thereafter indexed in line with prices only.[9] One therefore gets a picture of the numbers falling below both what are in effect relative income poverty lines (ranging from 40 to 100 per cent of average income), and below a range of income poverty lines held constant in real terms from the base year, which is now 1979.[10] While there are once again repeated official disclaimers about according the figures the status of poverty lines, public discussion has tended to focus on those below half average income as 'the poor'.

The proportion of the population below the half average income relative threshold has risen from 10 per cent in 1979 to 20 per cent in 1991/2 (DSS 1994: 37 and table F1).[11] Those concerned with a fixed threshold, on the other hand, can highlight the fact that there was a (small) fall in the proportion below half average 1979 income uprated for inflation, with a larger fall in the proportion below 60 per cent of that figure. The official HBAI series extends back only to 1979, but Goodman and Webb (1994) have applied the same methodology to FES data going back to 1961. This shows that the proportion of the population below half average equivalent income fluctuated between 9 and 12 per cent from 1961 to 1971, before falling to a

[9] The series also shows the composition of those falling into different decile groups in the income distribution, the numbers involved of course remaining unchanged.

[10] The base year used was initially 1981, but this was changed from DSS (1992).

[11] The HBAI series give results on the basis of income both before and after housing costs; the figures quoted here refer to before housing costs, which would be the most common usage internationally. With income after housing costs, the proportion below half average income rose even more, to about 25% by 1991/2.

low of 6–7 per cent in 1976–7, bouncing back to 8–10 per cent up to 1985, and then rising very sharply indeed to reach 20 per cent by 1991. Major changes in the composition of the households falling below that relative income line have occurred. In 1961, 44 per cent of the individuals below half average income were in pensioner families, 36 per cent were in families with children, and 20 per cent were in non-pensioner families without children.[12] In 1979 the corresponding figures were 35, 46, and 19 per cent, and by 1991 they were 27, 48, and 25 per cent.[13] As pensioners have made up a declining proportion of those below the relative lines, unemployment has become much more important as a cause of low income (see Goodman and Webb 1994: A31, fig. 3.19 table).

The methodology used to construct the HBAI figures has been reviewed and altered since its introduction, and looking at the main areas of concern helps to illustrate the issues that arise in empirically implementing the apparently straightforward relative income line approach, or in monitoring progress *vis-à-vis* lines fixed in real terms.[14] The DSS *Technical Review* (1988*b*), which gave rise to the new series, examined issues such as the best income measure and recipient unit and how to take differences in household size and composition into account. Its recommendations were adopted in moving to HBAI, so, compared with the Low Income Statistics, this involved a shift from the family/benefit unit to the household as income recipient unit, from the use of 'normal' work income for those in the survey who had been away from work for thirteen weeks or less when interviewed to current income, and from the equivalence scales implicit in SB rates to those estimated from expenditure patterns by McClements (1977). (Equivalence scales provide a method of adjusting income for differences in household size and composition, incorporating a value for the needs of different household types relative to a benchmark type.) This generated a certain scepticism in the reaction when the changeover was made, since these changes (particularly in recipient unit) reduced the numbers showing up as on low incomes (as Johnson and Webb 1989 show), although, faced with a straight choice, the arguments advanced in the *Technical Review* are in our view quite strong (see Nolan 1989). Subsequent concern about the

[12] While the household is used as income recipient unit, the family type and economic status classifications employed in HBAI categorize individuals according to the benefit unit of which they are a member.

[13] Goodman and Webb (1994: A20–1, table for fig. 3.7). The declining importance of pensioners among those below half average income to 1979 reflects a substantial fall in the number of pensioners below the line during the 1970s. From the early 1980s, by contrast, the number of pensioners below half average income rose substantially, as social security pensions were indexed to prices rather than earnings and fell behind average incomes; however, the number of non-pensioners below that line increased even more rapidly.

[14] We will not attempt to document the convoluted process whereby external critiques of the methodology (and in one case the accuracy) of the figures were taken into account (or sometimes not) in modifications to the official statistics. A series of studies by the Institute for Fiscal Studies (Johnson and Webb 1989, 1990, 1991) and the House of Commons Social Services Committee (1990) were particularly influential.

HBAI methodology has centred on the sensitivity of the results to the income measure, the equivalence scales and recipient unit used, and the reliability and representativeness of the data on which the results are based. An official 'stocktaking' exercise was carried out in 1991 (DSS 1991) and some changes in the methodology were implemented from the edition covering 1988/9 (DSS 1992).

Because of concerns that the annual FES may produce excessive year-to-year variation in incomes at both the top and the bottom of the distribution, it was decided to combine the results for two years in HBAI. Because outliers at the top of the income distribution can have a major impact on the mean and are subject to random sampling variation, an adjustment was incorporated whereby information from income tax records (from the Inland Revenue's Survey of Personal Incomes) is used for the top of the distribution. The sensitivity of the results to different equivalence scales is now examined in an appendix, and figures in the main tables that are particularly sensitive are identified as such. An appendix also shows where individuals would be located *vis-à-vis* the relative income thresholds if the benefit unit rather than the household were used as income recipient unit.[15] Both the original technical review and the stocktaking exercise discussed the question of using expenditure rather than income as the measure of living standards and concluded that income was preferable, primarily because expenditure as measured in the FES over a two-week period may fluctuate for reasons that do not reflect an underlying change in living standards.[16] However, attention has been drawn to the anomalous position of some of those on very low incomes, who are seen to have relatively high expenditure and levels of possessions of consumer durables (see also Davies 1994 and McGregor and Borooah 1992).[17] An appendix has been introduced comparing the decile position of persons in the income distribution with their position when expenditure is used as the ranking variable.

There has also been on-going debate about the use of the mean rather than the median, and of income before versus after housing costs, in HBAI. From the outset, mean equivalent income across all households has been the yardstick from which income thresholds were derived, but initially means were also used to show how the incomes of different decile groups were evolving. For the bottom (and top) of the income distribution, it was found that the mean was much less stable than the median from one year to

[15] This does not show the results that would be produced by a wholesale switch to the benefit unit, because the thresholds themselves remain those derived using the household as recipient unit.

[16] The *Technical Review* concluded that FES expenditure data 'appears to be a more volatile measure of an individual household's long-term expenditure than FES income data is of their long-term income' (DSS 1988b: 14–15).

[17] This appendix in DSS (1994: 141) shows e.g. that in 1991/2 2% of those in the bottom income decile are in the *top* decile ranked by expenditure. Davies (1994) shows that those at the very bottom of the income distribution—not the entire bottom decile—have relatively high expenditure levels and also higher levels of possession of certain consumer durables.

another, being much more affected by outliers which could be due to sampling variation or wrongly reported. Since the second edition of HBAI, the median rather than the mean has therefore been shown for each decile group.[18] The *Stocktaking Report* also considered whether the median rather than the mean should be used as the benchmark for income thresholds. While noting the problem of the impact of outliers on the mean, the conclusion reached was that, if the mean could be measured within an acceptable margin of error, it was preferable: the median and mean provide answers to different questions, and it is changes in position relative to the average for the population that are of greatest interest in this context (DSS 1991: 13).

Since its inception, HBAI has presented figures on two distinct bases: income before and income after housing costs. Income before housing costs is simply the sum of income from all sources including housing-related state benefits. Income after housing costs is that total less rent, local authority rates, mortgage interest, and structural insurance. The former would be the conventional measure of living standards in poverty studies, but is open to the objection that housing is a 'necessity' and for many households housing costs are effectively fixed, at least in the short term. Higher expenditure on housing may occur if rents or interest rates rise, with no improvement in housing quality but leaving less for other expenditure, so money left after housing costs may therefore be a better measure of general living standards. However, to the extent that expenditure on housing is a matter of choice, higher housing expenditure may in fact reflect better housing.[19] Both the *Technical Review* and the *Stocktaking Report* concluded that both measures have value and should be included in the series. The results show that focusing on one rather than the other can make a substantial difference to the numbers below relative income thresholds and, in some cases, to trends over time.

It is obvious from these brief descriptions that there are profound differences between the USA and the UK in official poverty/low-income measurement practices and preoccupations. These relate not simply to the approach to constructing income thresholds and the balance between relative thresholds versus ones that are fixed in real terms over time. The most striking difference is the confidence with which the extent of poverty is officially measured in the USA (despite the acknowledged scope for a range of estimates) compared with the uncertainty and unwillingness to arrive at such conclusions in the UK. An in-depth account of the historical contexts in which they evolved and the socio-political forces at work would be necessary to explain these differences, but they point up a central dilemma for official poverty measurement. As Tobin (1969) put it in discussing the

---

[18] Decile means were also reported in the second edition to show the effects of the change, but the *Stocktaking Report* recommended that this be discontinued.

[19] For an assessment of the merits of each approach and a suggested alternative, see Johnson and Webb (1990).

USA, 'Adoption of a specific quantitative measure, however arbitrary and debatable, will have durable and far-reaching political consequences. Administrations will be judged by their success or failure in reducing the officially measured prevalence of poverty.' While this may have overstated the actual impact this innovation was to have in the US case, having an official poverty measure (however constructed) does give a standard against which progress can be measured by policy-makers and public alike. (The various ways in which such an official poverty standard may affect policy are considered at a general level in Atkinson 1993*b*.)

In the UK, by contrast, the plethora of official statistics now published allows the user to arrive at conclusions which may differ depending on the extent to which he or she sees poverty in primarily relative terms, which threshold is regarded as most appropriate, which adjustment for household size, which recipient unit, and so on. This is much more congenial for the researcher, who will be conscious of the issues involved in making these choices, than for the general public (while it may in some circumstances also suit politicians). The flavour of the underlying approach is conveyed by the following quotation from the HBAI:

Besides the questions of comprehensiveness, consistency and accuracy, one should bear in mind that HBAI results relate to a particular set of income definitions and methods for calculating income and deriving results. . . . It would have been possible to employ alternative definitions or methods, which in some cases might be as respectable and relevant as those actually employed. It can sometimes happen that alternative approaches give significantly different results. (DSS 1992: 9–10)

Such a degree of agnosticism in how poverty is officially defined is likely to make policy formulation (much less political mobilization) to tackle poverty more difficult than if a consensus were achieved on a crude and necessarily over-simplified official measure.[20] This is one of the many issues raised by this discussion to which we return later, but now we move on to consider the 'official' measurement of poverty in the European Union.

The European Union

Research on poverty measurement sponsored by the Commission of the European Union and by Eurostat, the statistical office of the European Communities, has covered a considerable range. Cross-country studies have been carried out employing different approaches, including subjective income poverty lines and official minima, and the use of non-monetary indicators of poverty has also been explored recently, as we shall discuss. However, the main emphasis has been on relative income or expenditure

---

[20] Atkinson (1993*a*: 25), who advocates the adoption of official poverty standards in Britain and at EU level, suggests that such a standard may have to be set at a level which the majority regard as too low, but very few people regard as too high.

lines, and it is on those lines that official statements about the level and trends in poverty in the European Union have been based. We will therefore concentrate here for the most part on the way in which this methodology has been implemented and on the issues relating to it which have received most attention. (A substantial body of research on causes and consequences of poverty, and particularly on local-area-based strategies to combat it, has also been sponsored by the Commission but will not be discussed here.)

Poverty measurement initially arose in the context of the First Community Programme to Combat Poverty, which ran from 1976 to 1980. The Council of Ministers in 1975 defined the poor as 'individuals or families whose resources are so small as to exclude them from the minimum acceptable way of life of the Member State in which they live'. While this clearly owes much to Townsend's definition,[21] there is an interesting difference in emphasis between his reference to being excluded from 'ordinary living patterns, customs and activities' and the EC's potentially more restrictive reference to exclusion from the 'minimum acceptable way of life' of the society, to which we return. Resources were central to the definition, and the notion of a common European standard, applying across all member states, was implicitly rejected. Thus, poverty was seen as clearly relative, certainly across countries and presumably also over time, since one could expect what constituted a 'minimum acceptable way of life' to change as living standards in the country rose. The Final Report on the First Programme (Commission of the European Communities 1981) sought to measure the extent of poverty in the different member states by employing an income poverty line set at 50 per cent of average disposable equivalent income in the country in question. On this basis it was estimated that in the middle 1970s approximately 10 million households (11 per cent of the total), containing 30 million persons, were in poverty in the nine member states of the then Community. However, the data and details of the way this procedure was applied differed across countries, seriously compromising comparability.[22]

The Second Poverty Programme, which ran from 1985 to 1989, took as starting-point the definition of poverty adopted in the Decision of the Council of Ministers of 19 December 1984:

The poor shall be taken to mean persons, families and groups of persons whose resources (material, cultural and social) are so limited as to exclude them from the minimum acceptable way of life in the Member State in which they live.

Compared with the 1975 definition, lack of resources is now broadened to

[21] Townsend's formulation was published and widely discussed well before his 1979 book—see e.g. Townsend (1970).

[22] This is amply demonstrated by the Irish example. No details were given in the Report as to how the figure for Ireland was produced or even the data source employed, and it has not been possible to reproduce it independently—see Nolan (1991a).

explicitly include cultural and social as well as material resources. In the course of the Second Programme, the Commission sponsored a number of research studies with an emphasis on improving the information available and ensuring, as far as possible, that comparable data and methods were used across countries in measuring poverty. (This included part-financing the Irish household survey on which this book is based, as part of a seven-country study of methods of measuring poverty described in Deleeck *et al.* 1992.) Comparative poverty estimates for member states and the Community as a whole for the early/mid-1980s were produced for the Commission as part of the Second Poverty Programme by O'Higgins and Jenkins (1990), and a separate set of studies was carried out for Eurostat.

O'Higgins and Jenkins set out to measure poverty in the same way as the report on the First Programme, i.e. using proportions of national average income as the poverty line, but taking care to harmonize across countries as far as possible the data sources, definitions, and methods of derivation of the estimates. They also looked at the numbers under 40 per cent and 60 per cent as well as half average income, and at the sensitivity of the results to the equivalence scale used. The headline result from their exercise was that by 1985 the number of people below half average national income in the twelve countries that were then members of the Community had risen to 44 million, compared with 38 million in 1975 and 40 million in 1980. (While their overall figure for the mid-1970s for the then nine member states was not very different from that in the Report on the First Programme, there were major but mostly offsetting differences for individual countries.) On this basis, the statement that the number of poor people in the Community rose from 38 million to 44 million from the mid-1970s to the mid-1980s was made in various official Community documents.

The study *Poverty in Europe*, carried out for Eurostat by the Institute of Social Studies Advisory Service in The Hague (ISSAS 1990), again employed relative poverty lines but with household expenditure rather than income as the measure of resources. The data were taken from the family budget surveys carried out by the official statistics offices in each member country—not always the surveys that O'Higgins and Jenkins had used[23]—and the results were based on tabulations provided by the statistical offices rather than direct analysis of the microdata. The arguments presented for using expenditure rather than income were that income definitions in the surveys differed across countries, and that the income data are often un-reliable owing to underreporting, a serious problem for several countries (notably Greece). The distinction between a resources versus a standard of living concept of poverty is not made, the use of expenditure being justified as a better measure of resources available and of 'permanent income',

---

[23] In the case of Ireland, for example, the ESRI 1987 Survey was the source for O'Higgins and Jenkins, whereas the Household Budget Survey carried out in that year by the Central Statistics Office was used in the Eurostat study.

rather than in terms of a concern with living standards. Poverty lines set at 40 and 50 per cent of national average equivalent expenditure were applied. The use of the median rather than the mean was discussed, with the median seen as preferable since the mean is more sensitive to 'extreme obser- vations', but the mean was retained to conform with previous practice. Results were presented only for the main equivalence scale used by O'Higgins and Jenkins, though the possible sensitivity of the results to varying the scales was noted. The results showed that 50 million people, 15 per cent of the population of the Community, were below half the average for their country in the mid-1980s, and again this was widely referred to in official publications as the number in poverty at that date.

In addition to applying relative lines derived from national averages, the ISSAS (1990) study also estimated poverty rates for each country, taking 50 per cent of average equivalent expenditure across the Community as a whole as the standard. While noting that the Council definition explicitly takes the member state as the reference society, 'on the eve of the Single Market, which is expected to show an increased mobility of goods, services, capital and labour within the Community, it may be useful to complement the "*Member State*" option with the "*Community*" option as an illustrative exercise' (p. 6). The overall number in poverty is not then very different, but unsurprisingly, the rates for the countries with relatively high average income or expenditure are lower and those for the poorer member states are much higher. The spatial distribution of the poor across the Community thus looks rather different from that produced by country-specific poverty lines.

Demonstrating what can happen when important methodological differ- ences are ignored, the Final Report on the Second Poverty Programme (Commission of the European Communities 1991) brought together the ISSAS estimates on numbers below the 50 per cent country-specific relative lines for the mid-1980s with the figures on numbers below such lines in the mid-1970s presented in the Report on the First Programme. While both used the same relative poverty line approach, the major differences be- tween the two exercises in the way it was applied—particularly the use of expenditure versus income—made this an invalid and misleading compari- son.[24] Despite this, much more attention than heretofore is now being paid at EU level to the need to harmonize as far as possible across the member states the data, definitions, and methodology employed in measuring pov- erty. The ISSAS study itself notes in this context that, although their study employs a consistent methodology across countries, the family budget sur- veys of the member states are in fact far from being harmonized: income

[24] This is illustrated by the fact that this showed a substantial fall in the percentage of households below the 50% poverty line in Ireland over the period, whereas as we will show in Ch. 3 the percentage of households below that line was stable or rose when relative income poverty lines are applied consistently to the Irish data.

definitions are not always comparable, the sampled population is not always the same, and there are differences in the coverage and measurement of expenditure.

Within the Third Poverty Programme (which ran from 1990 to 1994), Eurostat continued to organize research on improving poverty measurement. One significant advance has been that the microdata from the family budget surveys have been brought together and directly analysed. Hagenaars *et al.* (1994) made use of these microdata for the period around 1987–9 to explore empirically the difference made by using income versus expenditure, alternative equivalence scales, and different proportions of the average as threshold. They were also able to achieve greater consistency across countries than previous studies in the way income and expenditure were defined (including imputed rent, for example), and to reweight samples to improve their representativeness. Hagenaars *et al.* state clearly their theoretical preference for income as a measure of resources, and for a resource-based concept of poverty. However, because of underreporting in a number of member states and possible measurement error in the survey income data, expenditure is considered to be the most reliable measure of resources. Their central results show 49 million persons living in households below half average equivalent expenditure in the country in question.[25] Using income rather than expenditure is shown to make a surprising large difference to the poverty rate in certain countries, dramatically altering the ranking of, for example, Italy and the UK (as will be detailed in Chapter 3). Using a Community-wide rather than country-specific standard, 53 million persons are in households below half average equivalent expenditure, but 37 per cent of these live in the four poorest member states, compared with 24 per cent of all those below the corresponding country-specific threshold.

In addition to this research with the family budget microdata, in the course of the Poverty-3 Programme Eurostat continued to sponsor research on subjective poverty lines by Van Praag and colleagues, looked at the matching of survey and administrative data, and also had several studies carried out on non-monetary indicators of poverty which will be discussed in Chapter 4. New opportunities in poverty research at EU level have been opened up by the launching in 1994 of the Europanel survey, whereby a harmonized panel survey with common questionnaire and procedures is being carried out for Eurostat in each member state. This will allow not only poverty at a point in time but the dynamics of income, labour force participation, and household formation over time to be analysed using a consistent microdata set. Poverty analysis based on the panel will measure resources primarily in terms of income, since expenditure is not being measured in the survey in any depth, but a range of non-monetary indi-

---

[25] The equivalence scale used for this estimate is 1 for the first adult, 0.5 for each additional adult, and 0.3 for each child, but results using the 1, 0.7, 0.5 scale employed by the ISS study and scales derived from the subjective poverty approach are also presented.

cators is also included, again to be discussed in depth later. Although a Fourth Poverty Programme has not been agreed as yet, research on poverty using the Europanel and other sources will be promoted by a Commission research initiative under the aegis of the Fourth Framework Programme for Research and Technological Development. These framework programmes are largely to encourage research on science and technology, but the Fourth Programme for the first time includes social sciences research under the title 'Targeted Social-economic Research', and one of the three research areas to be covered is 'Social Integration and Social Exclusion in Europe'.

In concluding the discussion of EU poverty measurement, it is worth noting the shift this illustrates towards use of 'social exclusion' rather than poverty in discussion and debate at EU level, particularly in official EU usage. The Council Decision that launched the Third Poverty Programme talked in terms of 'fostering economic and social integration of the least privileged groups', and during its period of operation the term social exclusion came to dominate official usage. Thus, in 1990 the Commission set up an 'Observatory' of independent experts to report regularly on national policies 'to combat social exclusion' (see Room *et al.* 1992, 1994), and the proposed successor to the Poverty-3 Programme is to 'combat exclusion and promote solidarity' (Commission of the European Communities 1993). As Room (1994: 6) remarks, 'How far these shifts reflected any more than the hostility of some governments to the language of poverty, and the enthusiasm of others to use the language of social exclusion, is a matter for debate'. None the less, substantive claims have been made for the merits of conceptualizing the issue in terms of social exclusion rather than poverty, the former being presented as relating more to multidimensional disadvantage, to dynamic processes, and to inadequate social participation and lack of power. As will be discussed in Chapter 8, the contrast is in our view based to a significant degree on a caricature of 'poverty' as a necessarily static and narrowly income-based concept, but there are underlying differences of substance and emphasis which it will be important to tease out.

2.5   Summary Poverty Measures

As we pointed out in Chapter 1, our concern in discussing the measurement of poverty is with the identification of the poor rather than with how best to summarize the extent of poverty—given a poverty line—in an aggregate measure. For that reason we do not review the burgeoning literature on the aggregation of the statistics regarding those identified as poor into a summary poverty measure. Sen (1976) highlighted the unsatisfactory features of the traditional head-count measure, and proposed a summary measure which takes into account not only the number of people below the poverty line but also the depth of their poverty. Alternative measures have been put forward by, among others, Anand (1977), Thon (1979), Blackorby and Donaldson (1980), Clark *et al.* (1981), and Foster *et al.* (1984)—a useful review is given by Foster (1984).[26] Particular attention has been paid to the development of axioms setting out desirable features for such summary measures, and on relating them to an underlying social welfare function. The family of measures proposed by Foster *et al.* has been shown by Foster and Shorrocks (1988*a*, 1988*b*, 1991) to have some particularly attractive features, in terms both of its decomposition properties and its relationship with social welfare orderings, and will be employed in Chapter 3. However, the value of sophisticated summary measures is predicated on having a satisfactory approach to the identification of the poor, and that is what we are concentrating on here.

2.6   Conclusion

This chapter has discussed the issues that have to be faced in conceptualizing poverty and in seeking to apply that concept empirically. It has critically reviewed the main approaches that have been used in developed countries in order to identify the poor, and a discussion of official practice in three quite different settings—the USA, the UK, and the European Union—has helped to highlight many of the problems and choices involved. There has been a very significant increase since the 1970s in the degree of sophistication and subtlety with which this topic is being addressed. Moving away from reliance on official poverty lines based on social security rates or on the food ratio or nutrition-based types of minima with their quasi-absolute background, the recent literature has brought central conceptual issues to the fore and has also opened up new ways of measuring poverty.

There is however no sign of a consensus emerging about how best to set and apply a poverty standard in developed countries. In these circumstances there are obvious attractions in Atkinson's (1985) 'intermediate path', which seeks to exploit the fact that partial orderings may be possible even when unanimity cannot be achieved. That has been an important influence on recent poverty research, with much more attention now being paid to the search for results that do not depend on—for example—precisely where the poverty line is set or how adjustment is made for household size. Even with that end in view, though, fundamental choices have to be made about what yardstick is to be employed in measuring poverty. There the debate is focused mainly on the use of income versus expenditure, with a good deal of confusion between arguments based on reliability of survey data on income or expenditure and those distinguishing a resource-based from a standard-of-living-based concept of poverty.

---

[26] For a comprehensive list of references on the topic, see Sen (1992: 106, n. 11).

Potentially one of the most important developments in that context, though still quite underdeveloped, is the use of non-monetary indicators in poverty measurement. The quite limited number of previous studies using non-monetary indicators in poverty measurement, briefly mentioned in this chapter, will be discussed in detail in Chapter 4 as a prelude to our own use of such indicators, which will be the central focus of this book. It is worth making the point here that these studies have produced as many questions as answers, and what has been learnt from them has not been adequately linked back with mainstream poverty measurement based on income or expenditure data. This is in our view a major gap, which we set out to fill, with implications not only for how the poor are identified but also for how the processes at work are understood. Before we reach that stage, though, we present in Chapter 3 the results of applying relative income poverty lines to the dataset on which this study is based. This is done precisely to facilitate the forging of links throughout the remainder of the volume between this conventional approach and the approach we develop to identifying the poor which also uses non-monetary indicators.

3

Income Poverty

3.1 Introduction

In this chapter we briefly describe the survey on which our empirical analysis is based, and apply relative income poverty lines to the sample to show the extent and composition of poverty as it would be measured by this widely used approach. We have seen in Chapter 2 that poverty in the rich countries is most often measured using income poverty lines, and that deriving these lines in a purely relative way, for example as proportions of average income, has a number of advantages. Spelling out how many and which households would be identified as poor using this method thus provides the background for the development in subsequent chapters of an alternative approach, which employs both income and indicators of deprivation. What will be most interesting, from the point of view of understanding poverty and framing policy responses, is whether the types of household seen to be below relative income lines are also those identified as poor by the alternative approach.

We begin the chapter with a discussion of the way income is measured in surveys such as the one employed here and the reliability of these measures. The issues that arise in using a current versus annual accounting period and the household versus family as recipient unit are also discussed. The way in which relative income poverty lines are derived is then described, including how differences in household size and composition are taken into account. Results using current household income are presented and compared with other countries and earlier years. The types of household falling below these relative income lines are then described. Finally, we assess how much difference using the family instead of the household as recipient unit, or using annual instead of current income, makes to the results.

3.2 Measuring Income

The survey on which our work is based, the Survey of Income Distribution, Poverty and Use of State Services, was carried out by the Economic and Social Research Institute (ESRI), Dublin, in 1987. As the title suggests, it was specially designed to produce information for a nationally representative sample of the population on incomes and other characteristics relevant to the analysis of poverty and inequality. The sampling frame was the Register of Electors, from which a multi-stage random sample was drawn. A sample of 3,294 households was obtained, representing an effective response rate of 64 per cent. This is comparable with those usually achieved in other in-depth surveys dealing with as sensitive a subject as income, such as the Household Budget Surveys (HBS) carried out by the Irish Central Statistics Office or the corresponding UK Family Expenditure Survey (FES).[1] Like the HBS, the sample is reweighted for analysis to correct for possible biases introduced by differential non-response across population groups.[2] Applying the reweighting scheme means that the sample for analysis accords with external information on the distribution of households in the population by size, urban/rural location, socio-economic group, and age of household head. Extensive validation of the data shows that the reweighted sample also represents the population well in terms of variables such as the age distribution, numbers in paid work, and numbers unemployed. A detailed description of the survey procedures, response, and validation is provided in Appendix 1.

Detailed information on the income of each household member from various sources was sought in the survey, the household being defined (as is standard) as a person or group of persons who live together and who share common catering arrangements. A range of questions covered income from employment or self-employment, rent, interest and dividends, private sick pay and pensions, social welfare payments, and other regular receipts such as transfers from other households. For most income sources, current income is measured as the amount received in the previous week (or the weekly equivalent, for those paid every fortnight or month). For the types of income that are particularly likely to fluctuate over the year or be received intermittently, this would not be satisfactory as a measure of the amount usually received, and the weekly average of the amount received over a longer period is used instead. For income from rent, interest and dividends information was sought on amounts received in the twelve-month period preceding the date of interview. For self-employment income, respondents were asked for a measure of pre-tax profit in the most recent twelve-month period for which they had accounts. Farm incomes were also measured over a twelve-month period, the calendar year 1986; they were estimated from information on farm outputs, inputs, costs, and receipts gathered on a special farm questionnaire (as outlined in Callan, Nolan, et al. 1989).

---

[1] The response rate in the FES is usually about 70%.

[2] In the UK the published FES reports do not involve reweighting, but reweighted FES samples have been used in various research studies; and in producing the HBAI statistics described in Ch. 2 the grossing-up factors employed in scaling up to estimated population totals vary by age and family type. Reweighting by number of adults in the household is essential for our survey because the sample from the Electoral Register is one of individuals (adults) rather than households.

Current income measured in this way is the main income concept employed in the survey, in line with many other such surveys including the UK Family Expenditure Survey and General Household Survey. Various income aggregates can then be derived, including:

income from work and property, before taxes and state transfers, often termed market or original income;
market income plus State cash transfer payments, that is gross income; and
gross income less income tax and employees' social insurance contributions, that is disposable income.[3]

Of these three concepts, in this study we focus mostly on disposable income, which is the most relevant to the household's spending power and standard of living. As we shall emphasize, though, current disposable income is by no means the sole determinant of command over resources, and much of our effort in subsequent chapters will go into demonstrating the importance of long-term income and broader measures of resources in influencing current living standards. This is not simply a matter of extending the period over which one measures income to annual rather than (largely) weekly, as some surveys do. We are able to construct estimates of annual income for our sample, and will see later in this chapter that this makes little difference to the results of applying relative income lines. Subsequent chapters will show that income and asset accumulation over a much longer period need to be taken into account in understanding current living standards. In addition, services provided by the State free or at subsidized rates, such as health, education, and housing, can have a major impact on living standards, and again will be discussed at a later stage. For the present, however, we concentrate on current disposable income.

How reliable are the income data obtained in such household surveys? Doubts about its reliability arise from the fact that total income reported in surveys often falls short of that shown by other sources such as the National Accounts, or that surveys also measuring expenditure usually find average expenditure significantly above average income for those with low reported incomes, or simply from the suspicion that people are often particularly unwilling to reveal their incomes to interviewers. Validation studies demonstrate that generalized scepticism is not warranted, though they do point to specific problem areas. For the UK, Atkinson and Micklewright (1983) carried out a detailed comparison between income as reported in the Family Expenditure Survey and the National Accounts aggregates, taking into account differences in definitions, concepts, and timing between the two. They found that, when appropriate adjustments had been made, divergences in the figures for employee earnings and social security benefits were

---

[3] Other amounts that may be deducted directly from pay by employers, such as superannuation contributions, trade union dues, or health insurance premia, are included in disposable income, which thus may differ substantially from take-home pay.

relatively small. However, for self-employment and investment income, the survey totals were significantly below the corresponding National Accounts figures, even after adjustments. Here they emphasize the role of under-representation in the sample of households receiving these income sources, especially those at the top of the income distribution, as well as understatement by respondents, which is what tends to receive most attention when reliability is discussed. Similarly, Atkinson *et al.*'s (1988) comparison of taxable incomes in the FES with the Survey of Personal Incomes, a large random sample from the UK income tax records, concluded that the very top of the distribution was not adequately represented in the FES. Other studies focusing on bias in response rates in the FES have pointed to the same conclusion.

The income data in the 1987 ESRI survey on which this book relies have been validated as far as possible by comparison with available external information. The numbers in receipt of the various social security transfers in the sample are close to those shown by administrative statistics, and the total income from these transfers in the sample is about 93 per cent of the corresponding administrative total (Callan 1991: 31–9). The distribution of tax units by range of taxable income in the survey was quite close to that published by the Revenue Commissioners, including towards the top of the distribution. The level and distribution of wage income was particularly close to that reported for income tax purposes. Perhaps surprisingly, incomes from farming and other self-employment were not lower in the survey than in the income tax statistics—in fact, if anything they were higher (Callan 1991: 39–54). However, investment income does appear to be underestimated in the sample, with one contributory factor being that interest accruing on deposits may often be neglected by survey respondents. The number of households in the sample in the (then) three means-tested categories for free or subsidized health care, and the number with private health insurance who tend to be on relatively high incomes, were also very close to the relevant percentages in the population.[4]

Validation checks such as these provide a basis for some confidence in the overall reliability of current income as measured in the survey, but reliability at household level will remain an issue when it comes to looking at the numbers and types of household reporting low incomes. In later chapters a range of other information obtained in the survey will allow us to see the relationships between reported incomes and other features of the household, such as possession of durables, other possessions and activities, and self-assessed financial strain, and the results will bear on the assessment of reliability of the income data. It is worth stressing here, though, that the fact that household budget surveys such as the FES or the HBS invariably

---

[4] Published Irish national accounts data do not distinguish the household sector but only the broader personal sector, so a comparison between the sample and the National Accounts similar to Atkinson and Micklewright's for the UK could not be carried out.

show average expenditure significantly above average income for those at the bottom of the income distribution does not necessarily mean that these incomes are mismeasured. Both income and expenditure are difficult to measure accurately in surveys, and their reliability relative to one another may vary from country to country and survey to survey. In addition, expenditure data may not cover the whole range of consumption items and may include 'lumpy' purchases which happen to fall within the recording period. Leaving aside data reliability and coverage, though, one would not *expect* all low-income households to have corresponding low levels of expenditure, because current income is not the only source of spending power. (As made clear in Chapter 2, using income versus expenditure in measuring poverty will also be influenced by how one conceptualizes poverty in the first place.) As we develop in subsequent chapters, divergences between household income and expenditure lead one to focus not simply on income reliability but also on income dynamics, and on the ways in which asset accumulation and erosion over a long period influence current living standards.

Before turning to the construction of relative income poverty lines, an issue that faces any attempt to measure living standards through incomes (or expenditure) must be faced: that is, the choice of recipient unit. Income generally accrues to individuals, but these individuals live in households, and the living standards of individuals are most often taken to depend on total household income rather than on their own income only. This assumes that resources are shared within the household, irrespective of who receives them. The extent to which this can been taken for granted has increasingly been questioned in recent years, particularly by those writing from a feminist perspective, who emphasize *inter alia* the possible under-counting of poverty for married women outside the labour force that this could produce if they do not fully share in the incomes earned by their husbands. Quite limited information is available on the extent to which incomes actually are shared within households, much of the research on the topic being based on very small samples from which it is difficult to generalize (see J. Pahl 1983, 1989, 1991; Glendinning and Millar 1987; and Jenkins 1991).

Moving to the other extreme and concentrating on an individual's own income would be clearly unsatisfactory, most obviously in giving a distorted picture of the living standards of children, most of whom have zero incomes. The principal alternative to the household as income recipient unit in practice is the narrower family unit of an adult together with his/her spouse and dependent children if any. (This is the unit of assessment for social security benefits in most countries, is often also used for income tax purposes, and so is often called the tax/benefit unit.) A household comprising a couple with two young children, one adult offspring, and a grandparent would then contain three such families. Using this family unit, the assumption is made in effect that income is shared fully within the family but not at all between two or more families living in the same household. This is also unlikely fully to reflect reality. In applying relative income lines in this chapter, we rely mainly on the household as recipient unit, but we also look at the difference made by using the narrower family unit.

3.3   Applying Relative Income Poverty Lines

The purely relative approach to constructing an income poverty line simply calculates the line as a proportion of mean or median household income, taking differences in household size and composition into account. Compared with alternative methods of deriving an income line, which as Chapter 2 made clear face a range of conceptual and empirical problems, this has a number of advantages. First, it incorporates the relative nature of the underlying concept directly and transparently. Secondly, exactly the same method can be applied to constructing lines for different countries, or for different points in time for a single country. Thirdly, within this framework a range of lines rather than a single line can be readily derived and applied, so that one can assess the sensitivity of the results to varying the poverty line. This is not to say that the purely relative approach is unproblematic. The two main challenges it faces are that it provides no basis for selection of one threshold rather than another, and that not everyone appears happy to see poverty in such unambiguously relative terms. Even in these terms, however, it provides a framework and a benchmark from which to begin, with scope for trying to narrow the range of lines considered relevant or introducing lines fixed in real terms from some base year, as discussed below.

The first step in constructing a relative income poverty line is to adjust the income of each household to reflect its size and composition, since the standard of living associated with a given income will obviously vary depending on how many people it must support. One could simply calculate average income per head for each household, but this would not take into account that adults generally have greater needs than children, and that there may be economies of scale for those living together, most importantly in accommodation costs, cooking, and heating. The standard procedure is instead to employ an equivalence scale, which incorporates a value for the needs of different household types relative to a benchmark type. Taking a single adult living alone as benchmark and giving it the value 1, for example, such a scale might state that a married couple has the value 1.6 and each child has the value 0.4. This allows one to calculate how many adult equivalents there are in each household, and by dividing total household income by the number of adult equivalents one arrives at equivalent income. The assumption being made is that a married couple with two children 'needs'

$[1 + 0.6 + 0.4 + 0.4] = 2.4$ times the income of a single adult to be at the same living standard.

Unlike some of the other methods of constructing income poverty lines, the purely relative approach does not itself derive this adjustment for household size/composition internally, as it were: the choice of scales is left open. Again, one could regard this as an advantage rather than a disadvantage, since the scales can be varied readily and the sensitivity of the results assessed. The problem, however, is that there is no consensus as to how best to produce such scales or which are most appropriate for different countries. A common approach is to try to derive scales from the spending patterns of different households. The scales most widely used in the UK, for example, are based on McClements's (1977) analysis of FES expenditure data. Unfortunately, the derivation of equivalence scales in this way remains hotly debated, with the extensive international literature containing many different techniques, each requiring different assumptions on how to identify economic well-being from observed behaviour (see Browning 1992; Banks and Johnson 1994 for reviews). An alternative is to base scales on the rates paid by the social security system to different family types. Again, the scales implicit in income support rates are commonly used in the UK (and do not differ enormously from the McClements's scales). This faces all the problems associated with deriving poverty lines from social security rates which were noted in Chapter 2. Whatever their initial justification, there is little or no research foundation for the current relativities in social security rates, and these have often been called into question (see e.g. Piachaud 1979; Bradshaw 1993 for the UK; Ruggles 1990 for the USA). In any case, what one wants is an independent basis for assessment of relative needs of different household types, rather than simply taking the 'official' ones for granted. The other methods of deriving poverty lines that produce equivalence scales internally, such as defining and costing minimum necessary consumption requirements for different household types or deriving scales from subjective assessments of the minimum income different households 'need' to get by, face the equally serious problems described in Chapter 2.

Given this uncertainty, the approach increasingly adopted in research studies, and indeed in some official statistics such as the UK HBAI series, is to look at results across a range of equivalence scales so that those that are particularly sensitive to the choice of scales can be identified. This is the procedure we adopt here in implementing relative income lines. Results based on three different scales are presented, ranging from one that makes rather generous allowance for the needs of children to one that is much less generous. With the first adult in the household taking the value 1, these scales are:

A 0.7 for each additional adult and 0.5 for each child: this scale has been one of the main ones used in poverty studies for the European Commission, for example by O'Higgins and Jenkins (1990), ISSAS (1990), Hagenaars *et al.* (1994);

B 0.6 for each additional adult and 0.4 for each child: this is similar to a simplified version of the scale implicit in UK income support, which has been used for example by the UK CSO in analysing the distribution of taxes and benefits;

C 0.66 for each additional adult and 0.33 for each child: this is close to the scale implicit in Irish safety-net social security support at the time of our survey.[5]

The next choice to be made is whether the mean or median of (equivalent) income is to be used as the measure of 'normal' living standards or central tendency of the income distribution, from which the relative poverty line is to be calculated. Each has been used for this purpose in cross-country poverty comparisons; for example, the mean was employed by O'Higgins and Jenkins (1990), ISSAS (1990) and Hagenaars *et al.* (1994), and the median by Buhman *et al.* (1988). The mean has the advantage that it can be more readily understood and is therefore more transparent than the median to the wide non-specialist audience to whom poverty studies are of interest. The disadvantage is that it is much more sensitive than the median to very high and very low incomes, which household surveys may have particular difficulties measuring accurately. Such surveys may therefore show excessive variation in the mean from year to year or country to country, whereas one would expect the median to be much more stable. Applying any particular proportion to median rather than mean income will results in lower values for the poverty line, since the median invariably lies below the mean of the income distribution, but this has no substantive implications since the choice of proportions is entirely open to the researcher. Here we rely primarily on the mean because this maximizes comparability with other published studies. The choice is not of particular significance in this study given that our primary focus is on the position of households *vis-à-vis* a range of income lines at a point in time.

We employ three proportionate cut-offs based on mean equivalent income, namely 40, 50, and 60 per cent. These three cut-offs have been widely employed elsewhere; for example, O'Higgins and Jenkins (1990), Hagenaars *et al.* (1994), and Goodman and Webb (1994) apply them to mean income and Buhman *et al.* (1988) apply them to the median. We noted in Chapter 2 that, while the HBAI series for the UK presents results for a

[5] Equivalence scales have been estimated from household expenditure patterns for Ireland by Conniffe and Keogh (1988), but these cover children only, not the relativities between households with different numbers of adults. They also employ a specification producing scales which vary with the income level of the household, unlike those most commonly employed in research on poverty and income inequality (on which see also Conniffe 1992). The impact of employing such scales in applying relative income lines to the 1987 ESRI data is examined in Nolan and Farrell (1990), but will not be pursued here.

range of cut-offs from 40 to 100 per cent of average income, the half mean income threshold tends to receive most attention: the numbers falling below that line are often referred to as 'the poor' by, among others, the Child Poverty Action Group. In the Irish case the 50 per cent line in 1987 was considerably below what an official Commission on Social Welfare (1986) recommended as a 'basic minimum income', so the 60 per cent line has also received a good deal of attention. In any case, presenting results for these three cut-offs allows one to see how much difference the choice of line makes to the numbers and types of household that would be identified as poor by this approach.

3.4 How Many Fall Below Relative Income Lines?

Table 3.1 shows the percentage of households in the 1987 Irish sample falling below 40, 50, and 60 per cent of mean equivalent income with each of the three equivalence scales described above. The numbers involved are very different depending on the cut-off chosen, but do not vary a great deal across the three equivalence scales. About 18 per cent of households are below half average income, whereas 8 to 10 per cent are below the 40 per cent cut-off and about 30 per cent are below the 60 per cent cut-off. The table also shows the percentage of persons in the households that are below each line, which in each case is greater than the percentage of households below that line—low-income households are larger than average. About one-fifth of all persons live in households below half average income.

Confidence in the reliability of these estimates from the ESRI 1987 survey is reinforced by the fact that another large household survey for the same year gives similar results. Applying the same methodology to the sample produced by the CSO's 1987 Household Budget Survey, we find a

Table 3.1 Percentages of households and persons below relative poverty lines, Ireland, 1987

	Relative income line		
	40%	50%	60%
Scale A			
% of households	10.0	18.9	29.0
% of persons	12.8	22.9	33.5
Scale B			
% of households	8.9	18.5	30.5
% of persons	10.5	21.2	32.2
Scale C			
% of households	7.5	17.5	30.0
% of persons	8.2	19.8	31.4

slightly lower percentage of persons in households below each of the lines—about 1 to 2 per cent less than the corresponding figures in Table 3.1. This difference is largely attributable to the fact that the farm income figures in the ESRI survey refer to 1986, which was a particularly bad year, whereas farm accounts in the HBS were kept through 1987. Average household size and mean household income in the two surveys are also similar.[6]

In seeing Ireland as an illustrative case, it will help the reader to know how it compares with other countries in terms of the extent of relative income poverty. Here one can draw on the cross-country poverty studies carried out for the EC Commission or Eurostat already described in Chapter 2 to see how Ireland compared with other EC member states in the mid-1980s. As we saw, O'Higgins and Jenkins (1990) used relative income poverty lines and a variety of data sources (including the ESRI survey itself for Ireland), whereas ISSAS (1990) applied the relative line approach but used household expenditure rather than income as the measure of welfare, with data from Household Budget Surveys for each country (in the Irish case, the 1987 Household Budget Survey). In each case Ireland was seen to have a level of relative poverty higher than most member states, similar to Spain and Greece but lower than Portugal (see Nolan and Callan 1994). The more recent estimates prepared for Eurostat by Hagenaars *et al.* (1994) for the late 1980s applied both income and expenditure lines, once again to Budget Survey data, and show a slightly different picture. Their main results, using a poverty line set at 50 per cent of average equivalent income or expenditure in the country in question, are presented in Table 3.2.

This table shows that on an income basis Ireland has about the same percentage of households in poverty as Spain, France, Germany, and Italy, lower than Greece, Portugal, and the UK, which now has the highest rate. On an expenditure basis, Ireland has a poverty rate similar to Spain, France, or the UK, and lower than Greece, Portugal, or Italy. It is not clear why there is such a large difference between income- and expenditure-based poverty rates for some countries, notably the UK, Italy, Denmark, and Portugal, but for Ireland that difference is relatively minor. The main reason why the income-based poverty rate for Ireland is considerably lower than those rates in Table 3.1 or in the earlier EC studies is the equivalence scale employed.[7] Hagenaars *et al.* in their main results use what they call the modified OECD scale, which assumes that for every additional adult a household needs 0.5 of the resources for the first adult and 0.3 for each additional child (under 14). The earlier ISSAS study for Eurostat used what

---

[6] There are some differences in the top half of the income distribution, with the top decile having a larger share in total income in the ESRI sample largely owing to several very high-income households (see Callan and Nolan 1995), but these have little impact on the relative poverty lines.

[7] The use of the Household Budget Survey rather than the ESRI sample is much less important in producing this variation across studies for Ireland.

Table 3.2 Percentages of households/persons below half national average equivalent income and expenditure, EC countries, late 1980s

Country	Income poverty % of households	Expenditure poverty	
		% of households	% of persons
Belgium	6.0	6.6	7.4
Netherlands	7.4	6.2	4.8
Germany	13.6	12.0	10.9
Italy	12.8	22.0	21.1
UK	22.4	17.0	14.8
Denmark	11.9	4.2	3.9
France	14.0	14.9	14.7
Spain	12.9	17.5	16.9
Ireland	**14.9**	**16.4**	**15.7**
Greece	18.6	20.8	18.7
Portugal	20.2	26.5	24.5

Source: Hagenaars *et al.* (1994: tables 1, 2, and 6).

we have called scale A, of 0.7 for each additional adult and 0.5 for each child, which was also the main scale employed by O'Higgins and Jenkins, and the other two scales we used in Table 3.1 also incorporate more generous allowances for the needs of extra adults and children than 0.5/0.3. As far as non-EC developed countries are concerned, the study by Buhman *et al.* (1988) applied relative income poverty lines based on the median to some countries in the (wave 1) LIS dataset. Applying such lines to the ESRI sample suggests that around 1987 the proportion of persons below half median income was higher in Ireland than in Sweden, Norway, or Switzerland, but lower than in the USA.

The implications of taking differences in real incomes into account in cross-country poverty comparisons are of interest: one may not want to ignore entirely the fact that mean income in one country is much higher than another. Going to the other extreme would involve applying a common line across all countries, and Hagenaars *et al.*'s comparative study for Eurostat allows one to see just how much difference this would make for the countries in the EU. As well as country-specific relative lines, they also present results for the percentages in each member country below a poverty line set at half average expenditure in the EU as a whole. The divergence in poverty rates across countries is then very much wider than with relative lines. The Irish poverty rate is in fact still about 20 per cent with such a line, but those for Greece and Portugal are very much higher and those for the richer member states much lower. One of the most useful features of the relative income line approach is that it provides a consistent basis for the analysis of trends over time, and once again these trends provide background relevant to the analysis of the 1987 survey on which we concentrate in subsequent chapters. The national samples produced by the CSO's Household Budget Surveys for 1973 and 1980 provide the only points of comparison currently available, since unfortunately that survey is carried out only every seven years. The 40, 50, and 60 per cent income lines have been calculated for these samples, and Table 3.3 shows the percentages of households and persons falling below each line compared with the 1987 ESRI sample using equivalence scale C (the one derived from Irish social security rates). The most striking aspect of the results is the consistent increase over the 1973–87 period in the percentage of persons living in households below the three relative lines. This reflects for the most part an increase in the average size of the households falling below the lines compared with other households, rather than an increase in the percentage of households in that position. The sensitivity of these trends to the equivalence scale was also tested by using scales A and B instead. This showed that the general pattern of broad stability in the percentages of households below the lines but an increase in the percentages of persons they contain held across all three scales (see Nolan and Callan 1989; Callan, Nolan, *et al.* 1989).

We have already noted the limitations of the head-count of the number of households below an income line as an aggregate measure of poverty, in that the extent to which these households fall below the line, i.e. the depth of their poverty, is not captured. Thus, if the number below a particular line was stable but they were moving closer to that line over time, this would have implications for poverty which would be missed by the head-count. As discussed in Chapter 2, this concern has given rise to an extensive sub-literature on summary measures of poverty, sparked off by Sen (1976). To give a more complete picture of the evolution of income poverty in Ireland,

Table 3.3   Percentages below relative poverty lines, Ireland, 1973, 1980, 1987[a]

	1973 HBS	1980 HBS	1987 ESRI
40% line			
% of households	8.3	8.0	7.5
% of persons	6.8	8.5	8.2
50% line			
% of households	17.7	16.8	17.5
% of persons	14.8	16.2	19.8
60% line			
% of households	26.0	27.6	30.0
% of persons	24.5	26.7	31.4

[a] Equivalence scale C.

two measures in addition to the head-count (which we may call P_1) were therefore also calculated for the 1973 and 1980 HBS and the 1987 ESRI survey with each of the three relative poverty lines. One is the per capita income gap, expressed as a proportion of the poverty line, which we will call P_2. It may be defined as:

$$P_2 = \frac{1}{n} \sum_{i=0}^{q} \frac{g_i}{z},$$

where n is the total number of households, q is the number of households below the threshold, z is the poverty line for household i, and g_i is the gap between household income and the poverty threshold for households below the line. The other, which we call P_3, is the distributionally sensitive poverty measure proposed by Foster, Greer, and Thorbecke (1984):

$$P_3 = \frac{1}{n} \sum_{i=1}^{q} \left(\frac{g_i}{z} \right)^2.$$

This again ranges between 0 and 1, and takes into account not only the depth of poverty but also its distribution among the poor, giving a particularly high weight to those with the lowest incomes and a lower weight to those near the poverty line. As can be seen from Table 3.4, both these measures consistently show an increase in measured poverty between 1973 and 1980, and between 1980 and 1987.[8]

It is important to place these trends in relative income poverty in the context of the evolution of average real incomes. This is particularly important in the Irish case in reaching conclusions about the 1970s and the 1980s, because the pattern of real income growth was very different in the two sub-periods analysed here, that is 1973–80 and 1980–7. Between 1973 and 1980 real incomes grew rapidly. Mean household income in the HBS in 1980 was 193 per cent higher than in 1973, when the Consumer Price Index had risen by 155 per cent, representing a 25 per cent rise in average income in real terms. Between 1980 and 1987, on the other hand, average incomes rose by 87 per cent in nominal terms but the CPI was 91 per cent higher by the end of the period, so real incomes actually fell. This means that poverty lines that were fixed in real terms, rather than changing *pari passu* with average income, would show very different patterns in the two sub-periods. Between 1973 and 1980 a substantial fall in the numbers below such absolute lines would be registered; in the 1980–7 period, on the other hand, there would be an increase in the number below absolute lines which was slightly greater than that seen with relative lines.

[8] Both income gaps and the Foster *et al.* (1984) measure were calculated on a household and a person basis, and the same pattern is shown in each case (see Nolan and Callan 1989).

Table 3.4   Summary poverty measures, Ireland, 1973, 1980, 1987[a]

	1973 HBS	1980 HBS	1987 ESRI
Average income gap			
40% line	0.018	0.027	0.030
50% line	0.036	0.046	0.054
60% line	0.062	0.074	0.087
FGT measure			
40% line	0.009	0.016	0.021
50% line	0.015	0.023	0.029
60% line	0.026	0.034	0.041

[a] Equivalence scale C.

Table 3.5   Risk and incidence of poverty (50% income line) by labour force status of head, 1987

Labour force status of head	% of all households in sample	Incidence: % of households below line in category	Risk: % of category falling below line
Employee	38.6	9.2	3.9
Farmer	11.8	23.9	34.9
Other self-employed	7.5	5.0	11.6
Unemployed	10.3	34.3	58.1
Ill	1.2	3.5	51.2
Retired	14.4	9.3	11.3
In home duties	11.3	7.6	11.8
Other (incl. disabled)	4.9	7.1	25.4
All	100.0	100.0	100.0

3.5   Who Falls Below Relative Income Poverty Lines?

We now look at the composition of households below the relative income lines in 1987, and at the major changes in composition that occurred between 1973 and 1987. Table 3.5 shows the breakdown of all households in the 1987 sample and those below the 50 per cent income line when categorized on the basis of the labour force status of the head. (Here and subsequently, when results for only one equivalence scale are presented it is scale C that is used: where substantively different results are given by scales A or B, this will be mentioned.) Households headed by an unemployed person accounted for only 10 per cent of all households in the sample but over one-third of those below the line. These are followed by farmer-headed households, which again accounted for only 10 per cent of the sample but one-quarter of those below the line. About 39 per cent all households were headed by an employee and 14 per cent were headed by a retired person, but these groups each made up only about 9 per cent of those below half average income. The table also shows the variation this implies across categories in the risk of falling below the line. Only 4 per cent of households headed by an employee are below half average income, but this rises to 35 per cent for farmer-headed ones and 58 per cent for those headed by an unemployed person.

While varying the equivalence scales does not substantially alter this picture, using the higher or lower relative line does make some difference. Using the 40 per cent rather than the 50 per cent line, farmer-headed households become even more important, accounting for 40 per cent of all those below the lower line. The levels of support paid by most of the social security programmes exceeded that lowest line, so among recipients only those dependent on safety-net or long-term means-tested unemployment assistance were likely to have been on incomes that low. It is unsurprising then that those not receiving support are most significant below that line, and as the income line is raised from 40 to 50 per cent the unemployed comprise a considerably larger proportion of the income-poor. With the 60 per cent line, on the other hand, the percentage below the line headed by an employee rises to about 14 per cent and those headed by someone in home duties or unable to work because of a disability also become more import-ant. The unemployed and farmers are less important than with the 50 per cent line but remain the largest groups.

Moving on to changes over time in composition, Table 3.6 shows the breakdown in 1973, 1980, and 1987 of households below half mean income by the labour force status of their head. In 1973, almost half those below the 50 per cent line had a head who was retired or 'in home duties', and only 10

Table 3.6 Households below 50% income line by labour force status of head, 1973–1987

Labour force status of head	Households below 50% line (%)		
	1973	1980	1987
Employee	9.0	10.3	9.2
Farmer	26.0	25.9	23.9
Other self-employed	3.6	3.5	5.0
Unemployed	9.6	14.7	34.3
Ill	5.7	7.3	3.5
Retired	17.0	18.9	9.3
In home duties	24.6	17.4	7.6
Other (incl. disabled)	4.5	2.0	7.1
All	100.0	100.0	100.0

per cent had an unemployed head. By 1980 the percentage of those below the corresponding line with a head retired or in home duties had fallen to 36 per cent and the unemployed now accounted for 15 per cent. By 1987, as we have seen, only about 20 per cent of the households below half mean income had a head who was retired or in home duties, while over one-third now had an unemployed head. Similar trends in composition are seen for households below the 40 and 60 per cent relative lines.

The fact that the level of unemployment increased dramatically, from about 6 per cent of the labour force in 1973 to 18 per cent in 1987, is therefore of central importance to understanding the evolution of poverty in Ireland in the 1970s and 1980s and the situation in 1987, when our survey was carried out. The *risk* of poverty for households headed by an unemployed person did not in fact rise between 1973 and 1987—about the same proportion of households with an unemployed head were below each of the relative lines in 1973 and 1987 (see Callan, Nolan, *et al*. 1989: ch. 7). It was the rise in the numbers unemployed in the population, not a worsening in the relative position of the unemployed, that produced the very substantial increase in the number of households headed by an unemployed person falling below the relative lines. At the same time, the relatively rapid rise in social welfare support levels for the elderly, as well as wider coverage of occupational pensions, and improved provision for widows and other lone parents, contributed to the decline in the proportion of those on low incomes coming from those groups. By 1987, then, households with an unemployed head had become the largest single group among those below the relative income lines.

This compositional change in terms of labour force status also explains why the average size of the households below the relative poverty lines rose so consistently and substantially over the period. Households with a retired head were effectively 'replaced' among the poor by those with an unemployed head, and far more of the latter contained two or more adults plus children. As Table 3.7 shows, there were substantial changes in the breakdown of the households below half average income when categorized by the number of adults and children they contain. There was a sharp decline in the importance of single-adult households among those below the line and a less marked but still substantial fall in the proportion of households consisting of a couple with no children. Conversely, households containing children accounted for 35 per cent of those below the line in 1973 but almost 60 per cent of the corresponding group in 1987. The result was a sharp rise in the risk of income poverty for children: in 1973, 16 per cent of children were in households below half average income, whereas by 1987 this had risen to 26 per cent. While the percentage of children in that situation at a point in time varies somewhat with the equivalence scale adopted, the increase over time is seen not to be sensitive to the choice of scale or

Table 3.7   Households below 50% income line by size/
composition, 1973–1987

Type of household	Households below 50% line (%)		
	1973	1980	1987
1 adult	32.4	29.5	12.6
2 adults	23.9	17.2	15.0
Other adult only	10.4	9.8	14.0
2 adults with children	14.6	22.3	36.2
Others with children	18.7	21.2	24.0
All	100.0	100.0	100.0

relative line.[9] By contrast, households comprising one or two adults without children, many of whom are elderly, saw a sharp decline in the risk of poverty. It is important to note that, although still falling over time, the risk of poverty for the elderly is a good deal higher when one moves to the 60 per cent relative line, because many such individuals are on state means-tested old age pension which was at a level between those two lines.[10]

These trends in the composition of low-income groups are not unique to Ireland. Very much the same pattern of an improvement in the position of the elderly and deterioration in that of children has been seen not only in the UK and the USA, as mentioned in Chapter 2, but also in countries such as Sweden, the Netherlands, and France. The percentage of US children in families below the official poverty line has risen from 14 per cent in 1969 to over 20 per cent in the early 1990s. In Britain the number of children in families on means-tested income support (or its predecessor, supplementary benefit) trebled between 1979 and 1993, and families with children became a substantially larger proportion of those below half average income.[11] While there are differences across countries, the improvement in old age and retirement pensions has been a key common factor for the elderly, while high unemployment or stagnant earnings growth has adversely affected the position of families with children. These changes in

[9] Nolan and Farrell (1990: 38–40) shows that the percentage of children below half average income in 1987 would be as high as 34% if scale A instead of C was used, but that the increasing risk for children between 1973 and 1987 holds across all three scales and for the 40%, 50% and 60% relative lines.
[10] This is a good example of how partial a picture focusing exclusively on a single income poverty line can give, as Goodman and Webb (1994) point out, having noted a similar pattern in the risk of poverty for British pensioners.
[11] Goodman and Webb (1994: A21) show that in the 1960s and 1970s individuals in families consisting of a single adult or couple together with children made up about 36% of those below half average income, but by 1991 they accounted for almost half that total.

composition have major implications for the design of tax and social security systems to alleviate poverty, and for combating poverty more broadly. For example, the fact that far more of the poor are now potentially in the labour force has served to bring the relationship between tax/transfer systems and work incentives to the fore. In addition, maintenance of the improved situation of the elderly cannot be taken for granted, since growing numbers depending on pensions will put pressure on the levels of support provided. The implications for tax/transfer and other policies of these changes are among the issues to be taken up in Chapter 9.

3.6   Family versus Household Recipient Unit

As noted earlier, using the household as income recipient unit means that all members of a given household have the same (equivalent) income; thus, either everyone in the household will be below any particular income poverty line, or no one will be. Since the assumption of full sharing within the household may not always be warranted, it is worth assessing the scope for error in measuring income poverty this introduces by looking at the results produced by adopting as recipient unit the narrower family or tax/ benefit unit, of an adult or couple together with dependent children if any. The assumption is now that all members of the family have the same income, but there is no sharing at all across families within the household. The presence of multiple family units within a household is sufficiently common for this to potentially make a difference to measured living standards: while two-thirds of households in our sample contain just one family/ tax unit, 21 per cent contain two and 13 per cent contain three or more. This means that, whereas there are 3,294 households in the sample, there are about 5,500 families.

We therefore apply exactly the same procedure as before to these families to calculate the three relative income lines, now as 40, 50, and 60 per cent of mean equivalent *family* income. The results show that the same percentage of persons is below the 40 per cent line whichever recipient unit is used, but that the percentages below the 50 and 60 per cent line are each about 2 percentage points higher with the family unit. (Thus, with equivalence scale A, for example, 25 rather than 23 per cent of persons are below half mean income.) This means that households above the poverty line but containing families with incomes below the line are more common than households below poverty thresholds but containing families with incomes above the corresponding poverty line. However, the overall picture in terms of the extent of relative income poverty is not very different when the family rather than the household is used.

In practice, it seems quite unlikely that the living standards of families living in the same household are usually independent. Given the practical choices, we would agree with Goodman and Webb's (1994) conclusion in this context that 'on balance the best working assumption is to presume that the living standard of a given individual is best measured by the income of the entire household'. Some support for this stance is provided by the results of Rottman's (1994a, 1994b) analysis of the way money is allocated within a sub-set of about 600 of the households in our own Irish sample, who were re-interviewed in 1989. His tentative conclusion was that, despite pervasive imbalances in power and control over resources between husbands and wives, the results did not lend credence to claims that substantial numbers of women and children in households above conventional poverty lines were living in poverty. This is based *inter alia* on the moderate differences between husbands and wives in reported access to personal spending money and opportunities for leisure. While relying on the household as recipient unit when measuring income, we will be able to address differences in living standards within the household directly in later chapters when we move on to the analysis of deprivation indicators, since some of these indicators relate to the individual's own situation rather than to the household.

3.8 Annual Incomes

The income measure employed up to this point has for most sources been current weekly income, though as we have seen income from self-employment and investment is measured over a longer period, usually a year. For those depending on employment income or social security when interviewed, income received in the previous week or month could be a particularly poor indicator of resources available if their situation has altered recently; for example, some of those currently in work could have been unemployed for much of the year, and some of those currently unemployed could have been in work for most of the year. It is therefore interesting to see whether adopting an annual rather than a weekly accounting period for all incomes—as some surveys such as the US CPS do—would make much difference to the measures of relative income poverty.

In addition to current income, the full individual questionnaire used in the ESRI 1987 Survey collected information on the pay last received by persons who were not currently at work but who had worked in the previous twelve months; on the number of weeks worked in the previous twelve months; and on the numbers of weeks for which payments under various social welfare schemes were received, together with the amounts of the most recent payment. This information has been used to construct an estimate of the income received by respondents during the twelve months preceding the date of interview (see Callan 1991). While it has limitations, this should capture the most important sources of variation over the year in these income types. Comparing current with estimated annual incomes showed that about 30 per cent of households had a difference of more than £5 per week between current and annual income (expressing the latter as a weekly average). These were about evenly divided into those for whom annual income was less than current and those for whom the opposite was true, and mean annual disposable income for the sample as a whole is almost identical to mean current income.

Lengthening the period over which income is measured is usually expected to improve the relative position of some of those on very low incomes and to disimprove the position of some of those on very high incomes, because they are only temporarily at those extremes, and thus produce a less skewed income distribution. Shorrocks (1978) points out how income mobility and the length of the accounting period are intimately related: the longer the period used to measure income, the more mobility is subsumed with the income measure. Thus, what would show up as mobility from week to week becomes subsumed within an annual income measure, and some of the income dynamics seen from one year to the next would be blurred if one moved to analysing inequalities in lifetime incomes. We find that moving from weekly to annual income does marginally reduce inequality in the distribution of equivalent disposable income: for most income deciles there is virtually no difference between the current and annual distributions, but the top two deciles have a slightly lower share in annual than current income, with the gains spread across various other deciles though not the bottom one. The Gini coefficient, a widely used aggregate inequality measure, is 0.377 for current and 0.372 for annual disposable household income.

The fact that the differences are so minor may be largely attributable to the way self-employment income is treated. Self-employment income is generally subject to a good deal of fluctuation from week to week, and recipients would show a great deal of mobility in their actual weekly incomes which would be smoothed on an annual basis. However, it is precisely for this reason that actual weekly income figures are not used for the self-employed in measuring current income. Thus, much of the difference between weekly and annual incomes is already removed from the estimates by the use of the longer accounting period for self-employment income throughout. The differences between current and annual incomes which are reflected in the estimates presented here arise primarily from interruptions to work or variations in social welfare receipt during the year. The substantial changes in household incomes these produce appear to have little impact on the shape of the distribution, with 'gainers' and 'losers' largely offsetting each other. It is important to note that, despite the overall stability in the shape of the distribution, moving from current to annual income does produce a good deal of reranking of households, with 20 per cent of households changing their decile ranking.

The same pattern is reflected in measures of poverty based on annual versus current income. Poverty lines based on 40, 50, and 60 per cent of average annual household equivalent disposable income were calculated for the sample. Since mean equivalent annual income is close to the corresponding current average, the levels of the poverty lines are little changed. The use of annual rather than current income was found to make no appreciable difference to the percentages falling below the lines: the use of the annual accounting period does not in itself lead to any significant change in the extent of income poverty based on the relative lines. It could still be the case that the depth of poverty for those below the line is affected by the choice of accounting period. However, when one moves from the head-count measure of poverty to the more sophisticated per capita income gap and the Foster *et al.* (1984) measures, the indices calculated on the basis of annual income are again very close to those calculated on the basis of current income (see Nolan *et al.* 1994: 51, table 4.5). The depth and distribution of relative income poverty, as well as its extent, are therefore very similar whether current or estimated annual incomes are used as the basis for the calculations.

This is consistent with the stability we found in the overall income distribution, but despite that stability there was considerable mobility in terms of reranking of households. In the context of the relative poverty lines, such mobility would mean that, although the numbers below current and annual income lines were similar, the households involved were not always the same. In fact, we find that about 10 per cent of the households below half mean current income had annual incomes above the corresponding line, and the same proportion of those below the annual line were above the current one. Thus, there is indeed some movement from below to above the poverty line and vice versa, but it is rather limited. Most of the households identified as in poverty using current income are also in that position using annual income. None the less, the fact that in addition to reported current income we have estimated annual incomes for our sample will be useful when we come to examining the relationship between income and indicators of deprivation in subsequent chapters.

3.8 Conclusions

In this chapter we have applied relative income poverty lines to our sample, and shown both the extent of poverty as it would be measured using those income lines, and the types of household identified as poor. In doing so, some particularly thorny issues that arise in using income poverty lines have been discussed, namely the period over which income is measured, the recipient unit, and the adjustment to take differences in size and composition into account. The results show that about 20 per cent of the persons in our sample were in households with current equivalent disposable income below half the average for the sample, a relative line widely employed in recent comparative poverty research. Using higher or lower lines, set at 60 or 40 per cent of the average, substantially alters the numbers who would be counted as poor, and also has some impact on the types of household involved. The numbers below the relative income lines do not however appear particularly sensitive to varying the equivalence scale over a significant range,[12] to using the tax/benefit unit rather than the household as recipient unit, or to using annual rather than current income.

This provides the point of departure for the use in the following chapters of indicators of deprivation, which allow us to see first of all the extent to which those falling below the relative income lines appear to be excluded from participation in the ordinary life of the society. We then go on to develop an approach to identifying the poor which makes use of both income and deprivation indicators. Drawing on the results presented in this chapter, we will then be in a position to see whether the types of household found below relative income lines are also those identified as poor by the alternative approach. This will provide a basis for assessing whether reliance on income poverty lines appears likely to mislead about the extent and nature of poverty in developed countries.

[12] The equivalence scales used here do not however cover the entire range one could envisage—as documented in e.g. Whiteford (1985), the scales produced by different approaches cover a very wide range indeed.

4

Measuring Deprivation

4.1 Introduction

As we have seen, poverty in industrialized countries is most commonly measured using income poverty lines. Such lines may be derived in a variety of different ways, as outlined in Chapter 2. It is not our aim here to adjudicate between these approaches, though purely relative income lines of the type applied in Chapter 3 have a number of advantages. Rather, our concern is with the use of income itself as the 'marker' which allows poor and non-poor households to be distinguished. Chapter 3 has explored a number of the well-known difficulties with the use of income, including the time period over which income is measured and the inherent difficulties in measuring income accurately by means of survey techniques. However, the fundamental issue about reliance on income is not simply one of measurement: it is whether income, properly measured, in fact tells us what we want to know when we set out to measure poverty.

As we have seen, poverty is now widely conceptualized in terms of exclusion from the life of society because of a lack of resources, and being 'excluded' in this context is generally taken to mean experiencing various forms of what that society regards as serious deprivation, both material and social. In relying on income to make statements about poverty defined in this way, it is necessary to assume that those falling below the specified income poverty line are not able to participate fully in the life of the community. This cannot be simply taken for granted, however: it requires validation. Indeed, Ringen's stringent critique of the use of income poverty lines is based precisely on the argument that low income is quite unreliable as an indicator of poverty, because it often fails to distinguish households experiencing deprivation and exclusion.

Assessing the validity of low income as a 'marker' for exclusion involves a comparison with direct measures of deprivation. How can we arrive at indicators of deprivation suitable for this purpose? That is the subject of this chapter. We begin with a review of the conceptual background and of how deprivation indicators have been derived and used in measuring poverty. We then outline and implement an approach which takes into account the fact that deprivation may best be treated as multidimensional rather than unidimensional and that various dimensions may behave rather differently. The indicators of life-style available to us are described and the relationships between the different indicators, and between them and income, are analysed. This allows us to distinguish a set of core indicators which, it is argued, are most likely to pick up the condition of generalized deprivation, the underlying latent variable in which we are interested. Chapters 5 and 6 will then make use of these results to look in depth at the relationship between dimensions of deprivation, income, and other household attributes, at the extent to which income alone is adequate as a summary indicator of poverty, and at the use of direct measures of deprivation together with income to identify those excluded owing to a lack of resources.

4.2   The Role of Deprivation Indicators in Measuring Poverty

Reliance on income in measuring poverty implicitly assumes in the first place that income is a valid indicator of the economic resources available to people. If poverty is conceptualized in terms of living standards rather than command over resources, it also assumes that those economic resources largely determine how well-off people are. We have seen in Chapter 2 that the alternative of using household expenditure rather than income has sometimes been adopted in poverty studies in both developed and developing countries, on the basis that it better reflects living standards. However, expenditure over a short period as measured in budget surveys can be low for quite different reasons, and may not be a particularly good indicator of exclusion resulting from lack of resources. This focuses our attention on the potential of *non-monetary* indicators of living standards and deprivation in the measurement of poverty.

National aggregates for non-monetary 'social indicators' such as life expectancy, infant and child mortality rates, literacy rates, educational participation, and housing conditions have long been used by international organizations and academic studies to complement per capita GDP in comparing welfare levels across countries. Most recently, dissatisfaction with per capita GDP as a measure of a country's welfare has led the United Nations Development Programme to develop its Human Development Index, a composite of GDP per capita, life expectancy, and literacy levels. In developed countries there has also been a long tradition of employing indicators such as unemployment rates and housing conditions in comparing welfare or deprivation levels across regions or areas within cities. In studies of household poverty, the living conditions of different income groups have also quite often been illustrated by non-monetary indicators. In the Scandinavian countries in particular, there has been an interest in measuring household 'levels of living' as well as income since the 1960s (see e.g. Erikson and Aberg 1987; Erikson *et al.* 1993). The OECD sought to promote and co-ordinate the collection of social indicators at household level in member states during the 1970s, drawing on the Scandinavian example, though these efforts petered out in the early 1980s.

However, such non-monetary indicators have seldom been used directly in measuring poverty in rich countries. (For developing countries by contrast, as noted in Chapter 2, there has been a substantial literature on identifying those unable to fulfil a range of 'basic needs'.) The impetus for focusing on patterns of living and deprivation in measuring poverty has come primarily from Townsend's (1979) pioneering British research. Townsend aimed at analysing styles of living and at developing indicators of objective deprivation, that is where households lack an amenity or do not participate in an activity which a majority of the population have or participate in. Twelve sub-categories or dimensions of deprivation were distinguished, namely dietary, clothing, fuel and light, household facilities, housing conditions, work conditions, health, education, environment, family activities, recreational, and social relations. Information on a total of sixty items across these domains was gathered for households in his survey (carried out in 1969). From these he selected a sub-set of twelve to cover the major aspects of deprivation, in order to construct a summary deprivation index. These items included having a refrigerator, an indoor WC, an evening out in the last fortnight, a week's holiday away from home in the last year, fresh meat at least four days a week, and a cooked breakfast most days. Townsend stated that a score of 5 or 6 or more on this index was highly suggestive of deprivation. However, scores on this index were not used directly to identify the poor. Rather, through relating scores on a deprivation index to resources, people with resources 'so seriously below those commanded by the average individual that they are, in effect, excluded from ordinary living patterns, customs and activities' could be identified (Townsend 1979: 31). This involved deriving an income threshold, representing the point below which deprivation scores, it was tentatively suggested, 'escalated disproportionately'. All those below that income threshold were then counted as poor, without reference to their deprivation scores.

Townsend's volume is a monumental one, crammed with illuminating discussion of the issues and concrete examples of what poverty and deprivation mean in the lives of people in his sample. Its discussion of the way living standards are affected by wider resources than current income, notably assets and public services, deserved more attention. Most of the reaction concentrated on the way he derived an income threshold and on the way deprivation indicators were selected and employed. Criticism of Townsend's methodology falls under two main heads. The first relates to the income threshold derived from the deprivation scores: the existence and indeed plausibility of such a threshold continue to be hotly debated. Piachaud (1981) and Mansfield (1986) criticized the procedure employed by Townsend, which involved plotting the mode of the deprivation score for different income groups against log income (expressed as a percentage of supplementary benefit entitlement to take differences in household size and composition into account). The use of both modal values and a logarithmic income score are questionable, and no statistical tests were applied. Desai (1986) defended Townsend's procedure and did apply such tests, but their value was questioned in turn by Piachaud (1987), who focused in particular on the implications of the functional form employed. Piachaud asserts that a threshold of the kind hypothesized by Townsend is intrinsically implausible, and that reality is more accurately described as a continuum from great wealth to chronic poverty.

The second major area of criticism relates to the selection of the deprivation indicators and the role of differences in tastes. The particular indicators used were chosen in a rather *ad hoc* manner from the wider set, and have been subjected to considerable criticism. While in principle Townsend argued that deprivation indicators should be possessed by a majority of the population, in fact this was not the case for three of the twelve items he selected—including, famously, having a cooked breakfast. The degree of judgement required on the part of the researcher in selecting items has been widely seen as a problem—Veit-Wilson (1987), for example, questions the justification for according the researcher this privileged status. At a more general level, Piachaud's influential critique and others have focused on the substantial variability in the deprivation scores of households at similar income levels (though moving up the income distribution average deprivation scores did generally rise as average income rose). If observed differences in living patterns may be largely attributable to differences in tastes rather than resources, the absence of a particular item or set of items cannot be taken to represent deprivation arising from resource constraints.

The study by Mack and Lansley (1985), based on a specially designed 'Breadline Britain' survey carried out in 1983, attempted to respond to these criticisms in a number of ways. While building on Townsend's approach, their study represented a significant departure in a number of respects. They defined poverty as an 'enforced lack of socially-perceived necessities', enforced in the sense of springing from lack of resources (p. 39): they are concerned with an inability to attain the *minimum acceptable* way of life in the society. Life-style items were selected for inclusion in their deprivation index on the basis of views in their sample as to what constituted a necessity, whereas Townsend's aim was to include items that reflected 'ordinary living patterns'. In the selection of items for inclusion in the deprivation index, they make use of respondents' stated views about whether particular items/activities constituted necessities. To assess the role of tastes, they also asked those who did not have a particular item or activity whether they 'would like, but can't afford' that item. To control for diversity arising simply from tastes, 'enforced lack' of an item was taken to be where the respondent lacked the item *and* said she would like it but could not afford it.

A deprivation index based on twenty-two items considered to be necessities by a majority of the sample, and also negatively correlated with income, was constructed. In a further and key departure from Townsend's method, they adopted a more direct approach, using deprivation indicators themselves to identify the poor, rejecting reliance on an income criterion because for a variety of reasons people with similar current incomes are found to have different living standards. Those who don't have and 'would like but can't afford' three or more items were counted as poor. Recognizing that there may be problems with taking at face value people's own evaluations of whether absence is enforced, they also looked at adjusting the estimated number in poverty so that households on high incomes were taken not to be experiencing enforced lack of an item even if they said that he would like but couldn't afford it, while those on low incomes lacking items were taken to be experiencing an enforced lack even if they said they were doing without by choice.[1] While income was taken into account in this way, Mack and Lansley's main thrust was to focus on deprivation indicators themselves. Once again, they found a good deal of variability in the deprivation scores of households at similar income levels.

The use of deprivation indicators in measuring poverty was placed in a formal setting by Desai and Shah (1988). They define a set of I 'consumption events' and a deprivation score Θ_{ij} representing the ith event for the jth person. They propose that the indicators reflect 'distance' from modal values in the sample in the frequency with which particular events are experienced by the respondent within a certain time period—rather than a simple 'did/did not do' dichotomy. These scores must be aggregated over different events, and Desai and Shah suggest that the weights employed be some inverse function of the proportion of the population actually deprived in terms of the 'event' in question; that is, being deprived of something that almost everyone has is more important than being deprived of something that most people do not have. This produces the aggregate deprivation measure

$$D_j = \frac{1}{I} \sum \beta_i \Theta_{ij}$$

for each individual j, where β_i is the weight for event i. They argue that information on personal characteristics can be used to separate econometrically the systematic effect on these events of socio-economic variables from the (assumed) random variation arising from tastes. Using

---

[1] For this purpose, those in the top half of the distribution were on 'high incomes', while those in the bottom four deciles were on 'low incomes'.

Townsend's original data, they implemented this approach in so far as that dataset allowed—which in practice principally entailed applying weights to the twelve indicators in constructing the index, since frequencies with which events were experienced were not available (or, for two indicators which referred to possession/absence of an item, did not apply). Current income was found to be a significant influence on deprivation scores, but so were family composition, wealth, and education. No attempt was made to specify a cut-off between poor and non-poor, in terms of either deprivation score or income; they suggest that their results 'do not contradict' Townsend's threshold level of income, but that not much should be made of this.

Townsend and Gordon (1989) developed Townsend's earlier work using data from a survey carried out in London in 1985–6 which covered a wider range of activities and items, with the objective of tapping multiple dimensions of deprivation. A distinction was drawn between material and social deprivation, a division into thirteen specific types of deprivation across these two was made, and a total of seventy-seven indicators or groups of indicators selected. The indicators used covered not only deprivation in terms of food, clothing, housing and home facilities, and family and recreational activities, but also local environment, working conditions, employment experience and rights, participation in social institutions, and education attained. Separate indices of material and of social deprivation were constructed and then aggregated, respondents being ranked according to the number of items on each of which they could be shown to be deprived. A further innovation was the use of discriminant analysis to identify the income level that best separates the 'deprived' and the 'nondeprived', which they argued can be considered to be the poverty line. The results produced a line that was at least 50 per cent higher than the means-tested social assistance rates at the time. Thus, like Townsend's original study, the core of the approach was to apply an income line, validated by the relationship with deprivation indicators, to identify the poor.

Hutton (1991) explored the possibility of combining information from two regular official UK surveys, the General Household Survey (GHS) and the Family Expenditure Survey (FES), to measure household living standards at different income levels. The two sources were linked to give a set of deprivation indicators, covering a wide range of possessions, activities, and expenditures, for five family types (reflecting stages in the family cycle) by income decile. Principal components analysis of twenty-two items applying across all family types was then used to develop a summary index of deprivation. These items included expenditure on food, clothing, alcohol, meals out and transport, possession of central heating, a telephone, and a fridge-freezer, and having income from investments. These items were assumed to be observable measures of the underlying single unobservable variable 'standard of living', and the first component from the principal components analysis was used as the summary index. Examining its relationship with income, the only evidence of a threshold was around the middle of the income distribution.

The 'Breadline Britain' survey on which Mack and Lansley (1985) based their work was repeated in 1990 and the main results were summarized in Frayman *et al.* (1991). (The main purpose of the survey was to provide the basis for a series of television programmes.) Among these findings were that the percentage of households experiencing an enforced lack of three or more socially prescribed necessities rose from 14 per cent in the 1983 survey to 20 per cent in 1990. More recently, the data have been used by Gordon, Pantazis, *et al.* (1995) to examine in more depth a number of issues raised by Mack and Lansley's work. They show, for example, that for most of the items included there was an increase between the two surveys in the percentage stating it was a necessity, consistent with expectations rising as average incomes rose, and also that there was a high degree of consensus in the 1990 survey between the multiply deprived and the rest of the sample, and across social classes and education levels, in what are regarded as necessities (see Chapter 3). A chapter in that report by Hallerod *et al.* (1995) uses the 1990 survey to compare scores on Mack and Lansley's deprivation index (consisting only of items regarded by 50 per cent or more as necessities) with an alternative index which includes all the items measured but weights each by the percentage in the relevant sex, age and family type regarding it as a necessity. (Desai and Shah also proposed weighting items in constructing a deprivation index, but used the proportion in the sample as a whole *possessing* the item as weight, and included only those possessed by a majority.) Their results show a high degree of overlap between the two deprivation indices, and also that with either index a significant proportion of those experiencing multiple deprivation are in the higher deciles of the income distribution.

Hallerod (1995) applies a similar approach to data on 'consumption items' for Sweden. He first constructs a consensual income poverty line using responses to the Minimum Income Question as described in Chapter 2, and finds that 21 per cent of his sample households had incomes below that line. A set of thirty-six items is then employed to construct a 'proportional deprivation index', with each weighted by the percentage of 'similar' households in the sample who stated it was a necessity.[2] Using the Mack–Lansley approach, it is only where the respondent states that he would like to have but cannot afford the item that absence contributes to the deprivation score. A cut-off on the deprivation index below which 21 per cent of households fall is then chosen, so that the same numbers as the consensual income line are identified as poor, facilitating comparison between the two groups. It is found that a substantial number of those below the deprivation cut-off are above the income line, and vice versa: those

---

[2] That is, the weights accorded to each item for a particular household are based on responses of those in the same age and sex group, household type, and geographical region.

meeting both criteria are termed the 'truly poor', accounting for 9 per cent of the population. Apart from the use of a consensual income poverty line, which is unsatisfactory for the reasons set out in Chapter 2, the principal problems with this approach are its inclusion of all the items in the deprivation index and the fact that there is no way to select a cut-off on that index. Items that are regarded as necessities by only a very small percentage of the population still go into the index, even if weighted accordingly: this does not seem appropriate in measuring enforced absence of socially defined necessities. It also means that there is no basis on which to say that those above a particular score are 'deprived': only by appealing to an income poverty line is a cut-off derived. While sharing the central aim of the present volume and its precursor, Callan *et al.* (1993), of identifying those on low income and experiencing deprivation as the 'truly poor', the way this is done in the Swedish study does not convince.

Mayer and Jencks (1988) represents a rare US poverty study in the Townsend mode. Material hardship in a sample of Chicago households was measured in terms of expenditure on food, whether the household said they could not afford food, could not pay the rent or gas/electricity bills, were in poor-quality housing, did not have health insurance, or did not visit the doctor because of lack of money. Constructing an eight-item hardship index, scores were found to decline continuously as (equivalent) income rose (with no clear breakpoint), and the log of income explained about one-quarter of the variance in number of hardships. Regression analysis found equivalent income to be a significant influence on deprivation, but so were age, non-cash benefits, home ownership, health status, and ease of access to credit. Mayer and Jencks (1993) also used indicators of material well-being for the USA, to compare what they show about trends in inequality with income and expenditure distributions. Mayer (1993) used housing conditions, possession of consumer durables, and health and use of health services as indicators of living standards to compare those on low incomes in the USA, Canada, Germany, and Sweden.

Muffels and Vrien (1991) use Dutch data to develop what they term a subjective deprivation scale. They adapt Desai and Shah's approach so that, in arriving at a scale, individual deprivation items are weighted not by the overall proportion of people who have the item but by the proportion in the household's 'reference group' who do so. A reference group is defined as 'the group in society with which an individual compares himself when evaluating one's own income situation or one's own situation in terms of consumption or deprivation' (p. 10), people with whom one has regular contacts, such as family, friends, and acquaintances. These are established following the methodology developed by Kapteyn *et al.* (1988), derived from preference formation theory. This approach is justified on the basis that it is relative deprivation that one wants to measure, and that the perception of the distribution of consumption is limited to one's own reference group. The items used were similar to those developed by Townsend (1979) and Mack and Lansley (1985). A summary index was constructed using forty-five items. (Principal components analysis was also carried out and identified fifteen components entering into the index, each of which was taken as representing a latent theoretical construct and labelled.) The correlations between variants of the summary index and income were very low, so that 'consumption deprivation measures seem to be quite different from income deprivation measures' (Muffels and Vrien 1991: 20). Regression analysis supported this conclusion, which the authors saw as arising because consumption deprivation is being defined and measured quite broadly rather than simply in terms of material goods.[3] This leads them to argue that in studying poverty the focus should be on income deprivation (i.e. low income) as well as on consumption deprivation (see also Muffels 1993).

Some interest in the use of non-monetary indicators in measuring poverty has also recently been shown at EU level. Our ESRI colleague Brendan Whelan co-ordinated a review for Eurostat of the availability of regular statistics on non-monetary indicators which might serve as poverty indicators in member states, particularly in the budget surveys, and looked at the way these have been used (summarized in B. J. Whelan 1993). He also illustrated the application of principal components analysis to the budget survey data on about twenty items for three countries to identify dimensions of poverty, drawing *inter alia* on our own work for Ireland. The CERC, Paris, was also contracted to examine data available on social indicators and to suggest how items for use as poverty indicators might be selected.

It will be clear from this review that to measure deprivation/exclusion directly in analysing poverty faces a number of serious problems. If we focus on Mack and Lansley (1985) as the most recent major poverty study in this vein for Britain, for example, we can see that these authors undoubtedly clarified some of the central problems posed by Townsend's pioneering study and developed a coherent approach to tackling many of them. None the less, the choice of a particular cut-off on their deprivation scale is problematic, and the way in which they combine actual life-style information, subjective assessments, and income to produce a poverty measure is also rather *ad hoc*. Further, no account is taken of the complex ways in which the relationship between possessions/activities and income or wider resources may vary across different types of item or different household types. Simply adding together items relating to everyday activities with those related to the possession of consumer durables or the quality of housing may also be unsatisfactory as a measure of current living standards/resource constraints.

---

[3] Their items include, for example, 'good heath', 'good use of rights on public provisions', 'living generally with a good temper', 'in general living the way one likes', and 'satisfaction with one's current conditions of life' (see Kapteyn *et al.* 1988: 30–1).

Hagenaars (1986) makes the important point in that context that there are systematic biases in the possession of, for example, consumer durables which are related to age, household size, and stage in the family cycle. Thus, absence of a particular durable item—for example a washing machine— may mean something quite different for a young single person than it does for a couple with children. Such items may therefore be inappropriate as general indicators of deprivation. More generally, aggregation of deprivation indicators into a single index implicitly assumes that poverty is unidimensional, but this may not be an accurate reflection of reality. For example, some households may be in poor-quality housing but are not otherwise experiencing deprivation, while others in good-quality housing may be experiencing a variety of other forms of deprivation.

This weakens the force of Ringen's own efforts to demonstrate what he asserts to be the mismatch between low income and observed deprivation, on which his critique of reliance on income poverty lines is based. He examined the relationship between income and consumption items using Swedish data to demonstrate that:

1. far from all members of the low-income groups suffer deprivations of consumption;
2. many who do not belong to low-income groups do suffer deprivations of consumption;
3. consumption deprivation does not occur much more frequently in the low-income groups than in the rest of the population;
4. the difference in consumption deprivation between low-income groups defined 'miserly' and 'generously' is not very large.

Ringen concludes on this basis that income is not a reliable indicator of deprivation and that consequently there are no acceptable criteria for determining the exact level of the poverty line. However, the set of indicators of consumption deprivation he employed was a very limited one—whether someone has a telephone, had a holiday last year, occasionally has friends or relatives in, and has crowded or low-standard housing.

An even more limited set of deprivation indicators was employed in McGregor and Borooah's (1992) comparison of income versus expenditure in measuring poverty using UK FES data, already mentioned in Chapter 2. They concluded that expenditure is a superior measure of welfare on the basis of the relationship between income and expenditure rankings, and between them and whether the household lives in a council house or owns a car, video, and freezer. As we shall see, our own results confirm Hagenaar's suspicion that indicators of deprivation related to housing and durables may be particularly weakly related to current income and may not be satisfactory as indicators of generalized exclusion.

Arising out of this review, the key issues that must be addressed in attempting to use indicators of deprivation in measuring poverty are in our view:

1. how to select items that are suitable to serve as deprivation indicators;
2. how to take into account the role of tastes versus resource constraints as determinants of living patterns;
3. how to aggregate deprivation items in a summary index or set of dimensions or otherwise to make use of the information they contain;
4. how to select a particular cut-off to distinguish the poor from the non-poor, either on the basis of deprivation scores or using both deprivation and income criteria; and
5. fundamentally, how to elucidate the ways in which the observed deprivation/income pattern comes about, which is essential if we are to have confidence that the deprivation indicators are measuring what we wish to measure.

In the next section we discuss the basis on which the first of these issues, the selection of items to serve as deprivation indicators, will be addressed.

4.3 Measuring Deprivation

Before considering how to select items to measure deprivation, we have to spell out our understanding of what one is seeking to measure. Like poverty, deprivation is a widely used term which is often applied without definition of the underlying concept, and significant differences can be seen across studies in the way it is interpreted. Townsend (1988), in a paper that sets out to clarify the meaning of deprivation and its relationship with poverty, defines it as a state of observable and demonstrable disadvantage relative to the local community or the wider society or nation to which an individual, family, or group belongs: 'People can be said to be deprived if they lack the types of diet, clothing, housing, household facilities and fuel and environmental, educational, working and social conditions, activities and facilities which are customary, or at least widely encouraged or approved, in the societies to which they belong' (pp. 125–6). He talks *inter alia* of people who lead restricted or stunted social lives, who do not or cannot enter into ordinary forms of family or other social relationships (p. 128).

In our view, this understates or misses entirely the importance of a central element in the concept of deprivation as it is widely understood, which is that it refers to being *denied* the opportunity to have or do something.[4] To constitute deprivation, lack of the item or failure to participate in the activity must reflect what most people would regard as *inability* to

---

[4] This is also, unsurprisingly, the dictionary definition.

participate. This inability could be attributable to various different factors, such as a lack of resources, ill-health, or discrimination, but it is not simply a matter of choice. Even if there is a societal consensus that something is an 'undesirable circumstance', one can still choose it freely and not then be considered deprived. One does not have to give extreme examples such as people who choose to be hermits in the desert to make the point: those who choose not to have a car or a television, or choose not socialize with their families, would not be seen by most people as deprived. Deprivation we therefore take to mean an inability to obtain the types of diet, clothing, housing, household facilities, and environmental, educational, working, and social conditions generally regarded as acceptable in the community in question. It refers to the results of the constraints on people's choices, not simply to the outcomes themselves.

However, the empirical reality is that the latter are much easier to observe than the former: we can measure whether people lack or fail to do particular things, but we face far greater difficulties determining why. One response to the difficulty of assessing opportunity sets rather than outcomes is to employ as deprivation indicators only those items/activities which we could reasonably expect most people to wish to avoid if possible. Thus, Erikson (1993) describes the Scandinavian surveys which sought to measure 'levels of living' across a wide range of different areas as measuring 'evil conditions' rather than welfare itself, because it is much easier to order such states in ways that most people would accept. However, distinguishing the impact of constraints from choices continues to be a central problem in measuring deprivation. This remains the case when one focuses on poverty: deprivation refers to conditions, while the Townsend definition of poverty is the situation obtaining when these conditions are attributable to a lack of resources rather than to other factors. We will therefore be devoting a great deal of attention to how to assess whether lack of a particular item or failing to participate in a particular activity is due to resource constraints. The point to be made at this stage, though, is that in measuring deprivation we will be interested in indicators where one might reasonably expect *a priori* that absence will most often be attributable to limited resources, rather than other constraints such as ill-health or simply differences in tastes. This may help to restrict the areas one seeks to cover in selecting indicators of deprivation, to concentrate on those that are likely to be directly affected by access to financial resources. This would not be true, for example, of education or health care where these services are provided free of charge by the state.

Several other points are worth making about the type of indicator that one is seeking for present purposes. Deprivation refers to conditions, covering both material and social aspects of life, and is multidimensional: a state of generalized or multiple deprivation exists when deprivation across a number of aspects of life is being experienced. In measuring deprivation here we are not trying to provide a full picture of the occurrence of deprivation across all these aspects of people's lives, but rather to identify indicators that will tap into the underlying latent variable of generalized deprivation. For our present purposes, then, we are not interested in deprivation that is likely to occur only in an isolated area of life. Once again, this may help to restrict the range of aspects of life one seeks to cover through indicators of deprivation for current purposes to a narrower range than that covered by for example the Scandinavian levels of living surveys (as we discuss further in Chapter 8).

Finally, the question arises as to whether indicators of deprivation are to reflect items and activities that most people have or do, or whether we are to take *views* in the society about what constitutes necessities as the touchstone. Townsend (1988), discussing the distinction between what he terms objective versus socially approved standards, notes that the two do not always coincide and that differences between them are an important matter for enquiry. However, he also emphasizes the dangers of the social scientist becoming 'the unwitting servant of contemporary social values' (Townsend 1979: 46), and in employing deprivation indicators sought to reflect 'ordinary living patterns' by choosing items which (in principle) were possessed by at least half his sample. As we have seen, Mack and Lansley (1985) take a different stance, aiming instead to identify 'socially-perceived necessities', and therefore selecting items for inclusion in their deprivation index on the basis of views in their sample as to which constituted a necessity. They argue that items become 'necessities' only when they are socially perceived to be so: 'needs' has no meaning outside that of the perceptions of the people. These meanings are of course socially constructed, and the manner in which this occurs is itself a subject for study. However, it is perceptions that 'determine the importance and significance that can be attached to the various aspects of our living standards' (p. 38).

We find their arguments convincing. It is precisely because what are generally seen as needs change over time that poverty can be meaningfully seen only in the context of the society in question; it is in that sense relative. The underlying concept of poverty is itself based on the notion that expectations are culturally conditioned: when forced by lack of resources to do without what are generally regarded as necessities, people are then likely to be regarded as (and generally though not invariably to feel) deprived. Harking back to Adam Smith, necessities are items which the 'custom of the country renders it indecent' for someone to be seen without. Something that most people have but do not regard as a necessity does not fit that definition, and having to do without such an item should not in general be a matter of shame, which Sen sees as the core of poverty. While, as we shall see, using views rather than extent of possession of items does not make a great deal of difference to the empirical results, it is worth making our position on the aim of the exercise clear at the outset. Like Mack and

Lansley, we are attempting to identify those who (owing to lack of resources) fail to meet what are seen as the minimum standards in the society as evidenced by enforced lack of socially defined necessities.

4.4   Deprivation as Measured in the 1987 ESRI Survey

We now proceed to describe the information available on life-styles in the 1987 ESRI survey, and to discuss how this may best be used in order to measure deprivation and analyse its relationship with current income and the longer-term accumulation of resources. In the Irish survey respondents were given a list of twenty items or activities, most of which had been selected for inclusion in the survey on the basis that they had proved useful in previous studies such as Townsend (1979) and Mack and Lansley (1985). These indicators apply across all household types; some items applying only to particular types of household have been employed in other studies, but the complications involved in using them in our view outweigh the possible benefits. (For this reason a further four items, included in our survey but relevant only to households with children, are not employed here.) Following Mack and Lansley (1985), respondents were asked which items they believed were 'Necessities, that is things which every household (or person) should be able to have and that nobody should have to do without', which items they did not themselves have/avail themselves of, and which of these they would like to have but had to do without because of lack of money. Table 4.1 lists the items and shows the sample responses (taking those of the household head where available as representing the household and, where these are missing, using the spouse's responses).

Looking first at the extent to which different items are possessed and regarded as necessities, we see that 18 of the 20 items are possessed by at least half the sample, and 16 are regarded as a necessity by at least half. The widely possessed items are generally also those widely regarded as necessities—with, for example, a fridge, heating for the living rooms, indoor toilet, and bath or shower possessed by most and felt by nearly all respondents to be necessities. However, there are exceptions: 4 of the 18 items possessed by at least half the sample are not regarded by the majority as a necessity. A colour TV is possessed by 80 per cent of the population but only 37 per cent said they regarded it as a necessity. Much less dramatically, a daily newspaper, central heating, and a telephone are possessed by a bare majority of households but regarded as necessities by less than 50 per cent. Conversely, of the 16 items regarded as a necessity by at least half the sample, 2—an annual holiday away from home and being able to save—are possessed by less than half.

Thus, a total of 14 items are both possessed *and* regarded as a necessity by at least half the sample. A stricter criterion whereby the item is both

Table 4.1   Indicators of actual style of living and socially defined necessities

Item	% lacking	% enforced lack	% stating necessity
Refrigerator	5	3	92
Washing machine	20	10	82
Telephone	48	31	45
Car	38	22	59
Colour TV	20	11	37
A week's annual holiday away from home	68	49	50
A dry damp-free dwelling	10	9	99
Heating for the living rooms when it is cold	3	2	99
Central heating in the house	45	30	49
An indoor toilet in the dwelling	7	6	98
Bath or shower	9	7	98
A meal with meat, chicken, or fish every second day	13	9	84
A warm, waterproof overcoat	13	8	93
Two pairs of strong shoes	16	11	88
To be able to save	57	55	88
A daily newspaper	45	16	39
A roast meat joint or equivalent once a week	24	13	64
A hobby or leisure activity	33	12	73
New, not secondhand, clothes	10	8	77
Presents for friends or family once a year	24	13	60

possessed and regarded as a necessity by at least three-quarters of the sample would produce a more limited set of 10 items. This means that deciding whether deprivation indicators are selected on the basis that they are possessed by a majority of the sample or that they are regarded as a necessity by a majority does make some difference to the items selected. Deciding whether a bare or significant majority is required in either case will also make a difference. However, a core of 10 out of the 20 items would be selected with either criterion and with a bare or significant majority.

If the items selected as deprivation indicators are intended to reflect socially perceived necessities, the next issue is whether there does in fact appear to be a broad consensus in the sample about what constitute necessities, or whether views vary widely between different groups. Views and attitudes often vary substantially across social classes, so that is an obvious place to start. We divide the sample into four classes derived from the

14-group Erikson–Goldthorpe social class schema (see Erikson and Goldthorpe 1992): professional and managerial, other non-manual, upper working class, and lower working class. (This class categorization is discussed in more detail in the next chapter.) Table 4.2 shows for the 20 items the percentage in each class stating that the item in question is a necessity.

A remarkable degree of uniformity across the classes is seen. An overwhelming majority in each class regard a refrigerator, a damp-free dwelling, an indoor toilet, a bath or shower, a meal with meat chicken or fish every second day, a warm overcoat, and two pairs of shoes as necessities, with very little difference across the classes in the actual percentage giving that

Table 4.2   Percentages stating item is a necessity, by social class

Item	Social class			
	Professional/ managerial	Other non-manual	Upper working class	Lower working class
Refrigerator	93	93	93	92
Washing machine	80	86	83	74
Telephone	50	51	40	36
Car	59	74	54	50
Colour TV	30	33	39	48
A week's annual holiday away from home	52	44	55	44
A dry damp-free dwelling	99	99	99	100
Heating for the living rooms when it is cold	99	99	98	98
Central heating in the house	46	52	51	53
An indoor toilet in the dwelling	99	99	98	96
Bath or shower	99	98	98	95
A meal with meat, chicken, or fish every second day	84	85	84	84
A warm, waterproof overcoat	95	94	92	93
Two pairs of strong shoes	91	87	88	89
To be able to save	80	90	87	92
A daily newspaper	44	36	40	38
A roast meat joint or equivalent once a week	52	66	70	64
A hobby or leisure activity	85	68	75	66
New, not secondhand, clothes	71	79	81	78
Presents for friends or family once a year	59	59	60	56

response. Mack and Lansley found a similar degree of agreement across classes, though like us they also found some interesting variations. One might expect those in the higher social classes to be conditioned by their own relatively prosperous living standards to be more 'generous' in their assessment of what constitutes a necessity. A washing machine, a telephone, a car and a hobby are regarded as necessities by a somewhat higher proportion of households in the professional/managerial class than the lower working-class one; on the other hand, the opposite is true for a television, a roast meat joint or equivalent once a week, and being able to save. It is not difficult to see how this could reflect differences in life-style— the crucial role that the television, for example, plays as a cheap form of entertainment in less prosperous households. Overall, though, it is the degree of uniformity across the classes that is striking. Of the 16 items regarded as a necessity by at least half the sample, 15 are regarded as such by a majority within each of the four social classes (the exception being a holiday, which is in any case viewed as a necessity by a bare 50 per cent of the sample), with very similar rankings of the items.

Some variation in attitudes by age might be expected, but Table 4.3 shows that this is also quite limited. In this case 14 out of the 16 items regarded by at least half the sample as necessities are regarded as such by a majority within each age group, the exceptions now being a holiday and a car. The elderly are less likely than others to regard a car and a washing machine as a necessity, but this does not appear to reflect any general tendency for the elderly to hark back to earlier times and have a more stringent attitude to what constitutes a necessity. Indeed, and again for entirely understandable practical reasons, the elderly are more likely than others to regard a telephone as a necessity. In a similar manner, urban versus rural location can also obviously affect attitudes because of differences in needs: the main difference in responses there was that 78 per cent of rural dwellers compared with only 47 per cent of urban households regarded a car as a necessity.[5]

Finally, one would expect responses to be affected by whether the household itself in fact possessed the item in question. Table 4.4 shows the percentage stating each item is a necessity for each of three groups: (1) those who have the item, (2) those who do not have it but say that they could afford it, and (3) those who do not have it and say this is because they cannot afford it. The pattern revealed is entirely consistent across all the items. Those who possess the item are most prone to declare it a necessity— indeed, for every item except a television, i.e. 19 out of the 20, a majority of those possessing it also said it was a necessity. Those who do not possess the item and say this is a matter of choice are least likely to regard it as a necessity. It is hardly surprising that for most items the percentage of this

---

[5] Rural households were also somewhat less likely than urban ones to regard a television, a newspaper, or a holiday as necessities.

Table 4.3   Percentages stating item is a necessity, by age

Item	Age					
	<25	25–34	35–44	45–54	55–64	65+
Refrigerator	96	95	94	92	91	90
Washing machine	94	89	86	87	80	70
Telephone	32	32	40	42	47	61
Car	60	64	68	63	57	46
Colour TV	39	37	35	40	35	38
A week's annual holiday away from home	31	51	50	54	52	48
A dry damp-free dwelling	98	99	100	99	99	99
Heating for the living rooms when it is cold	100	98	99	99	98	99
Central heating in the house	46	58	52	49	49	44
An indoor toilet in the dwelling	100	97	100	99	97	98
Bath or shower	100	99	98	99	96	97
A meal with meat, chicken, or fish every second day	89	83	84	85	84	86
A warm, waterproof overcoat	87	90	92	95	94	95
Two pairs of strong shoes	83	89	86	90	88	90
To be able to save	84	85	88	87	89	89
A daily newspaper	18	36	37	46	39	39
A roast meat joint or equivalent once a week	52	63	65	71	61	60
A hobby or leisure activity	70	79	78	79	67	64
New, not secondhand, clothes	81	76	77	78	78	81
Presents for friends or family once a year	60	58	59	61	55	64

group stating it was a necessity is very low. (Most of the exceptions related to basic housing quality and facilities.) The intermediate group were those who did not have the item in question and stated this was because they could not afford it. It is understandable that people in this situation, who have had to get by without the item, are less likely to state that it is a necessity than those who possess it.[6] It is therefore all the more striking that 13 of the 16 items regarded as a necessity by at least half the sample are also

---

[6] Among those who did not possess an item and said they could not afford it, those stating that the item was not a necessity did not appear to have distinctive characteristics compared with those stating that it was a necessity. Average income, equivalent income, and wealth levels of the two groups for each item were generally similar.

Table 4.4 Percentages stating item is a necessity by possession/lack of item

Item	Possess	Lack and state:	
		Can afford	Cannot afford
Refrigerator	94	31	64
Washing machine	91	32	63
Telephone	62	11	31
Car	77	16	38
Colour TV	43	2	21
A week's annual holiday away from home	69	21	50
A dry damp-free dwelling	100	86	96
Heating for the living rooms when it is cold	99	66	87
Central heating in the house	63	9	46
An indoor toilet in the dwelling	99	70	90
Bath or shower	99	54	88
A meal with meat, chicken, or fish every second day	89	17	64
A warm, waterproof overcoat	97	39	86
Two pairs of strong shoes	93	32	74
To be able to save	91	58	86
A daily newspaper	60	7	24
A roast meat joint or equivalent once a week	74	14	43
A hobby or leisure activity	89	29	60
New, not secondhand, clothes	81	25	51
Presents for friends or family once a year	69	8	41

stated to be necessities by at least half of those who say they are doing without them because of a lack of money.

Formal regression analysis of the responses as to whether items were considered a necessity was carried out on an item-by-item basis, and showed very much the same picture.[7] Possession of the item itself is a significant positive influence on the probability that it will be regarded as a necessity, and so is the number of other items regarded by the household as a necessity. When these two variables are included, social class, age, and urban/rural location are not generally significant. The most important exceptions are the ones already revealed by the cross-tabulations—rural lo-

[7] Logistic regression was employed, the dependent variable taking the value 1 when the respondent stated the item in question was a necessity and 0 when he or she stated it was not.

cation makes it more likely a car will be regarded as a necessity, unskilled manual social class more likely that a television will be, and age 65 or over more likely that a telephone will be. Overall, though, it is the the absence of significant variation in responses across these characteristics that is most common. The responses given by the sample therefore show a very substantial degree of consensus across social classes and age groups, as to whether particular items are regarded as necessities. While we do not rely to the same extent as Mack and Lansley on these responses alone in selecting items to use as indicators of generalized deprivation, it is important to be able to establish that many of them are widely regarded as part of a minimum acceptable standard of living.

4.5   The Relationship with Income

In assessing which of these items are suitable as indicators of deprivation, we are interested not only in whether they are regarded as a necessity or possessed by most of the sample, but also in their relationship with income. We have already emphasized that simply measuring the absence of an item cannot in itself be taken to represent deprivation, much less poverty: it is absence that is enforced rather than a matter of choice, and enforced by lack of resources rather than other factors, which we want to measure. The information obtained in the survey allows us to distinguish, among those who lack the item, those who said that it was because they could not afford it. We will refer to this situation as 'enforced lack', but emphasize that 'enforcement' in this sense is self-assessed, and these subjective assessments have to be interpreted with care. A particular concern for our purposes is that, as Mack and Lansley note, some low-income households may have grown accustomed to doing without or be reluctant to admit that they cannot afford something that most people have, which could result in deprivation being under-counted. (The fact that some households with relatively high incomes none the less say they are forced to do without an item can be more easily dealt with in measuring poverty by imposing an income criterion, as we shall see.) We will return in Chapter 5 to the question of whether these subjective assessments appear consistent with the standards that most people, rather than simply the respondents themselves, would apply, but for the present will concentrate on what we have called enforced lack.

Table 4.5 shows the correlation between enforced lack of each item and current disposable household income. The correlation coefficients are all negative, and lie in the range −0.05 to −0.18. The items whose enforced absence is most highly correlated with income are 'capital' ones such as a washing machine, a telephone, a car, and central heating, and consumption

Table 4.5 Correlation between enforced lack of indicators and income

Item	Correlation between enforced lack and:	
	Income	Equivalent income
Refrigerator	−0.08	−0.07
Washing machine	−0.14	−0.11
Telephone	−0.18	−0.21
Car	−0.14	−0.16
Colour TV	−0.14	−0.13
A week's annual holiday away from home	−0.16	−0.24
A dry damp-free dwelling	−0.08	−0.10
Heating for the living rooms when it is cold	−0.05	−0.06
Central heating in the house	−0.15	−0.19
An indoor toilet in the dwelling	−0.11	−0.09
Bath or shower	−0.11	−0.10
A meal with meat, chicken, or fish every second day	−0.12	−0.14
A warm, waterproof overcoat	−0.10	−0.12
Two pairs of strong shoes	−0.11	−0.15
To be able to save	−0.19	−0.25
A daily newspaper	−0.12	−0.14
A roast meat joint or equivalent once a week	−0.14	−0.16
A hobby or leisure activity	−0.09	−0.13
New, not secondhand, clothes	−0.10	−0.13
Presents for friends or family once a year	−0.14	−0.16

items such as a holiday, a weekly roast, and presents for friends or family. Those whose enforced absence is least highly correlated with income also include capital or housing quality items—a refrigerator, a damp-free dwelling, and heating for the living rooms. The average correlation across the 20 items is −0.13. Using the annual income estimates described in Chapter 3 rather than current income makes little difference to these correlations. Current or annual household income does not take into account differences in 'needs' associated with household composition, which one would expect to affect ability to afford necessities.

As discussed in detail in Chapter 3, it is customary to adjust household income for such differences in the number and ages of household members by the use of adult equivalence scales. Employing the scale that allows 1 for the household head, 0.66 for each additional adult, and 0.33 for each child, Table 4.5 also shows the correlation between enforced absence of each of the 20 items and equivalent current income. This produces lower correlation coefficients for some items and higher coefficients for others, the average across the 20 items being marginally higher at –0.14.[8]

Finally, we might not expect the likelihood of absence of an item to fall steadily as income rises throughout the range—a linear relationship may not be the most plausible *a priori*. Substituting the log of income, so that a given increase has a smaller impact at higher income levels, does in fact produce generally higher correlation coefficients, with the average across the twenty items rising to –0.17 for log equivalent income.

These correlations are similar to those we find with simple absence rather than enforced absence, and to those reported by previous studies such as Townsend (1979), Mack and Lansley (1985), and Mayer and Jencks (1988).[9] While Townsend emphasized the fact that his deprivation indicators are indeed correlated with income (and other measures of resources), some other authors (for example Mayer and Jencks) have focused on the fact that the correlation is so far below 1—in their case, how little of the variation in scores on a deprivation index is explained by equivalent income. One of our main aims in this study is to explore these relationships in a systematic way, using a regression framework and taking into account not only income but also broader resources and a range of household characteristics in attempting to explain deprivation scores. That is the subject of Chapter 5. However, before reaching that stage we have some distance to go in considering how best to construct summary indices from our indicators. In the remainder of this chapter we concentrate on the relationships between the different items themselves and the implications for construction of such indices.

From this point on we are able to include four additional items which can be constructed from the survey information, but were not obtained in the format of has/lacks, can/cannot afford, and does/does not regard as a necessity employed for the twenty items, and so could not be included in the earlier analysis. These four items were constructed as follows:

1. whether there was a day during the previous two weeks when the 'household manager' did not have a substantial meal at all—from getting up to going to bed;
2. whether the household manager had to go without heating during the last year through lack of money, i.e. having to go without a fire on a

---

[8] Once again, although perhaps surprising at first sight, this is consistent with Townsend's results. For the 12 items in Townsend's summary index, the correlation with income is shown in his Table 6.3 (Townsend 1979: 250), and for all 60 of his items the correlation with income equivalized using supplementary benefit scale rates is shown in his Appendix 13. Comparison of the two for the 12 items shows that the correlations are in fact mostly higher—often considerably higher—when income is not equivalized.

[9] For reference, the corresponding correlations between simple absence and unadjusted and equivalent income are shown in Appendix 2 below, Table A2.1. The average correlation between annual income and absence of the 12 items Townsend used in his summary deprivation index was –0.12, while Mack and Lansley found very similar average correlation between enforced lack and income.

cold day, or go to bed early to keep warm, or light the fire late because
of lack of coal/fuel;

3. whether the respondent has not had an afternoon or evening out in the
    last fortnight, 'something that costs money', and this was stated to be
    because they had not enough money;

4. whether the household has experienced debt problems in terms of any
    of the following:

    (a) it is currently in arrears on rent, mortgage, electricity or gas;
    (b) it has had to go into debt in the last twelve months to meet
         ordinary living expenses (such as rent, food, Christmas, or back-
         to-school expenses);
    (c) it has had to sell or pawn anything worth £50 or more to meet
         ordinary living expenses; or
    (d) it has received assistance from a private charity in the past year.

It is the *presence* of these items that would potentially indicate deprivation, whereas for the twenty items in Table 4.1 it was of course *absence*
that would do so. These additional items, though not available in the preferred format, nevertheless prove particularly valuable and are incorporated in the analysis for that reason. For items 2 and 3, the question explicitly
states that experiencing the problem is to be attributable to lack of money,
and for the other two the nature of the problem makes it overwhelmingly
likely that this is the case. We will therefore take it that 'cannot afford'
subjective assessments apply in all cases. About 4 per cent of the sample had
a day without a proper meal in the last two weeks, 7 per cent had to go
without heat, 15 per cent had experienced severe debt problems of the sort
detailed under item 3, and 17 per cent had not had a night out in the previous
fortnight because of lack of money. The correlations with equivalent disposable household income were −0.08, −0.10, −0.14, and −0.17 respectively (and
the correlations with unadjusted income were slightly lower).

It is on these twenty-four items that we base our analysis. A broader
range of indicators might be helpful, though we were able to make use of
Townsend and Mack and Lansley's results in selecting items for inclusion in
our survey in the first place, and we have also discussed why for present
purposes one might not want to cover as broad a range as, for example,
Townsend and Gordon (1989). This focused set of items will allow us to
make substantial progress in teasing out whether different dimensions of
deprivation are involved and determining their relationship with income.

4.6   Dimensions of Deprivation

From the set of twenty-four items available in our survey, how should
indicators be selected and aggregated to measure deprivation? Townsend

Table 4.6   Distribution of scores on 24-item enforced
lack summary index

Score	% of households
0	21.3
1–3	37.7
4–6	21.9
7–9	11.6
10–12	4.6
13–15	1.9
16 or more	1.0
All	100.0

used a sub-set of the items in his survey, selected on the basis of the extent to which they were possessed in the sample, to construct a summary deprivation index, while Mack and Lansley constructed such an index with items regarded by the majority as a necessity. The items involved may however relate to rather different aspects or dimensions of deprivation, and simply adding them in a single index without taking this into account may not be the most appropriate procedure. We therefore look first at how similar summary indices could be constructed from the items in our sample, but proceed to an examination of the relationships between the items and the implications for such an exercise.

We begin by simply constructing an aggregate 24-item deprivation index where a household scores 1 for each of the 20 items in Table 4.1 which respondents do not have and say they would like but cannot afford, and one for each of the 4 additional items which they do experience. The pattern of scores on this index is shown in Table 4.6. About 21 per cent of households score zero, 41 per cent score 4 or more, and 7 per cent score 10 or more.

How do scores on this summary index vary with current household income? The mean scores on this 'enforced lack' summary index for households ranked by current equivalent disposable income decile are shown in Table 4.7. (The pattern with unequivalized income is very similar and so is not shown separately.) The mean score does not vary much across the bottom three deciles, peaking at over 6 in the second rather than the bottom decile. It then falls fairly steadily as we move up the income distribution, to under 1 for the top decile. However, the table also shows that there is a good deal of variability in scores within each decile, with some low-income households having very low scores and some high income ones reporting substantial enforced lack. For example, while the mean score for households in the bottom decile is 6, about one-third of these households have scores of 10 or more and another third have scores of 5 or under. At the top,

Table 4.7   Scores on 24-item enforced lack index, by household equivalent income

Equivalent income decile[a]	Mean score on index	% with score of 10 or higher	% with score of 5 or less
Bottom	5.8	34.8	30.7
2	6.3	36.0	31.0
3	5.5	29.8	27.5
4	4.5	20.6	42.9
5	3.6	15.9	52.7
6	3.6	11.9	65.4
7	2.5	4.8	75.3
8	2.2	7.6	72.5
9	1.6	3.2	87.3
Top	0.9	1.7	92.3

[a] Equivalence scale 1 for household head, 0.66 for each other adult, 0.33 for each child.

about 8 per cent of households in the top decile score over 5.[10] The regularity of that relationship should be emphasized: fully 97 per cent of the variance between the deciles in mean deprivation scores is explained by the simple linear relationship with decile rank.[11]

The main deviation from that linear relationship is the fact that the mean deprivation score for the bottom decile is lower than that for the second one. How might this come about? One explanation could be that it is attributable to households reporting zero or extremely low incomes: they will generally be self-employed reporting zero profit (or indeed losses) for the year, and if this is a particularly poor reflection of their command over resources over any substantial period, they may have relatively low deprivation scores, bringing down the average score for the bottom decile as a whole. This is not in fact the explanation, however: excluding those on zero or very low incomes makes little difference to the mean score for the bottom decile. What is important is the fact that farm households (that is, those headed by a farmer) make up about one-third of the bottom decile, compared with 15 per cent of the sample as a whole, and have low deprivation scores compared with other households in that decile. If one excludes all farm households, the mean deprivation scores for the bottom two deciles are then identical—at 6.5—while those for the other deciles are virtually unchanged from those shown in Table 4.7. The relationship between reported income and deprivation scores is therefore somewhat different for low-income farmers than for others on similar income levels. This

[10] The pattern shown by a 24–item index constructed on the basis of simple absence rather than enforced absence of items is very similar, as shown in Appendix 2, Table A2.2.
[11] In other words, out of a total sum of squares of 9,074, 8,800 are accounted for by linearity and only 274 by deviation from linearity.

could be partly because the year in question was a remarkably poor one for farmers—as already mentioned—but those affected were more likely to have some other resources to fall back on. Farm incomes are in any case particularly difficult to measure accurately, and this assumes greater importance in the Irish case than in most other developed countries given the size of the farming population. The point of more general significance is that, having excluded farmers altogether, we find no variation in deprivation scores across the bottom two deciles, followed by a fairly steady decline in mean scores as one moves up the distribution.

The correlation between scores on the 24-item summary index and equivalent income, at −0.33, is higher than that between income and any of the individual items, as one would expect, since aggregation should reduce the relative importance of random versus non-random influences. One would presumably have greater confidence in the reliability of the income data in measuring income decile position than precise income level, so it is interesting that the correlation between scores on the index and the household's income decile rank is even higher, at −0.50. Clearly, although there is a strong relationship between current income and scores on the summary index, as one would expect, current disposable income would be inadequate as the sole predictor of life-style or deprivation—among other things, stage in the life-cycle and experiences and resources over a longer period would be expected to play a central role, as we will be investigating in Chapter 5.

However, there are a number of reasons why simply proceeding to apply this 24-item summary index might not be satisfactory. The first and most obvious is that not all the 24 items may be considered appropriate as indicators of deprivation: not all are either possessed by or regarded as necessities by the majority of the sample. One could therefore select the sub-set which a majority or most households consider to be necessities or possess, which, depending on the precise cut-off applied, would produce a set of between 14 and 22 items.[12] The second point, though, is that simply aggregating them in a single index ignores the fact that different items may reflect different dimensions of deprivation and adding them together may lose valuable information. This is an issue which has not received much attention in the UK literature on deprivation indicators, though as we have seen Muffels and Vrien (1991) have addressed it using Dutch data. As Buck puts it,

the mainstream of research on non-monetary poverty indicators in the UK has focused on testing the robustness of single index measures, mainly constructed additively. The main concerns have been to establish the conceptual integrity of the scale, to investigate the nature of the relationship with income, and in particular to discover whether a single threshold exists. (Buck 1992: 7)

---

[12] This assumes that the 4 additional items on which we do not have direct responses concerning whether they are regarded as necessities would be included.

Townsend and others have discussed the different aspects or dimensions of deprivation which indicators are intended to pick up, but little attention has been paid to the relationship between the different indicators, or to assessing whether it is in fact appropriate to add them together in constructing a single summary index. A priority in this volume is therefore systematically to examine the dimensions of deprivation, to see whether the items cluster into distinct groups.

In order to do so, we apply factor analysis to the 24 items. In the case of the 20 items in Table 4.1, we once again concentrate at this stage on absence which was stated by the respondent to be due to lack of resources, returning later to the issue of the reliability of these subjective assessments. The enforced absence of particular items is of interest in so far as it reflects what Ringen (1987) refers to as a state of generalized deprivation and what Coates and Silburn (1970) termed an interrelated network of deprivation. The first stage in the analysis therefore, before attempting to select items that would be appropriate as indicators of such generalized deprivation, is to examine systematically our range of deprivation items to see whether the items cluster into distinct groups. Factor analysis enables us to identify such clusters of interrelated variables. Each factor or dimension is defined by those items that are more highly correlated with each other than with the other items. A statistical indication of the extent to which each item is correlated with each factor is given by the factor loadings on what is termed the rotated factor solution. Based on a preliminary examination of the items and their correlations with each other, three underlying dimensions of deprivation were hypothesized:

1. basic life-style deprivation—consisting of basic items such as food and clothes;
2. secondary life-style deprivation—consisting of items such as leisure activities;
3. housing deprivation—consisting of items related to housing quality and facilities.

The manner in which factor analysis was applied to the set of dichotomous items employing Muthen's (1988) procedure is described in C. T. Whelan et al. (1991). The results of the factor analysis when a three-factor solution was specified are shown in Table 4.8. Informed by the results of the factor analysis, the 24 items were categorized into three groups in the manner shown in the table: 8 items are taken to be indicators of basic deprivation, 9 as indicators of secondary deprivation, and 7 as indicators of housing deprivation. While the results of the factor analysis were taken as the general guide, judgement was applied where the loadings were similar—for example in categorizing presents for friends and family and having a hobby as secondary rather than basic items. Heating for the living room when it is cold is included in the housing group although it loads more

Table 4.8   Factor solution for life-style deprivation items

	Basic life-style deprivation	Secondary life-style deprivation	Housing/ household capital deprivation
Basic items			
Go without heat	*0.81*	0.33	0.11
Go without substantial meal	*0.89*	0.09	0.20
Arrears/debt	*0.76*	0.25	0.04
New not second-hand clothes	*0.74*	0.30	0.29
Meal with meat/chicken/fish	*0.74*	0.30	0.40
Warm waterproof overcoat	*0.76*	0.16	0.42
Two pairs of strong shoes	*0.75*	0.25	0.38
Roast or equivalent weekly	*0.73*	0.33	0.25
Secondary items			
Annual holiday away frome home	0.39	*0.69*	0.01
Able to save regularly	0.49	*0.54*	0.18
Daily newspaper	0.48	*0.50*	0.11
Telephone	0.25	*0.65*	0.28
Hobby or leisure activity	0.59	*0.44*	0.08
Central heating	0.19	*0.59*	0.40
Presents for friends/family yearly	0.58	*0.44*	0.20
Car	0.26	*0.60*	0.20
Afford afternoon/evening out	0.43	*0.38*	0.08
Housing items			
Bath or shower	0.17	−0.01	*0.99*
Indoor toilet	0.16	−0.01	*0.98*
Washing machine	0.02	0.46	*0.63*
Refrigerator	0.26	0.23	*0.62*
Colour TV	0.21	0.30	*0.53*
Dry damp free dwelling	0.27	0.30	*0.47*
Heating for the living room	0.48	0.25	*0.30*

heavily on the basic one, because the latter already includes having to go without heating through lack of money.

Looking back at Table 4.1 with these categorizations of the items in mind, levels of absence are generally low for the basic deprivation items—each item except the weekly roast is possessed by 84 per cent or more of the sample. Where these items are lacked, for most of the households this is considered by the respondent to be 'enforced'. The extent of possession is generally even higher for the housing items (except for the washing machine and television), and absence is even more likely to be attributed to lack of resources rather than choice. The secondary items are generally much less widely possessed than those in the other two dimensions, and absence is less often considered to be enforced. As far as attitudes in the

Table 4.9 Distribution of scores on basic, housing, and secondary summary indices

Score[a]	Basic index (% of households)	Housing index (% of households)	Secondary index (% of households)
0	67.2	73.9	24.2
1	15.1	14.7	17.1
2	7.0	6.0	16.0
3	4.1	3.2	13.4
4	3.1	1.3	10.7
5	1.9	0.5	8.4
6	0.6	0.3	5.1
7 or more	1.1	—	5.2
All	100.0	100.0	100.0

[a] There are 8 items in the basic index, 7 in the housing etc. index, and 9 in the secondary index.

sample to the items are concerned, the five basic items for which we have the information are considered necessities by at least two-thirds of the sample. An even higher percentage regard the housing items as necessities, with the exception of a colour television. The items included in the second-ary deprivation group, on the other hand, are regarded as necessities by much lower percentages, with the exception again of being able to save regularly.

The sample evidence thus suggests that it is useful to distinguish these three dimensions, instead of simply aggregating items across the factors into a summary index—rather different households or types of household are lacking each type, suggesting that the processes producing each may also be somewhat different. On the basis of these groupings we now construct, rather than a single summary index, three separate indices for enforced lack of basic, housing, and secondary items respectively.[13] The distribution of scores on the three indices for the sample is shown in Table 4.9. For the basic deprivation index, 68 per cent of households score 0, 15 per cent score 1, and 17 per cent are experiencing enforced lack of two or more basic items. On the housing index, almost three-quarters of sample households score 0, 15 per cent score 1, and 11 per cent score 2 or more. On the secondary index, by contrast, only one-quarter of sample households score 0, 46 per cent score 1–3, and 30 per cent score 4 or higher.

Before proceeding to employ these measures, it is necessary to assess their reliability. Fundamentally, reliability concerns the extent to which a procedure yields the same result on repeated trials. The measurement of

[13] For the 4 items not obtained in the standard format, as argued earlier, the wording of the question and the nature of the experience involved suggests that lack is likely to be enforced in that sense in most cases, so simply experiencing the problem adds to the basic enforced deprivation index.

any phenomenon is always subject to a certain amount of chance error. However, while repeated measurements of the same phenomenon never duplicate each other precisely, they do tend to be consistent from measurement to measurement. The tendency towards consistency found in repeated measurement is referred to as reliability. By far the most popular measure of reliability is Cronbach's coefficient alpha, which can be expressed as follows:

$$\alpha = N\bar{\rho}\left[1 + \bar{\rho}(N - 1)\right],$$

where n is equal to the number of items and p is equal to the mean inter-item correlation. In most situations α provides a conservative estimate of reliability.

Cronbach's alpha can be interpreted as the correlation between an index based on this particular set of items and all other possible indices containing the same number of items which could be constructed from a hypothetical universe of items that measure the characteristic of interest. The alpha reliability coefficients for the deprivation scales are as follows:

- Basic deprivation   0.76
- Secondary deprivation   0.74
- Housing deprivation   0.62

Our results suggest that the basic index exhibits a high degree of reliability and that rather similar results would be observed if any alternative set of eight indicators from the potentially infinite set of indicators tapping basic deprivation had been chosen. This holds equally for the secondary deprivation dimension, though for the housing scale the level of reliability falls slightly below what we would ideally like. Further evidence of the fact that the results do not depend on idiosyncratic factors associated with any particular item is provided by the relationship between the specific items and the overall index. Focusing on the eight-item basic deprivation dimension, in the first place the correlations between each of the items and the overall score excluding that item fall in the range 0.38–0.54. This is consistent with the size of the factor loadings we found for each of the items. Furthermore, while the exclusion of any of the items would reduce the level of reliability of the index, in each case the effect is extremely modest: for the set of possible seven-point scales, the alpha coefficients range from 0.72 to 0.75. A similar pattern of results is observed in relation to the other two indices. The evidence thus suggests that neither the addition of comparable indicators nor the deletion of any one of our current indicators would substantially alter the conclusions we are likely to reach regarding the determinants and consequences of the dimensions of deprivation reflected in our indices.

The next stage in our analysis is to look at the influences on household scores for each of these indices, to see for example what distinguishes the type of household experiencing basic deprivation from the type experiencing housing deprivation. In the next chapter therefore we examine the relationship between these indices and household income, and then introduce a range of other variables relating to the household, from resources to needs to previous experiences, which help in explaining the observed variation in life-styles and deprivation across these three dimensions. It is important to be clear at this point about what our aim has been in applying factor analysis. We are not suggesting that three and only three dimensions of poverty have to be distinguished: it would undoubtedly be possible to distinguish within each further sub-groups which might refer to for example food poverty, heat poverty, and so on. (Thus, Muffels and Vrien (1991), for example, distinguish fifteen different dimensions in their Dutch data.) Our aim here is not exhaustively to categorize and measure different aspects of deprivation, but rather to identify indicators that are likely to reflect the underlying latent variable of generalized deprivation across various aspects. What the factor analysis we have carried out achieves in this context is to show which of the indicators we have available do *not* cluster together, and on this basis we can form a judgement as to which are best suited to our fundamental objective. The analysis in Chapter 5 of the three broad dimensions we have identified will be helpful in this context, but it is worth signalling at this stage that the results of that analysis, taken together with the pattern of views about necessities and possession of the items presented in this chapter, lead us to concentrate in Chapter 6 on what we have called the basic dimension as the one most likely to reflect an underlying situation of generalized deprivation and therefore the most relevant to poverty measurement.

4.7 Conclusions

In this chapter we have discussed the definition and measurement of deprivation. The definition of poverty in common use in developed countries is that it constitutes exclusion from the life of society arising from a lack of resources. Being 'excluded' in this context is generally taken to mean experiencing various forms of what the society in question regards as serious deprivation, and the reliability of the common practice of using low income as a 'marker' for exclusion can be assessed only by comparison with direct measures of deprivation. Reviewing the limited number of previous studies employing non-monetary indicators in poverty measurement, a number of serious problems were noted. Townsend's influential British study remains a central point of reference in this area, but both the way he selected items to serve as indicators of deprivation and the way in which he then used these indicators to derive an income poverty line have been subject to searching criticism. The substantial variability in deprivation scores of households at similar income levels also led some to argue that observed differences in living patterns may be largely attributable to differences in tastes rather than resources.

Mack and Lansley developed a coherent approach to the selection of items widely regarded as necessities, sought to control for differences in tastes by asking respondents whether the reason they did not have an item was because they could not afford it, and did not attempt to derive an income threshold. However, the choice of a particular cut-off on their deprivation scale and the way in which they combined deprivation indicators, subjective assessments and income to produce a poverty measure were rather *ad hoc*. Further, no account was taken of the fact that simply adding together items relating to everyday activities and those related to the possession of consumer durables or the quality of housing may be unsatisfactory. More recent studies have illuminated the issues but have failed to mark out a satisfactory way to tackle the two key ones: what criteria are to be employed in selecting suitable indicators, and how they are then best aggregated in order to provide a measure of deprivation?

We have made clear that our approach to these issues is governed by the use to which we wish to put deprivation indicators. We are not intending to provide a comprehensive picture of deprivation in all its aspects, attributable to a range of different factors. Instead, our aim is to be able to identify households experiencing generalized deprivation enforced by lack of resources. From this perspective, Mack and Lansley's argument that deprivation indicators should be items widely regarded as necessities appears to us a persuasive one, since the underlying concept of poverty is itself based on the notion that expectations are culturally conditioned. However, it is not enough that items be regarded as necessities: the relationships between the items themselves also need to be taken into account if they are to be indicative of generalized deprivation. For that reason, having described the twenty-four items on which we have information in our survey and how they relate (individually and in the form of a summary index) to income, we subjected them to factor analysis. Three sets of items that cluster together, which we have called the basic, secondary, and housing dimensions, were distinguished.

Having distinguished these dimensions, separate indices for each were then constructed, each household's score showing how many of the items in question it lacked and had said that it was because they could not afford them. In the next chapter we go on to analyse the determinants of households' scores on each of these indices. As we shall see, this adds considerably to our understanding of the processes at work, and also helps in deciding which indicators are most useful in measuring poverty.

5

Income, Resources, and Deprivation

5.1 Introduction

We have argued in earlier chapters that household deprivation indicators are valuable not only because they help to show in a graphic way what it means to be poor, but also because they may help in identifying the poor more accurately in the first place. Before they can safely be used for that purpose, however, we must have confidence that the indicators being employed are themselves satisfactory. By 'satisfactory', we mean in this context that they are likely to serve as indicators of an underlying state of generalized deprivation. In the previous chapter, analysis of the set of potential deprivation indicators on which we have information has suggested that the choice of indicators should not be governed simply by whether they are possessed by most people, or regarded by most people as a necessity. The interrelationships between the potential indicators, the way they cluster together, suggest that different dimensions are being picked up by different indicators. In this chapter we consider how this comes about and how it affects the way deprivation indicators are best employed in measuring poverty.

Since it is exclusion arising from a lack of resources that we wish to measure, the relationship between deprivation indicators and income is of central importance. Like previous studies, we have found rather weak correlations between individual life-style items and household income. How does this arise, and what are the implications for the value of such indicators? To pursue this, we examine first of all the relationship between the different dimensions or clusters and household income. Since current income has serious limitations as a measure of the resources available to a household, a priority is then to broaden the measure of resources by making use of information about household savings and other assets, as well as variables likely to affect the longer-term or 'permanent' income of the household. In addition, households differ in the demands on their resources for a variety of reasons, which will affect their consumption patterns and observed life-styles. This chapter sets out to examine the extent to which household scores on the summary indices for the different dimensions can be explained in terms of a wide range of variables relating to resources and 'needs'.

By demonstrating that deprivation scores are in fact strongly related to

Table 5.1 Scores on basic, housing, and secondary enforced lack indices, by household equivalent income

Equivalent income decile[a]	Basic		Housing		Secondary	
	Mean score on index	% scoring > 0	Mean score on index	% scoring > 0	Mean score on index	% scoring > 0
Bottom	1.5	56.8	0.6	35.0	3.6	90.2
2	1.7	60.3	0.7	39.0	3.9	95.5
3	1.2	54.0	0.8	45.7	3.4	92.3
4	0.8	42.1	0.7	38.0	3.0	87.8
5	0.5	25.4	0.5	28.5	2.6	80.2
6	0.7	28.0	0.4	21.7	2.5	75.6
7	0.4	22.1	0.2	16.8	1.8	76.6
8	0.3	18.5	0.3	19.1	1.6	65.2
9	0.2	12.3	0.2	12.6	1.2	56.9
Top	0.1	10.5	0.1	5.7	0.7	38.9
All	0.8	32.8	0.5	26.1	2.4	75.8

[a] Equivalence scale 1 for household head, 0.66 for each other adult, 0.33 for each
child.

such variables, in a way that varies across the dimensions, we achieve a
number of objectives in this chapter. First, the indicators themselves can be
taken with much greater confidence knowing that the counsel of despair
that they are primarily a product of tastes rather than resource constraints
is unfounded. Secondly, the value of distinguishing between the different
dimensions is reinforced. Finally, the results underpin the use of a particular
sub-set of indicators, together with income, in measuring poverty, to which
we turn in Chapter 6.

5.2 The Relationship between Life-Style Dimensions and Income

To examine the relationship between the three dimensions and current
income, we first show in Table 5.1 the pattern of scores on the basic,
housing, and secondary enforced lack indices by equivalent income decile.
We see that for the basic and secondary indices the mean score is highest in
the second rather than the bottom decile, and then declines fairly steadily as
one moves up the distribution, though with a 'spike' in the sixth decile. For
the housing index the highest mean score is for the third decile, again
followed by a reasonably steady decline. The table also shows the percentage in each decile scoring one or more on each index, which is also of
particular interest. For the basic index, one sees that about 55–60 per cent
of the households in the bottom three deciles register a score of 1 or

Table 5.2   Correlation between income and indices of enforced lack of basic, housing, secondary, and all items

Income concept	Correlation with income of scores on:			
	Basic index	Housing index	Secondary index	24-item index
Disposable	−0.17	−0.19	−0.26	−0.27
Equivalent	−0.22	−0.17	−0.33	−0.33
ln(disposable)	−0.22	−0.28	−0.30	−0.34
ln(equivalent)	−0.29	−0.20	−0.38	−0.39

higher—so about 35–40 per cent of the households at these relatively low income levels display no such enforced deprivation. In the upper reaches of the income distribution, on the other hand, while the percentages reporting enforced basic deprivation are much lower, they are none the less sizeable, accounting for about one-quarter of those around the middle of the distribution and 10–20 per cent of those towards the top. Both the other indices also show substantial numbers reporting enforced lack in the top half of the distribution, though considerably higher percentages do so in the bottom half.

This pattern is reflected in the rather low level of correlation between scores on these indices and income. We have already seen in Chapter 4 that, like previous studies, the correlation between household income and individual life-style/deprivation indicators is low. The average correlation between equivalent disposable income and (simple or subjectively enforced) absence of the twenty-four items on which we have information for our Irish sample is about −0.14, very similar to those reported by Townsend, Mack and Lansley, and Mayer and Jencks.[1] Aggregating items into a summary index significantly increases the correlation with income: again as already noted, the correlation coefficient between equivalent income and the summary index constructed using self-assessed enforced lack of the twenty-four items is −0.33. We now look in Table 5.2 at the correlations between various income measures and the indices for the enforced lack of basic, housing, and secondary dimensions, together with the twenty-four-item summary enforced lack index. (Once again, using lack versus enforced lack would make little difference to the pattern, the correlations with income generally being slightly lower with the latter.) We see that the index for the secondary items is a good deal more strongly correlated with income than either the basic or the housing indices. The variants on the income measure shown are disposable household income, equivalent disposable

[1] As we saw in Ch. 4, Townsend's and Mayer and Jencks's results refer to simple lack of items, whereas Mack and Lansley's refer to subjectively assessed enforced lack: we found little difference between the two in the mean correlation with income.

income, the natural log of unadjusted income, and the log of equivalent income. For the basic and secondary indices the correlations with equivalent income are higher than with unadjusted income, but the opposite is true with the housing dimension. The correlations are higher for all three indices when the log of income is used, suggesting that a given absolute increase in income has a larger impact on enforced lack of these items at low than at higher incomes.

These levels of correlation, of the strength of the relationship between current income and life-style/deprivation outcomes, do not take into account the fact that neither is measured with perfect accuracy, and it is worth noting the impact this may have on the measured correlations. Given estimates of the reliability of two variables, one can 'correct' the correlation between them for unreliability arising from measurement error to determine what the correlation would be if they were made perfectly reliable (Carmines and Zeller 1979). In relation to the life-style items, we saw in Chapter 4 how one can assess statistically the reliability of the indices, where 'reliability' refers to the extent to which any measurement procedure yields the same result in repeated trials, with the widely used estimator of reliability, Cronbach's alpha. Income as measured in household surveys is subject to well-known problems, particularly with respect to self-employment income and income from capital, on which we have touched in Chapter 3. While we cannot assess the reliability of the income measure in the same way as we can for the deprivation indices, it might be expected that a household's position in the decile income distribution is measured more accurately than income itself. This is consistent with the finding that the indices for the life-style dimensions are more highly correlatied with decile rank than with income (or log income) itself. Employing the decile (equivalent income) rank and correcting for less than perfect reliability of the life-style measures, one finds the following corrected coefficients:

−0.41 for the basic index;
−0.29 for the housing index;
−0.54 for the secondary index;
−0.52 for the overall 24-item index.

The relationship between income and life-style indicators is thus rather stronger than it might appear at first sight—and stronger than those sceptical about the value of deprivation indicators appear to believe. However, other variables also clearly play a major role in determining the scores on these indices, as indeed one would expect, and we will shortly seek to identify the key variables at work.

This will help to explain the consistent finding, which may seem surprising, that the basic and housing indices, made up of items possessed by most of the sample and regarded by most as necessities, are less highly correlated with income than the secondary dimension, which includes items much less widely held and less strongly regarded as necessities. This is not in fact an implausible pattern, given the nature of the items in each dimension. The housing and household capital items are of a type that would be accumulated over a long period, so that stage in the life-cycle and permanent income would be expected to play a particularly important role. Current income would therefore be less important than it is for the items of current consumption which make up the majority of those in the secondary index. The items in the basic index, on the other hand, though relating largely to current consumption, represent rather more extreme forms of deprivation than the secondary items (in the sense that more people regard them as necessities and fewer lack them). One might therefore expect that people would go to considerable lengths, drawing not only on current income but also on savings and other accumulated resources and on available social support from extended family and friends, to avoid these forms of deprivation. It is thus precisely for the items in the secondary index, such as holidays, presents, and nights out, on which a greater degree of choice is likely to be exercised, that current income itself may have its most pronounced effect. To show how factors such as savings, social support, the duration of low income, previous experiences, and differences in needs impact on current life-style but in ways that differ across the dimensions, we move in the next section to a multiple regression framework.

5.3   Determinants of Life-Style and Deprivation Scores: the Variables to be Employed

One would expect current life-style and deprivation to be influenced by many factors other than current income. Households at a similar current income level will have arrived at that position in a variety of different ways, which may profoundly affect their current life-style and the extent to which they experience deprivation. Most obviously, households on low income over a prolonged period are in a very different situation from those who have only recently seen their income fall, particularly in the resources they can call on over and above current income; and expectations of how long low income will be sustained into the future will also affect current behaviour. (Indeed, our results will show that experiences over a very long period can influence current behaviour, particularly factors likely to have affected the accumulation and erosion of resources.) In addition, the demands on a particular level of income will vary across households not only owing to differences in the number of adults and children, but also because 'needs' can be affected by factors such as age, illness, and location.

We now use the information available for our sample on a particularly wide range of potentially relevant variables to explore the determinants of household life-style/deprivation patterns through regression analysis. This type of analysis was not carried out by Townsend or Mack and Lansley on their indicators/indices, but Desai and Shah (1988) did use Townsend's data to model econometrically eight deprivation items (from the twelve in Townsend's summary index), and they looked at the implications for an index comprised of these items. The independent variables used were family composition type, income, wealth, region, education level of household head, and whether he/she was ill: family type was the most consistently significant as an explanatory variable, followed by income, then education, then wealth (which is significant only for half the items). Mayer and Jencks (1988) regressed scores on their hardship index on income, family size, age, sex, and health of head, housing tenure, and whether social assistance in the form of food stamps or Medicare was being received. Here we are able to include a considerably wider range of deprivation indicators and of potentially important explanatory variables, and our approach is distinguished by the focus on separate indices for the different dimensions.[2] The fact that we found the indicators clustered into groups, that distinct dimensions of life-style/deprivation emerged from the factor analysis, implies that the explanatory variables should not operate in exactly the same way across the dimensions, and it will be particularly important to identify these differences.

The explanatory variables we employ can usefully be grouped into a number of broad categories relating for example to current command over resources, 'needs', or demands on these resources, and how the household arrived at its present situation. Although the allocation of variables to categories is not always clear-cut, as we shall see, they relate to:

1. current income;
2. needs;
3. non-income resources;
4. current relationship with labour force;
5. permanent income;
6. background/history.

We now describe the variables we have available falling into each of these groups, and discuss how they are hypothesized to influence life-style/deprivation scores, how they are measured in our survey, and how they are used in the regression analysis.

---

[2] Muffels and Vrien (1991) and Muffels (1993) carry out multivariate analysis of scores on a summary deprivation index, although they show that the items included represent different dimensions. In addition, their analysis is based on the concept of reference groups, so in addition to income and family size they include reference group factors as explanatory variables.

Current Income

Current disposable household income is central to command over resources and would obviously be expected to be negatively related to deprivation. The way in which income has been measured for our sample has already been described in detail in Chapter 3. It could be entered into the analysis in various guises—for example as a continuous variable, as a set of dummy variables, or in logarithmic form—depending on the form one expected the income-deprivation relationship to take.[3] Here we adopt the logarithmic specification, building in a declining response of deprivation to a given absolute increase in income as income rises. Overlapping with the next category, the issue also arises as to whether the income variable is to be equivalized in order to take differences in household size and composition into account, and, if so, using what equivalence scales. Here we follow previous studies in entering equivalized income into the equations, using the scales already outlined which allow 1 for the household head, 0.66 for each additional adult, and 0.33 for each child,[4] and testing the sensitivity of the results to varying the scales.

'Needs'

The living standards associated with a given level of household resources will be affected most obviously by the number of people in the household, with the chances of experiencing deprivation at any given income level rising with *household size*. The ages of household members will also matter, with children needing fewer resources than adults to avoid deprivation, and perhaps with the elderly requiring greater resources than younger adults. Differences in 'needs' arising from differences in household size and composition can be taken into account by adjusting income through equivalization as already discussed, or by entering measures of size and composition as separate explanatory variables, or both. Equivalization alone may not suffice for a number of reasons. First, we do not know which equivalence scales are the 'right' ones for our purpose, and no consensus exists as to how best to derive them. Secondly, the equivalence scales may not take all relevant differences in composition into account—some scales are based simply on size with no variation by age, for example, and most distinguish children and adults but not the elderly, who may have particular needs. Thirdly, the impact of differences in household composition may itself depend on other variables such as income level. Thus, in addition to equivalizing income, we assess whether also including variables for the number of adults and children, and

[3] Mack and Lansley used ln(*income*), for example, whereas Desai and Shah used a set of dummy variables for different income ranges.
[4] We take child to be aged under 15.

interactions between these and other variables such as income, add to explanatory power.

Illness or disability can create special needs, drawing resources from other areas and increasing the chances of deprivation, in addition to impacting on life-styles directly. Adults in our sample were asked whether they had a 'major illness, physical disability or infirmity that has troubled you for at least the past year or that is likely to go on troubling you in the future?' In the analysis we test both a dummy variable taking the value 1 when the household head said he/she was ill and 0 otherwise, and the number of adults in the household who said they were ill, to see whether these affect deprivation scores.

Location, for example living in a rural versus an urban area, may in itself increase needs and the chances of experiencing deprivation through differential access to public transport, services, or social support; we include a dummy variable taking the value 1 for households located in a rural area (defined as in open country or a village of fewer than 1,500 people), 0 otherwise.

Resources Other than Current Income

Apart from current income, the extent to which it can *draw down savings* or *borrow* are the main factors one would expect to influence a household's current spending power or command over resources, with the probability of experiencing deprivation being highest for those with little or no savings or capacity to borrow. In our survey respondents were asked to specify the range in which their deposits in banks or building societies fell, the mid-point of the range then being taken as a point estimate of the level of deposits. (While such asset data are notoriously difficult to obtain, particular attention was paid to this topic in our survey with a battery of detailed questions about deposits in different types of financial institution: Appendix 1 describes the data obtained and discusses its reliability.) As with income, and for the same reason, the variable we enter is the log of this figure. Ability to borrow is particularly difficult to measure; although we had information available on outstanding debts and current repayments on bank loans being made by households, the capacity to borrow further could be positively or negatively related to the level of current loans in different circumstances. We were therefore not able to include a measure of capacity to borrow, though some of the deprivation indicators themselves which we are seeking to explain are likely to reflect this indirectly.[5]

In addition to the household's own savings, availability of *support from family, friends, or neighbours* could be an important means of avoiding or

---

[5] The item 'debt problems' includes whether the household has had to go into debt in the last 12 months to meet ordinary living expenses, and whether it has had to sell or pawn anything worth £50 or more.

minimizing deprivation for a time for those with very limited access to other resources. Respondents in our sample were asked whether, if they were to get into financial difficulty, they thought relatives (outside the household) would help out, and we employ a dummy variable taking the value 1 where they said it would as an (admittedly imperfect) indicator of whether such help is likely to be currently available.

Other Aspects of the Current Situation

Marital status and current *labour force status* may affect both resources and needs in ways that are not reflected in income or the needs-related variables already mentioned. Income fluctuates much more for the self-employed, for example, while a household headed by a retired person or someone in home duties may have rather different needs from one where the head is in full-time employment. For labour force status we take the situation where the household head is an employee as the reference category, and include separate dummy variables for when he or she is a farmer, unemployed, retired, and in home duties. In addition to the labour force status of the household head, we also include a dummy variable taking the value 1 where the spouse of the head is at work. Being married versus single may also affect the way resources are accumulated over time, as well as patterns of expenditure, so we also include a dummy variable taking the value 1 when the household head is single.

Permanent Income

Income over a long period may affect current life-style and deprivation in a variety of ways other than through its impact on savings (which will already be included in our deposits variable). Most obviously, one would expect it to have had the major role in the household's acquisition of housing and durables over time. The effects probably go rather deeper, though, as reflected in economic theory's emphasis on the importance of permanent rather than transitory income in influencing consumers' current expenditure patterns. We therefore include in the regression analysis a number of variables that are likely to be indicators of permanent income, and hypothesize an inverse relationship between them and current deprivation .

Social class of household head, generally used to categorize households by class, should also be strongly associated with permanent income (as well as potentially picking up class-related differences in behaviour arising from cultural factors). Here we use a greatly simplified version of the CASMIN class schema developed by Erikson and Goldthorpe (1992) to classify households into four classes:

Class 1: the managerial/professional salariat or service class (CASMIN classes I and II);

Class 2: the intermediate non-manual and higher *petit bourgeoisie* class, comprising higher-grade routine white-collar workers, technicians, and supervisors of manual workers, self-employed with employees, and farmers with 50 acres or more (CASMIN IIIa, IVa, IVc 50 acres+, V);

Class 3: the upper working class and lower *petit bourgeoisie*, comprising lower-grade white-collar workers, skilled and semi-skilled manual workers, self-employed without employees, and farmers with less than 50 acres (CASMIN IIIb, IVb, IVc less than 50 acres, VI, VIIa semi-skilled);

Class 4: the lower working class, comprising unskilled manual workers and agricultural workers (CASMIN VIIa unskilled and VIIc).

With class 1 as the reference category, we include dummy variables for each of the other three classes.

The other variable we employ which may act as an indicator of permanent income represents the major form of asset accumulated by most households, namely the *value of their house* net of outstanding house-related debt. This has a positive value only for owner-occupiers, with those renting their dwelling (whether it is owned by a private landlord or public authority) having zero. An estimate of the market value of their house was sought from owner-occupiers in the survey, as were details of current mortgage repayments if any, the amount originally borrowed, and the terms of the loan. On this basis, the outstanding housing debt is estimated and subtracted from the market value of the house. Unlike deposits, assets in this form are not readily convertible into purchasing power which could be used to offset a temporary fall in income, but the amount accumulated is likely to be a good indicator of the household's expectations with regard to long-term income. Like income and deposits, we enter the variable in the equations in log form.

Background/History

The final group of variables included relate to long-term experiences and background which might have an impact on current life-style. To some extent these could reflect the impact of permanent income, over and above the variables in the preceding sub-section, but it may also be that there are other deep-seated processes whereby socio-economic background and labour market experiences affect current life-style and the probability of experiencing deprivation. We include three variables to test for such effects.

The first is the *education level* attained by the household head, since this is a key determinant of career earning power. A range of dummy variables representing different attainment levels—i.e. none beyond primary, intermediate second-level, completed second-level, and third-level—was tested, but the simple dichotomy between those with no educational qualifications and all others proved to have as much as explanatory power and so that is what is included in the results we report.

The *social class origin* of the household head might also be important. Respondents were asked whether their father or mother was the main breadwinner when they were growing up, and what his or her principal occupation was at that time. On this basis, the social class from which the household head comes is identified, using the four class categories outlined above. Respondents were also asked *how their family was able to manage financially when they were growing up*; that is, was it able to make ends meet with great difficulty, some difficulty, a little difficulty, fairly easily, easily, or very easily? We use this to construct a dummy variable taking the value 1 for those who responded that their family was able to make ends meet 'with great difficulty'. In each case we are interested in testing whether a dis-advantaged background increases the probability of currently experiencing deprivation even when one controls for current income, current social class, and other characteristics.

Being separated, divorced, or widowed may not only affect needs but also have a long-term impact on the ability of the household to accumulate resources, over and above its impact on current income. Adults in the sample were asked their marital status and we include a dummy variable taking the value 1 where the household head said they were separated, divorced, or widowed and 0 otherwise.

Finally, respondents were asked about their experiences since entering the labour market, specifically how many years of that time they spent in employment, self-employment, unemployment, illness, home duties, re-tired, or in return to education. To reflect long-term difficulties in the labour market, we use the *proportion of time in the labour force that was spent unemployed*, hypothesizing that substantial unemployment experience could be associated with a higher probability of current deprivation in ways not fully picked up by our other variables.

5.4 Determinants of Life-Style and Deprivation Scores: Results

We now proceed to the regression analysis itself. We analyse in turn the determinants of scores on the indices representing the three life-style/ deprivation dimensions identified in Chapter 4, that is the basic, housing, and secondary dimensions. We then bring these results together with a similar analysis of the summary index comprising all twenty-four items. A total of 2,400 households are included in the analysis, the remainder being excluded because of missing information on one or more of the explanatory variables.[6] (The households omitted on this basis do not differ substantially

---

[6] This arises primarily because some of the explanatory variables, such as unemployment experience during one's career or social class origins, were not included in a shortened version of the questionnaire which was administered when a full questionnaire could not be com-pleted, and was in some cases filled in by another household member—e.g. when the individual concerned was ill or never at home or reluctant to co-operate fully.

from those that could be retained, in terms of such characteristics as income, composition, or age of household head.) The analysis consists of ordinary least squares regression of household (enforced lack) index scores, for the various indices, on the explanatory variables we have just described. We first show the results when only income is entered as an independent variable, and then progressively widen the set to include the variables related to needs, other resources, other aspects of current situation, permanent income, and finally background/history. This allows us to demonstrate the extent to which these different groups of variables add to the explanatory power of the equation.

The Basic Index

Table 5.3 presents the results for the basic deprivation index. We see in column (1) that income alone clearly has a substantial negative impact on basic deprivation scores, but explains a relatively low proportion of the variance in scores as reflected in the R^2 of 0.09. Even though income is equivalized, when the number of children in the household is added to the equation column (2) shows it is significant, the predicted deprivation score rising with the number of children. However, an interaction term between income and number of children is also significant but negative, indicating that the impact of an additional child on basic deprivation falls as income rises. (Number of adults was also tested, but it is not significant in this or any of the other results and is thus not shown in the table.) Basic deprivation appears to be inversely related to the age of the household head (with the nonlinear term insignificant, so this effect does not fall away for the elderly). Urban location and having a chronically ill household head also significantly add to the predicted score. The explanatory power of the equation is considerably higher, the R^2 doubling to 0.17.

When the measures of the level of deposits the household has in financial institutions and the availability of financial support from friends or relatives are included in column (3), both are significant and the coefficients have the hypothesized negative sign.

Column (4) shows the results when marital and labour force status of the household head, whether the spouse is at work, social class, and the value of the house are added to the equation. Marital status is not significant, but several of the labour force status dummy variables are highly significant. The reference labour force category omitted from the equation is 'Employee': compared with that, where the household head is unemployed, away from work because of illness or disability, or in home duties, this adds significantly to the predicted basic deprivation score. Interestingly, having a farmer or retired person as head does not do so. Where the spouse of the head is in work the predicted score is lower. Of the social class dummies, only that for the lower working class is significant, with a positive

Independent variable	(1)	(2)	(3)	(4)	(5)
Constant	3.17	2.55	2.69	2.02	1.55
Equivalent income	-0.58***	-0.39***	-0.33***	-0.20***	-0.16***
Number of children		0.38***	0.38***	0.29***	0.25***
Income children		-0.23***	-0.22***	-0.15***	-0.12***
Age		-0.008***	-0.01***	0.24***	-0.01*
Age^2		—	—	—	—
Chronic illness		0.34***	0.33***	0.17**	0.15*
Urban		0.24***	0.27***	0.24***	0.25***
Deposits			-0.0001***	-0.0001*	-0.0001
Support from relatives etc.			-0.44***	-0.40***	-0.34***
Single				0.67***	0.41***
Unemployed				0.48***	0.43***
Sick				0.51***	0.42***
Home duties				—	—
Retired				—	—
Farmer				—	—
Spouse at work				-0.16*	-0.13*
Intermediate non-manual class				—	—
Upper working class				—	—
Lower working class				0.29**	0.16*
House value				-0.00001***	-0.00001***
No qualifications					0.12*
Difficulties growing up					0.27***
Separated/divorced/widowed					0.98***
Proportion of time unemployed					1.96***
Multiple R	0.299	0.420	0.451	0.525	0.562
Adjusted R^2	0.089	0.174	0.201	0.271	0.310

$*p < 0.1$ $**p < 0.01$ $***p < 0.001$

coefficient as one would expect. Net house value is also highly significant and negative.

Finally, adding in the other background/history variables in column (5), we find significant coefficients for all four of these. Having a head who has no educational qualifications, was raised in a family under financial strain, is separated/divorced/widowed, or has had substantial unemployment experience in his or her career—all raise the predicted basic deprivation score. Thus, as well as household income, most of the other explanatory variables available to us have proved significant in explaining current basic deprivation. It is worth emphasizing how much they have increased our ability to explain the observed variation across households in basic deprivation scores: the adjusted R^2 has risen from 0.09 with income alone to 0.31 with the full set of explanatory variables. As variables are added and the explanatory power of the equation increases, income remains highly significant but its coefficient falls, from −0.58 when it is the only independent variable to −0.16 when the full set of variables are included.

The Housing Index

Moving on to the housing dimension, Table 5.4 shows the corresponding regression results when the dependent variable is the household's score on the index for enforced lack of housing items. Once again, in column (1) current equivalent income is the only explanatory variable. It is seen to have a substantial negative impact on basic deprivation scores, but explains an even lower proportion of the variance in scores than with the basic index, as reflected in the R^2 of 0.04.

Adding needs-related variables in column (2), the number of children in the household and the interaction term between income and number of children are not now significant. The age of the household head and age-squared are now both significant, the former with a negative coefficient and the latter with a positive one. This pattern, and the size of the estimated coefficients, mean that, *ceteris paribus*, the predicted housing deprivation score falls as the age of the head rises but at a declining rate until, after age 75, it begins to go up again. Having a chronically ill household head significantly adds to the predicted score, but urban location now reduces the predicted score. The inclusion of these variables leads to a doubling of the R^2, to 0.08.

When the measures of savings and availability of support are included in column (3), both are again are significant with negative coefficients. Column (4) shows that being single is now highly significant with a positive coefficient. The labour force status dummy variables also show quite a different pattern from that seen with the basic index: it is now having as head a farmer or person engaged in home duties that adds significantly to the predicted score, with being unemployed insignificant. Having the

Independent variable	(1)	(2)	(3)	(4)	(5)
Constant	1.69	2.11	2.33	1.91	1.51
Equivalent income	-0.29***	-0.28***	-0.23***	-0.16***	-0.11***
Number of children		—	—	—	—
Income children		—	—	—	—
Age		-0.03***	-0.03***	-0.03***	-0.03***
Age^2		0.0004***	0.0004***	0.0004***	0.0004***
Chronic illness		0.17***	0.16***	0.15***	0.13***
Urban		-0.12***	-0.12***	-0.12***	-0.12**
Deposits			-0.0001***	-0.0001***	-0.0001***
Support from relatives etc.			-0.34***	-0.27***	-0.23***
Single				0.60***	0.62***
Unemployed				—	—
Sick				0.34***	0.33***
Home duties					
Retired					
Farmer				0.18***	0.18**
Spouse at work				-0.10*	-0.08*
Intermediate non-manual class				—	—
Upper working class				0.33***	0.23***
Lower working class					
House value					
No qualifications					0.11*
Difficulties growing up					0.15***
Separated/divorced/widowed					0.21*
Proportion of time unemployed					0.74***
Multiple R	0.207	0.290	0.337	0.424	0.443
Adjusted R^2	0.043	0.082	0.111	0.176	0.191

*$p < 0.1$ **$p < 0.01$ ***$p < 0.001$

spouse of the head in work reduces the predicted score, and being in the lower working class increases it. Net house value is, perhaps surprisingly, not significant. Adding in the other background/history variables in column (5), all are significant with positive coefficients, as was the case for the basic index. When all the additional significant variables are included, we see that the R^2 is now up to 0.19.

The Secondary Index

Table 5.5 shows the corresponding regression results for scores on the index for enforced lack of secondary items. Current equivalent income has a substantially greater impact on this than on basic or housing deprivation scores, as seen in its much higher coefficient in column (1), and alone explains a considerably higher proportion of the variance in secondary deprivation scores, with an R^2 of 0.15. Adding needs-related variables in column (2), the number of children in the household and interaction term between income and number of children are now significant, as they were for the basic index. The age of the household head is not significant, and neither is having a chronically ill household head or an urban location.

When the measures of savings and availability of support are added in column (3), both are significant with negative coefficients. In column (4) we see that being single is in this case insignificant, and the significant labour force status dummy variables are being unemployed, sick/disabled, or in home duties. Having the spouse of the head in work reduces the predicted score. Now each of the three social class dummies, not just the lower working class, are significant, with the predicted score rising steadily as one moves down from the reference category omitted from the equation, the higher managerial/professional class. Net house value is now highly significant with a negative coefficient.

In column (5) one sees that, when the other background/history variables are added, all are again significant with positive coefficients. The R^2 increases steadily as the groups of explanatory variables are added, reaching 0.38 when the full set is included.

The Twenty-Four-Item Index

Before further discussion of the estimated equations for the different dimensions, it is worth also looking at the results produced by a similar analysis of the enforced lack summary index which simply aggregates across all twenty-four items, ignoring the existence of the different dimensions. These results are shown in Table 5.6. Income alone is highly significant, with an R^2 of 0.16. Adding in the different groups of explanatory variables shows that almost all are significant, the only exceptions being the quadratic age term, urban location, marital status, and the intermediate non-manual

Independent variable	(1)	(2)	(3)	(4)	(5)
Constant	7.67	6.40	6.36	4.56	3.87
Equivalent income	-1.23***	-0.95***	-0.79***	-0.46***	-0.39***
Number of children		0.48***	0.47***	0.28***	0.26***
Income children		-0.29***	-0.29***	-0.14***	-0.11***
Age					—
Age^2					—
Chronic illness					—
Urban					—
Deposits ($\div$ 1000)			-0.00004***	-0.00004***	-0.00004***
Support from relaives etc.			-0.64***	-0.52***	-0.44***
Single					—
Unemployed				0.95***	0.90***
Sick				0.89***	0.84***
Home duties				0.83***	0.69***
Retired					—
Farmer					—
Spouse at work				-0.22**	-0.18
Intermediate non-manual class				0.39***	0.26*
Upper working class				0.76***	0.56***
Lower working class				1.30***	0.98***
House value ($\div$ 1000)				-0.00002***	-0.00002***
No qualifications					0.40***
Difficulties growing up					0.38***
Separated/divorced/widowed					0.94***
Proportion of time unemployed					0.88*
Multiple R	0.386	0.426	0.484	0.603	0.618
Adjusted R^2	0.149	0.180	0.232	0.360	0.377

$*p < 0.1$ $**p < 0.01$ $***p < 0.001$

Table 5.6 Determinants of scores on 24-item enforced lack index

Independent variable	(1)	(2)	(3)	(4)	(5)
Constant	12.53	10.80	10.88	7.92	6.96
Equivalent income	-2.10***	-1.59***	-1.31***	-0.69***	-0.60***
Number of children		0.80***	0.78***	0.47***	0.39***
Income children		-0.53***	-0.52***	-0.25***	-0.20***
Age		-0.02**	-0.01**	-0.01*	-0.02**
Age^2					
Ill		1.11***	1.08***	0.55***	0.51***
Urban		—	—	—	—
Deposits			-0.00008***	-0.00005***	-0.00005***
Support from relatives etc.			-1.37***	-1.17***	-1.04***
Single				—	—
Unemployed				1.84***	1.39***
Sick				1.39***	1.22***
Home duties				1.98***	1.72***
Retired				0.57***	0.48*
Farmer				0.88***	0.68***
Spouse at work				-0.64***	-0.56***
Intermediate non-manual class				—	—
Upper working class				0.66***	0.43***
Lower working class				1.74***	1.27***
House value				-0.00004***	-0.00004***
No qualifications					0.59***
Difficulties growing up					0.77***
Separated/divorced/widowed					1.94***
Proportion of time unemployed					3.38***
Multiple R	0.404	0.468	0.525	0.643	0.665
Adjusted R^2	0.163	0.218	0.274	0.409	0.438

*$p < 0.1$ **$p < 0.01$ ***$p < 0.001$

class dummy. When all the significant variables are included, the R^2 for the full set has risen very substantially, to 0.44.

Comparing the Results for the Different Dimensions

To highlight the similarities and differences between the estimation results for the basic, housing and secondary indices, we now bring together the full estimated equation for each with that for the aggregate twenty-four-item index, which is done in Table 5.7. Focusing first on the similarities, the most striking is that, although income is significant in each case, it falls very far short of exhausting our ability to predict deprivation scores. Second, the measures of wider resources add significantly to predictive power across all the equations. Third, the same is true of variables related to permanent income and background, that is membership of the unskilled manual social class, having no educational qualifications, having substantial unemployment experience, being separated/divorced or widowed, and having been raised in a household undergoing financial difficulties. It is remarkable that, even when one controls for current income and a variety of other factors relating to current situation, such long-term characteristics are seen to underpin the pattern of current deprivation. Finally, having the household head in home duties raises the predicted scores on all three indices.

Now turning to the differences, the first is the varying extent to which the equations explain the different aspects of deprivation. We saw earlier that the simple correlation with income was highest for the secondary dimension, and considerably lower for the basic and housing ones. Employing the full set of explanatory variables, we are once again most successful in accounting for the variation in secondary dimension scores, with an R^2 of 0.38. The ability to explain scores on the basic deprivation increases more, however, and the R^2 achieved in the full equation is not very much lower than that, at 0.31. We are now least successful in explaining scores on the housing index, with an R^2 in the full equation of 0.19.

Important differences across the indices also emerged in the impact of a substantial number of the independent variables. Having equivalized income, the number of children (and the interaction between this and income) were significant for basic and secondary scores but not for housing. Age was not significant for secondary scores and was significant for basic and housing ones, but differed between them in its impact since the quadratic term was significant only for housing. Being in an urban rather than a rural area was significant for basic deprivation scores only, as was being chronically ill or disabled. Being single was a significant predictor of housing deprivation but not of the other two dimensions. The pattern for labour force status also varied, with current unemployment or illness being significant predictors of basic and secondary but not housing deprivation, while being a farmer added to the probability of housing but not basic or second-

Table 5.7 Summary of results for determinants of scores on basic, housing, secondary and all items indices

Independent variable	Basic	Housing	Secondary	Aggregate
Constant	1.55	1.51	3.87	6.96
Equivalent income	-0.16***	-0.11***	-0.39***	-0.60***
Number of children	0.25***	—	0.26***	0.39***
Income children	-0.12***	—	-0.11***	-0.20***
Age	-0.01*	-0.03***	—	-0.02**
Age^2	—	0.0004***	—	—
Chronic illness	0.15*	0.13**	—	0.51***
Urban	0.25***	-0.12**	—	—
Deposits	-0.00001	-0.0001***	-0.00004***	-0.00005***
Support from relatives etc.	-0.34***	-0.23***	-0.44***	-1.04***
Single	—	0.62***	—	—
Unemployed	0.41***	—	0.90***	1.39***
Sick	0.43***	—	0.84***	1.22***
Home duties	0.42***	0.33***	0.69***	1.72***
Retired	—	—	—	0.48*
Farmer	—	0.18**	—	0.68***
Spouse at work	-0.13*	-0.08*	-0.18	-0.56***
Intermediate non-manual class	—	—	0.26*	—
Upper working class	—	—	0.56***	0.43***
Lower working class	0.16*	0.23***	0.98***	1.27***
House value	-0.00001***	—	-0.00002***	-0.00004***
No qualifications	0.12*	0.11*	0.40***	0.59***
Difficulties growing up	0.27***	0.15***	0.38***	0.77***
Separated/divorced/widowed	0.98***	0.21*	0.94***	1.94***
Proportion of time unemployed	1.96***	0.74***	0.88*	3.38***
Multiple R	0.562	0.443	0.618	0.665
Adjusted R^2	0.310	0.191	0.377	0.438

*$p < 0.01$ **$p < 0.001$ ***$p < 0.001$

ary deprivation. While being in the lower working class was significant for all three indices, distinguishing between the other three classes was helpful only in predicting secondary deprivation. While the four variables related to background/history are significant for all three indices, unemployment experience is seen to have a greater impact on basic deprivation than on scores on the other two indices.

Overall, then, the equations suggest that basic deprivation is associated with low current equivalent income and membership of the lower working class but is also particularly likely where the household has little or no savings to fall back on, where there are children, where there is chronic illness/disability, and where there is not only current unemployment but a history of unemployment experience. The secondary deprivation index, on the other hand, behaves rather more like an overall indicator of living standards, being the most strongly influenced by current income, current labour force status, and the gradations of social class, and being highly correlated with assets accumulated in the form of housing. The housing index is quite distinctive: while income and social class do of course play a role, the relationship with current labour force status, age, marital status, and family type is different from the other dimensions, with single people and farm households particularly likely to experience this but not the other forms of deprivation.

5.5 Conclusions

The levels of correlation between current income reported in surveys and indicators of life-style or deprivation are rather modest in our own survey, as in previous studies. This has been taken by some to mean on the one hand that these indicators primarily reflect differences in tastes, or on the other that reported income is entirely unreliable. Without understanding this relationship, one cannot then be confident about how best to measure poverty or understand the processes producing it. This chapter has presented an in-depth analysis of the determinants of the scores of our sample households on deprivation indices reflecting the three distinct clusters of indicators we have identified. Regression analysis has estimated the relationships between these scores and a wide range of independent variables, covering current income, savings and other assets, factors affecting demands on household resources, labour force status, social class and class background, education, and experience of unemployment. We take a number of key messages from the results of this analysis.

The first conclusion is that current income is an important influence on deprivation, but so are many other aspects of a household's current situation and how they arrived there. The fact that the income–deprivation relationship is not more pronounced does *not* mean that differences in tastes are dominating life-style and thus undermining the use of indicators of life-style and deprivation in measuring poverty. When a wide range of other explanatory variables is included, the surprise is how much rather than how little of the variance in deprivation scores we can explain (by comparison with the levels of explanatory power usually attained in the social sciences).

This does mean that it is important that current income not be taken as the sole indicator of current living standards and/or command over resources in measuring poverty. Rather than discarding it entirely, though, it should be possible to combine income and direct measures of deprivation to improve the way poverty is measured, as we explore in Chapter 6.

The results highlight the role of long-term factors in influencing a household's current situation even when one controls for current income level, relating most importantly to the way resources have been accumulated or eroded over time. The recent literature, drawing on panel survey data for a number of countries, has highlighted the importance of adopting a dynamic perspective to understanding unemployment and poverty, focusing on for example the duration of unemployment and poverty spells. Our results reinforce the crucial role of dynamics, but suggest that the focus also needs to be longer-term, rather than simply on dynamics from one year to the next.

Finally, the fact that the various explanatory variables were seen to impact rather differently on the basic, housing, and secondary indices shows how important it can be to distinguish between different dimensions in using deprivation indicators to measure poverty. This has implications for the type of indicators one would wish to employ in applying combined income and deprivation criteria to identify poor households, which are also taken up in the next chapter.

6

Income, Deprivation, and Poverty

6.1 Introduction

The relationship between current income, wider resources, and experience of deprivation is a complex one. We have seen in Chapter 5 that there is indeed considerable variation in the extent of deprivation being experienced by households at a similar level of current income, which is consistent with earlier studies such as Townsend (1979), Mack and Lansley (1985), and Mayer and Jencks (1988). What we have been able to show, going beyond these studies, is that this variation is to a significant degree explicable in terms of household characteristics and previous experiences. Shifting from a static to a dynamic perspective, not only current income but the accumulation and erosion of resources over a long period are seen to affect current living standards. The criticism of the use of deprivation indicators that they must primarily reflect differences in tastes rather than resources because they are relatively weakly related to current income thus loses much of its force. In understanding why people are poor and how to alleviate poverty, this focuses attention on the dynamic processes at work, particularly in the labour market, and we turn our attention to the implications for framing policy in Chapter 9.

Before doing so, it is necessary to grasp the nettle and ask, in the light of what we have learned, how deprivation indicators can best employed in measuring poverty. As outlined back in Chapter 1, our aim is to take as starting-point the definition of poverty as *exclusion* arising from *lack of resources*, and to see how information on deprivation indicators and income can be used to incorporate both exclusion and lack of resources directly into the poverty measure. Ringen's critique of reliance on income in measuring poverty is based on the argument that income is not a *satisfactory* measure of poverty because many of those not on low income suffer deprivation in consumption, and far from all the members of low income groups suffer such deprivation. One key implication of the results of our analysis in Chapters 4 and 5 of the relationship between income and a much broader and more satisfactory set of deprivation indicators than were available to Ringen is that this critique is well founded.

We now follow through on his conclusion that, if poverty is defined as exclusion resulting from lack of resources, the poor must therefore ident-ified using both a consumption/deprivation and an income criterion: exclusion is to be measured directly, together with an income criterion to exclude those who have a low standard of living for reasons other than low income. As we have seen in Chapter 4, this is not the approach to poverty measurement adopted even by most of the studies that have attempted to measure deprivation directly. Townsend (1979) used scores on his deprivation index to try to identify an income poverty line, corresponding to the point below which deprivation escalated, and Townsend and Gordon (1989) also sought to identify an income cut-off. Mack and Lansley (1985) focused on those who were experiencing self-assessed enforced lack of three or more out of a set of twenty-two necessities, although they did look at the difference made by excluding those on 'high' incomes even if they were reporting such deprivation.[1]

If the objective is to identify exclusion resulting from lack of resources, neither of these approaches is adequate. Using an income threshold alone, even one identified on the basis of the extent of observed deprivation at different income levels, is unsatisfactory because a substantial proportion of those below any such line are not experiencing such deprivation. In addition, in our judgement the theoretical and empirical support for the existence of a Townsend-type threshold below which deprivation escalates is itself unconvincing: as we discuss below, the fact that factors other than current income have been shown here to have such a substantial impact on current deprivation scores makes the notion of such a threshold somewhat implausible. Using deprivation scores to identify the poor directly, on the other hand, faces the opposite problem that a substantial proportion of those reporting (what they consider to be enforced) deprivation are not on low current incomes. Mack and Lansley's imposition of additional income criteria is rather *ad hoc* and still gives more weight to deprivation scores than income in identifying the poor. Here, by contrast, we will give equal weight to both elements in seeking to identify those who are experiencing deprivation because of low income/low command over resources.

As mentioned in Chapter 4, Ringen (1988) himself briefly illustrates the joint use of consumption and income criteria with data from Sweden, but with a very limited and unsatisfactory set of indicators of consumption deprivation. In addition, he adds to the general confusion by applying relative income lines together with an unchanged 'absolute' consumption deprivation standard to 1968 and 1981, on the grounds that poverty should be measured by some combination of relative and absolute standards (p. 361). The logic behind this suggestion is far from clear, and the issue of how best to employ deprivation indicators over time will be pursued later: we concentrate at this stage simply on the use of combined income/deprivation criteria at a point in time.

[1] They also look at the difference made by including as poor those on low incomes lacking three or more items even where they said they were doing without by choice—see Mack and Lansley (1985: 175–83).

It is important to be clear about the purpose of the exercise. Veit-Wilson (1989) has distinguished between aiming to *count* the numbers defined as poor, to *explain* why people are poor, and to *prescribe*, *report*, or *discover* an income poverty line. If the relationship between current income and deprivation is not so strong, then counting those excluded because of a lack of resources and discovering an income poverty line (presumably defined as an income level below which 'most' people are excluded because of a lack of resources and above which they are not) become distinct exercises. Our aim is to identify and count those who are excluded because of a lack of resources. We see this as a crucial first step in explaining the processes that lead to people being in that situation, which *may* also allow conclusions to be drawn about the minimum resources necessary to avoid such exclusion. We explore in Chapter 9 the implications of the results for assessing the adequacy of social security support rates, but the objective is not to discover an income poverty line. Rather, it is to follow through the logic of incorporating both exclusion and lack of resources in identifying the poor.

In this chapter, we first discuss how the deprivation indicators developed in Chapters 4 and 5 are best employed together with income information with this aim in view. For reasons to be explained, the basic deprivation index is felt to be more appropriate than the housing or secondary index, or the summary index encompassing all three dimensions, for this purpose. We therefore focus on households that are both below income thresholds and appear to be experiencing enforced basic deprivation. The number and characteristics of these households are compared with those who fall below relative income poverty lines, described in Chapter 3, so that one can see how much difference the use of combined income 'plus' deprivation criteria makes. Multivariate analysis is then employed to look at the factors distinguishing households which (1) have low incomes and are experiencing enforced basic deprivation, (2) report enforced deprivation but do not have low incomes, (3) have low incomes but do not report enforced deprivation, and (4) do not have low incomes and do not report basic deprivation. The validity of this categorization is assessed by reference to a number of other characteristics of the households, and the explanations for how households find themselves in the 'inconsistent' groups are discussed. Finally, the levels of enforced deprivation of housing and secondary items being experienced by each of these groups is described, and the relationship between these items, resources, and generalized exclusion discussed.

6.2   Combining Income and Deprivation Criteria:
The Approach

In seeking to identify those excluded owing to lack of resources, we have to decide how best to use the indicators of deprivation and the income data available to us. As far as deprivation is concerned, one option would be to use the full set of twenty-four indicators on which we have information. This could involve simply using the summary index constructed from all twenty-four items described in Chapter 5, where absence of any item adds 1 to the household's score. Alternatively, we could follow Hallerod (1995) and construct a weighted index, where each item is weighted by the proportion in the sample regarding it as a necessity. In that way, all the items contribute to the deprivation measure but those whose absence is likely to be most severely felt add more to the index. However, some of the items included by Hallerod were neither possessed nor regarded as necessities by a majority of the sample. While we can see some logic in including such items in a measure of living standards, they do not appear to us to have a role to play—even with a low weighting—as indicators of generalized deprivation. Our aim, as spelt out earlier, is to measure inability to afford socially defined necessities: knowing that a household cannot afford an item regarded as a necessity by only 10 per cent of the population (such as access to a summer cottage, in Hallerod's Swedish sample) tells us something about that household's living standards but nothing at all about its ability to obtain such necessities.

The second option, followed by Townsend and by Mack and Lansley, is to select the sub-set of items possessed by a majority (Townsend) or re-garded as a necessity by a majority (Mack and Lansley) as suitable to represent deprivation, and aggregate those in an index. We have already noted that Mack and Lansley's case for selecting items perceived as necessi-ties, rather than applying a criterion in terms of possession, is in our view a strong one, because it is consistent with the social construction of expec-tations underlying the notion of poverty as exclusion. One could object that a bare majority seems a rather modest criterion: to be a 'socially defined necessity', it would seem more reasonable that an item be regarded as a necessity by 'most' people. However, the more fundamental objection is that the results of our factor analysis clearly showed that these items cluster into different dimensions, and that simply selecting items regarded as necessities and adding them across these dimensions fails to take this into account.

Each dimension contains important information about life-styles and living standards, but here, given our objective, we concentrate on what we have termed the basic dimension. As we have seen, the items in the basic deprivation index clearly represent socially perceived necessities and are possessed by most people,[2] they reflect rather basic aspects of current

---

[2] Information on three of the items in the basic index—going without heat, going without a substantial meal all day, and running into debt to meet ordinary living expenses, etc.—was obtained under a different format from the others, and avoiding rather than 'possessing' them indicates absence of deprivation, but for convenience we refer to 'possessing' across all the items. For these items also we do not have the views of the respondents as to whether they constitute necessities, but as argued in Ch. 4 the nature of the items makes it likely that they are so regarded by most people.

material deprivation, and they cluster together, which lends support to the notion that they are useful as indicators of the underlying generalized deprivation we are trying to measure. Most of the items in the secondary dimension, on the other hand, are not overwhelmingly regarded as necessities. (Less than 60 per cent on average see them as necessities, as against an average of over 80 per cent for the items in the 'basic' set.[3]) The housing and durables items are possessed by most people and regarded as necessities by almost everyone (except for the TV). However, we have seen that they do not relate to the current resources and extent of exclusion of the household in the same way as the basic items. The fact that they do not cluster with the basic items itself means that rather different households and causal processes are involved. Deprivation in terms of housing and related durables appears to be a product of very specific factors, and so the housing items, though providing valuable information about one aspect of living standards, are not satisfactory as indicators of current generalized exclusion.

It must be emphasized that this will not necessarily hold for all types of housing indicator, or for other societies where the housing market is structured differently. (Indeed, at a more general level, our anxiety to avoid reification of the particular dimensions we have identified is to be emphasized: our interest is in analytical approaches to the identification of satisfactory measures of generalized deprivation). Returning to the housing and secondary items towards the end of this chapter, we proceed by concentrating on the items in the basic dimension. It is important to be clear about why we do so: it is not because we wish to prescribe in a normative fashion a hierarchy in which people *should* satisfy their needs, or to focus exclusively on a particular set of items. Rather, the respondents' evaluations, the results of the factor analysis, and the analysis of the relationship between the different items and household resources leads us to believe that these are the best indicators available to us of the generalized underlying deprivation we are trying to measure.

The first stage in identifying households that are excluded because of a lack of resources is therefore to look at scores on the eight-item index of enforced basic deprivation. So far, for this and the other indices, we have been using household responses as to whether they were doing without the item because they could not afford it or by choice to indicate if lack was 'enforced'. By using these responses for the five items in the basic index for which that information is available, we know that the household in question states that absence of the item is enforced by lack of resources. However,

---

[3] 'Being able to save regularly', although stated to be a necessity by most people, we do not regard as satisfactory as an indicator of generalized exclusion in the Irish context because it is lacked by 57% of the sample. Having a hobby or leisure activity is also widely considered a necessity and is possessed by 67% (and in fact loads more heavily on the basic dimension in the factor analysis). We do not include it in our preferred measure of deprivation principally because of its vagueness and ambiguity: a hobby or leisure activity could mean quite different things to different people, involving a very different commitment of resources.

this is helpful but not sufficient as a measure of resource constraints, since these responses apply individual rather than societal standards to what constitutes 'enforced'. Simply relying on individual assessments gives rise to two concerns in this context. The first is that some of the households that lack basic items but say this is by choice may have grown accustomed to doing without, or may be reluctant to admit they cannot afford something most people have, whereas by societal standards they are doing without because of lack of resources. The second is that, conversely, some of those reporting enforced basic deprivation are on relatively high incomes, and by societal standards would be regarded as able to afford the item.

Focusing first on those who are lacking one or more of the basic items but say this is by choice, it is helpful to look at their average income compared with households that have the item, and with households which are reporting enforced lack. What we find is that their mean income is much closer to the former than the latter. About 12 per cent of the sample lack one or more of the basic items but do not report an enforced lack of any, and these households have a mean equivalent income of £92 per week. The 58 per cent of the sample that do not lack any of the items have a mean equivalent income of £99 per week. The remaining 30 per cent of the sample, which report enforced lack of at least one of the basic items, have a mean income of only £62 per week. This provides some basis for accepting at face value the subjective assessments of those who say they are doing without basic items by choice. (It is worth mentioning that this contrast is less pronounced for some of our other items, and so this should not be taken as a general validation of the 'doing without by choice' responses across all items.) Some of the households reporting that they are doing without basic items by choice are on low incomes, but their low incomes alone are not sufficient to make us discount their subjective assessments precisely because a significant number on similar income levels do not lack any of the items. We therefore feel justified in concentrating on those reporting enforced lack of basic items, rather than on all those lacking such items. Any resulting downward bias in our estimate of the extent of exclusion arising from lack of resources could not be large, as we shall see. Given what we have learnt about the relationship between current income and deprivation, the alternative (looked at by Mack and Lansley) of counting lack as necessarily enforced for all those on low incomes appears more likely to over-estimate the numbers experiencing exclusion arising from lack of resources.

What about the second and more substantial area of concern, which is that—as we saw in Chapter 5—many of the households reporting enforced lack of basic items are on relatively high incomes? Enforcement owing to lack of resources needs to relate to societal rather than simply individual standards and expectations, and needs to be taken into account directly if the poverty measure is to be fully consistent with the definition. This provides the rationale for focusing on those households that are experiencing both basic deprivation and relatively low incomes. Such a focus was justified by Ringen in the following terms:

A state of general deprivation cannot be measured with either resource indicators or way of life indicators alone ... Resource indicators alone can only say something about the probability of deprivation in way of life. Low income, for example, may represent only a temporary and atypical situation which does not force the person in question to change his life style—he may for a while live off savings—and there may be ways of avoiding a life in deprivation in spite of low income, such as to live on someone else's income. To ascertain poverty we need to identify directly the consequences we normally expect to follow from low income. On the other hand, to rely on way of life indicators alone, that is, to go all out for direct measurement, is also insufficient since people may live as if they were poor without being poor ... We need to establish not only that people live as if they were poor but that they do so because they do not have the means to avoid it. (Ringen 1987: 161–2)

We will therefore identify as excluded owing to lack of resources only those reporting enforced lack of basic items *and* on low income. But what constitutes low income? Rather than seek to derive an income threshold, using a range of income lines at this stage allows us to see the consequences of varying the income criterion for the numbers and types of household identified as poor. For this purpose we employ relative income lines derived from average equivalent disposable income in the sample in the manner described in Chapter 3; lines going from 40 to 80 per cent of that mean are employed for illustration.

6.3 Combining Income and Deprivation Criteria: the Results

Table 6.1 shows the percentage of households in the sample falling below each of these income thresholds *and* experiencing enforced deprivation of at least one basic item. This ranges from 3 per cent using the lowest, i.e. 40 per cent , relative income line to 23 per cent of all households using 80 per

Table 6.1 Percentages of households below relative income thresholds and experiencing basic deprivation

Relative income line	% below income line and:	
	Experiencing enforced basic deprivation	Experiencing enforced lack of 2 or more basic items
40%	3.3	2.0
50%	9.8	6.6
60%	16.0	10.7
70%	20.9	12.7
80%	23.2	14.0

cent of mean equivalent income as the cut-off. Before seeking to narrow the income range that one might consider relevant, we have to ask whether a score of 1 on the basic index should suffice to indicate exclusion for current purposes, or whether higher scores should be taken. To see how sensitive the results are to such a choice, Table 6.1 also shows the percentage reporting enforced lack of two or more basic items who are below each income line. We see that, using for example the 60 per cent income line, a score of 2 or more would identify 11 per cent of households as 'poor', whereas 16 per cent are below that line and scoring 1 or more.

Here it is essential to emphasize that the presence or absence of a *particular* item in itself is not crucial. The set of items measured is intended to serve as an indicator of pervasive exclusion from ordinary living patterns—what Ringen describes as a state of general deprivation—which is the latent or underlying variable one is trying to measure. On conceptual grounds, we would argue that genuinely enforced deprivation of even one socially defined necessity should be sufficient to indicate such pervasive exclusion. Given the way in which the basic index has been constructed—the nature of the items themselves, the fact that the factor analysis showed that they cluster together, and that only subjectively assessed enforced lack is counted—and that an income criterion is also to be applied, we would argue that even a score of 1 on that index should be employed to indicate generalized deprivation.

One measure of the reliability of our measure is again to calculate Cronbach's alpha, which as we saw in Chapter 4 can be interpreted as the correlation between an index based on this particular set of items and all other possible indices containing the same number of items which could be constructed from a hypothetical universe of items that measure the characteristic of interest. Variation in the size of the alpha coefficient can also provide evidence relevant to the validity of our measure. As we impose increasingly stringent conditions in order to ensure that the items are lacking because of resource constraints, we would expect that the increased precision of our measure should be reflected in the size of the alpha coefficient, and this is indeed what happens. When we focus simply on absence of the items in the basic index, the alpha coefficient is 0.71; restricting our attention to what is stated to be enforced absence raises this to 0.76; finally, as one imposes income conditions employing the 70, 60, and 50 per cent lines respectively, the coefficient increases from 0.80 to 0.82 and finally to 0.85.

Our confidence that the conclusions regarding levels of enforced deprivation are not dependent on random factors associated with specific indicators is consequently extremely high. Our conclusions regarding levels of poverty are dependent, however, not simply on the position on a continuum of deprivation, but on our choice of criterion of the enforced absence of one basic item. Once again, however, the removal of any particular item has little effect on our conclusions. As we might expect, given its more general nature, it is the item relating to entering debt in order to provide for ordinary living expenses that produces the highest number of households reporting deprivation. Even so, the exclusion of this item has only a modest effect, changing our estimate of the percentage of households below the 60% income line and experiencing basic deprivations from 16 to 14.6 per cent. For all other estimates employing seven rather than eight indicators, the poverty rate remains in the range 15–16 per cent. Our conclusions relating to the extent of poverty thus remain extremely robust, and conclusions about the types of household affected by poverty are even less dependent on any specific indicator in our set.

Turning to the income threshold, it may be possible to apply sensible upper and lower limits to the range to be considered. In broad terms, for our sample such a range may be bounded by the 50 and 70 per cent relative lines. Below the 50 per cent line, the income levels involved are lower than most of the existing social welfare support rates. Further, households below the 40 per cent line have lower levels of basic deprivation and are less likely to state that they are having extreme difficulty making ends meet than those between the 40 and 50 per cent thresholds. This is related to the nature of the households involved and in particular to their resources over the longer term, as will be shown. Above the 70 per cent income threshold, on the other hand, the income levels involved are significantly higher than most of the social welfare system's support rates. Most of the households between the 70 and 80 per cent lines are not experiencing primary deprivation, and the proportion reporting extreme difficulty in making ends meet is considerably lower than for households between the 60% and 70 per cent lines. We will therefore proceed to focus on this income range, and generally present results using the 60 per cent line where the conclusions would not be substantially altered by substituting the 50 or 70 per cent ones.

Combining enforced basic deprivation and an income line of between 50 and 70 per cent of the mean, Table 6.1 would thus identify between 10 and 20 per cent of the households in our sample as excluded because of a lack of resources. These poverty rates produced by the combined income/basic deprivation criteria can be contrasted with the total numbers below the relative income poverty lines, discussed in Chapter 3. We saw there that between 10 and 30 per cent of households would be counted as poor, depending on the choice of an income cut-off between 40 and 60 per cent of average equivalent income which is the range conventionally employed in applying these lines. Approximately half the households below these income lines are also reporting enforced basic deprivation, so simply adding the basic deprivation criterion to these lines would cut the estimated poverty rates in half. However, we are focusing on the higher income range of 50–70 per cent with our combined income-plus-deprivation criteria, for the reasons just outlined, and so our range of estimated poverty rates goes up to two-thirds of the level produced by the relative income lines alone.

It would of course be convenient if a single income line rather than a range could be employed, together with deprivation scores, to produce a single estimate of the numbers in poverty. The basic deprivation scores themselves do not in our view provide a basis for identifying a particular income line *à la* Townsend. As we saw in Chapter 5, apart from the anomalous position of the bottom decile, mean basic deprivation scores decline fairly steadily as one moves up the income distribution. Indeed, a simple linear relationship with income decile accounts for almost 90 per cent of the variation across the deciles in mean basic income scores, with no evidence of an income threshold below which deprivation 'escalates disproportionately'. In any case, all that we have learned from our regression results in Chapter 5 about the importance of factors other than current income in determining basic deprivation scores makes the idea that one could detect such a threshold via the income–deprivation relationship rather implausible: a model explaining deprivation scores that does not include a wide range of other variables is simply seen to be misspecified. Given the problems with other approaches to deriving income poverty lines noted in our review in Chapter 2, we also do not believe that such a line can usefully be identified on some other basis and then used together with deprivation scores in measuring poverty. We will not therefore pursue the search for a single-income threshold, and will instead assess the sensitivity of our results to the location of the income cut-off between 50 and 70 per cent of the mean. This is in keeping with the strategy advocated by Atkinson (1987) with respect to income poverty lines *per se*, of seeking to highlight robust results which do not depend on reaching consensus about where to 'draw the line'.

Table 6.2 shows which items are in fact lacked by those experiencing basic deprivation and having an income that falls below these lines, distinguishing households below the 50 per cent line, those between the 50 and 60 per cent lines, and those between the 60 and 70 per cent lines. The table also shows the responses of each set of households to the question in the survey about whether they were having difficulty 'making ends meet'. For the households below the 50 per cent line, 55 per cent were in debt to meet everyday expenses, and about 40 per cent said they could not afford two pairs of shoes, a roast or equivalent once a week, or a meal with meat or fish every second day. More than three-quarters of these households said they were having extreme difficulty in making ends meet. Looking at those between the 50 and 60 per cent lines and experiencing basic deprivation, lower but still very substantial numbers are experiencing debt, and cannot afford new clothes or a second pair of shoes, or a roast every week or meat/ fish every second day. About 60 per cent stated they were having extreme difficulty making ends meet. For the final group, between the 60 and 70 per

Table 6.2   Experience of basic deprivation for households at different income levels and lacking at least one basic item

	% of households experiencing basic deprivation and		
	below the 50% line	between the 50% and 60% lines	between the 60% and 70% lines
Debt	54.5	44.0	33.9
Main meal	17.0	13.8	11.7
Heat	27.4	23.7	11.8
Enforced lack of:			
New clothes	33.6	22.3	14.7
Two pairs of shoes	43.7	36.2	28.0
Coat	24.4	31.7	25.5
Roast or equivalent	44.7	37.2	44.4
Meat, fish or equivalent	39.3	29.7	24.5
Experiencing extreme difficulty in making ends meet	77.7	60.9	54.2

Table 6.3   Composition of households experiencing basic deprivation and below income thresholds in terms of labour force status of head

Labour force status of head	% of households experiencing basic deprivation and below:		
	50% line	60% line	70% line
Employee	8.8	11.7	14.9
Farmer	16.7	12.4	11.1
Self-employed	2.2	2.1	2.8
Unemployed	49.5	36.5	29.9
Ill/disabled	11.9	16.6	14.0
Retired	3.8	5.6	8.3
Home duties	6.7	15.0	18.9
All	100.0	100.0	100.0

cent income lines, the levels of deprivation are again lower and 55 per cent say they are having extreme difficulty making ends meet. So as the income threshold is raised the level of basic deprivation declines, but even for the group between 60 and 70 per cent of average income, about one-quarter cannot afford a warm overcoat or two pairs of shoes.

What are the characteristics of the households identified as poor by the joint income–deprivation criteria? Table 6.3 shows the labour force status of the household head for those reporting enforced basic deprivation and below the 50, 60, and 70 per cent income lines respectively. With the lowest line half the households are headed by an unemployed person, though this falls to 30 per cent as the income threshold is raised. Much lower but still substantial numbers have a head who is sick/disabled, in home duties, a farmer, or an employee. Very few are headed by a self-employed or retired person. In terms of the *risk* of being poor, these figures imply very substantial variation across the groups. Focusing for illustration on those experiencing basic deprivation and below the middle 60 per cent income line, half of all households with an unemployed head would then be counted as poor. The risk of poverty would be 42 per cent for those with a sick/disabled head, 25 per cent for those with a head in home duties, and 16 per cent for farmer-headed households, but only 7 per cent for those with a retired head and 4 per cent for those with an employee or self-employed person as head.

6.4   The Impact on Composition

We have argued that the application of criteria in terms of both basic deprivation and current income serves to identify a set of households that merit the description 'poor' in accordance with the Townsend definition, i.e. are excluded because of a lack of resources. Does applying these income-plus-deprivation criteria rather than purely income cut-offs make much difference to the composition of the group involved? In other words, are different types of household identified as poor? This is crucial, since it will indicate the extent to which income lines alone are likely to mislead policy-makers about the main types of household towards which their efforts should be directed, and will also affect how we understand poverty and the processes generating it. About 16 per cent of households in the sample are below the 60 per cent line and experiencing basic deprivation, which is approximately the same as the overall percentage below the 50 per cent income line, so it is convenient to compare the composition of these two groups. We find that the fact that the same number of households are involved does not in fact mean that the same households are identified as poor in each case. Overall, about 77 per cent of all households in the sample are not poor on either basis while 10 per cent are poor on both; however, 7 per cent fall below the 50 per cent line but are not experiencing basic deprivation, and 6 per cent fall between the 50 and 60 per cent income lines and do experience such deprivation. Thus, about 60 per cent of the households counted as poor on one basis would also be poor under the other, but 40 per cent would not.

It is therefore important to explore the characteristics of the households that would be categorized as poor on one basis versus the other, beginning with labour force status of the household head. The main difference made

Table 6.4 Risk of poverty by labour force status of head of income and combined income–deprivation criteria

Labour force status of head	% below 50% income line	% below 60% income line and experiencing basic deprivation
Employee	3.4	4.6
Farmer	32.0	17.6
Other self-employed	10.6	6.0
Unemployed	58.0	52.8
Retired	9.2	7.4
Ill/disabled	25.5	44.5
Full-time home duties	13.4	30.5

by adopting the combined income–deprivation criteria rather than (lower) income line is that farmers account for a much smaller proportion of 'the poor'—12 versus 23 per cent—while the ill/disabled and especially households headed by someone in home duties form a higher proportion. Households headed by an unemployed person remain the most important single group, accounting for more than half all 'poor' households in each case. Although the overall percentages headed by an unemployed person or employee do not change very much when we move from the income to the income-deprivation measure, it is noteworthy that the actual households within a particular group are not always the same. Focusing on those below the 50 per cent line and *not* experiencing basic deprivation, about half these households are headed by someone who is either a farmer, self-employed, or retired, but one-quarter have an unemployed head. While households with an unemployed head account for about the same percentage of the poor using either approach, then, the households involved are not identical.

The differences in composition imply substantial differences in the risk of poverty by labour force status of the head of household when the two approaches are compared, as shown in Table 6.4. While almost one in three farmers falls below the 50 per cent relative income line, this drops to one in six for the combined 60 per cent income–basic deprivation criteria. The risk for non-farm self-employed also falls, from 10 to 4 per cent. There is a slight increase in the risk for employers and a slight decrease in that for the unemployed and the retired. The most striking increases in risk of poverty when we move to the combined income–deprivation criteria are for households headed by someone who is ill/disabled or in full-time home duties: for the former the risk level rises from 25 to nearly 50 per cent, and for the latter from 10 to 25 per cent.

There also turn out to be interesting differences between the two groups in terms of both current social class and class origins. Table 6.5 shows the risk of poverty on each basis for households classified first by current social

Table 6.5 Risk of poverty by social class and class origins for income and combined income–deprivation criteria

	Social class		class origins	
	% below 50% income line	% below 60% income line and experiencing basic deprivation	% below 50% income line	% below 60% income line and experiencing basic deprivation
Professional and managerial	2.8	1.8	4.9	3.4
Intermediate non-manual	14.2	8.5	15.8	8.5
Upper working class	19.9	21.1	17.9	18.4
Lower working class	29.6	32.3	21.4	26.4

class and then by class origins of the household head, using the four class categories described in Chapter 5. Both for current class and class origins, using the combined income–deprivation criteria produces a higher risk for the two lower classes and substantially lower risks for the other two classes than the 50 per cent income line. As a result, the disparity in risk levels between the professional/managerial class and the lower working class is much greater, and the division between the middle (intermediate non-manual) class and working class groups is much more pronounced, with the combined criteria. While the lower working class are almost eleven times more likely than the professional/managerial one to fall below the income line, the disparity rises to over eighteen to one for the combined criteria. For class origins, the corresponding figure goes from four to one up to seven to one when we move from the 50 per cent line to the combined criteria.

The different approaches also identify somewhat different groups as poor in terms of sex and marital status of the household head. Table 6.6 shows that with the 50 per cent income line households headed by a separated or divorced woman display the highest level of risk, with more than one in three falling below that income threshold. In contrast, for households headed by a man who is separated or divorced the poverty rate is actually lower than for households headed by a married or (even more so) a single man. Households headed by a single woman face a very low risk, much lower than those headed by a single man.[4] Moving to the combined income–deprivation poverty line, however, the pattern is rather different. The risk of poverty falls for households headed by a married or a single man—constituting a majority of all households—and rises for all the other cat-

---

[4] Where both spouses are present the husband is taken here as the household head.

Table 6.6   Risk of poverty by marital status by sex of household head for income and combined income–deprivation criteria

	% below 50% income line		% below 60% income line and experiencing basic deprivation	
	Male	Female	Male	Female
Married	18.6	—	16.3	—
Separated, divorced	14.1	34.9	31.7	40.2
Widowed	11.9	5.8	19.0	14.4
Single	22.9	8.3	16.1	17.9

egories. Although separated or divorced women continue to display the highest poverty rate, now reaching 40 per cent, the risk for households headed by a separated or divorced man is also high, at 32 per cent. Furthermore, there is now little difference between single men and women. Finally, the risk for households headed by a widow was remarkably low with the 50 per cent income line, at 6 per cent, but moving to the combined income–deprivation criteria this rises to 14 per cent.

These findings are consistent with the notion that the combined income-and-deprivation measure is more successful than the (lower) income line in capturing the households that are experiencing enforced deprivation because their resources have been eroded over a long period, and/or because there have been above-average demands on the household income. We can explore these links more formally by carrying out a multivariate analysis of the determinants of each 'type' of poverty. This is done by logistic regression of the dichotomous dependent variable 'is/is not poor', for both methods of identifying the poor, on a set of independent variables similar to those already employed in the analysis of deprivation scores in Chapter 5. The results are set out in Table 6.7, with column (1) referring to whether a household falls below the 50 per cent income line and column (2) to whether it falls below the 60 per cent line and is experiencing enforced basic deprivation.

Column (1) shows that the variables that play the greatest role in determining whether the household falls below the 50 per cent income line are the current labour force status of the household head—with an unemployed person, farmer, or to a lesser extent ill or disabled head all having significant and sizeable positive coefficients—the proportion of time the head spent unemployed in his/her career, whether the head's spouse is at work, and the number of household members at work. The risk of income poverty rises and then falls with age, and is also higher where the household head has no formal educational qualification. While neither number of children in the

Table 6.7 Logistic regression of determinants of falling below 50% income poverty line, and of meeting combined 60% income and enforced basic deprivation criteria

	50% income line:	60% income and enforced deprivation line:
Labour force status		
Farmer	1.14***	—
Unemployed	1.80***	1.30***
Ill or disabled	0.51*	1.28**
In home duties	—	1.26***
Age	0.22***	0.06*
Age^2	−0.002***	−0.007*
Working class	0.10	0.24
Number of Children	0.02	0.15
Working class number of children	0.36***	0.30***
Proportion of time unemployed	2.08***	4.09***
Spouse at work or retired	−0.59*	−0.65***
Number employed in household	−1.78***	−1.44***
Absence of educational qualifications	0.29*	0.60*
Separated or divorced	1.93***	0.93**
Men	0.70*	—
Separated or divorced × men	−2.93***	—
Working class origins	—	0.69***
Major illness or disability	—	0.52***
Household experienced extreme difficulty making ends meet when head was growing up	—	0.43**
Constant	−7.70	−4.49
Model chi-square	927.1	915.7
McFadden pseudo R^2	0.380	0.388

$*p < 0.1$ $**p < 0.01$ $***p < 0.001$

household nor social class has a significant impact, the interaction between them has: this means that being in the unskilled manual working class is associated with a heightened risk of income poverty when there are children, which increases with the number of children. Being headed by a separated or divorced woman significantly increases the likelihood that the household falls below the income threshold, even controlling for the other variables in the equation, whereas being headed by a separated or divorced man actually reduces that probability.[5] Taken together, this set of variables gives a model chi-square of 927 with 16 degrees of freedom and gives a

---

[5] This is compared with the omitted category, which includes households headed by a married or single man, a single woman, or a widow(er).

value of 0.380 for McFadden's pseudo R^2, indicating a reasonably high degree of explanatory power.[6]

The picture for the combined income–deprivation line shown in column (2) is somewhat different, as might be expected from the cross-tabulations. The major contrast in terms of labour force status is now between those households where the household head is at work and all others. Being a farmer is no longer significant, whereas being unemployed, away from work because ill/disabled, or in home duties are all significant and now have very similar coefficients. The coefficients on age and age-squared now mean that the net impact is a falling risk of poverty as age increases. The impact of being in the lower working class is again greater as the number of children in the household rises. The influence of the spouse of the head being at work and the number of persons in the household in employment are also quite similar to the income poverty results. However, separation/divorce is now equally important for men and women, and a variety of longer-term factors that influence command over resources or permanent income emerge as substantially more important in the case of the combined poverty line. These include the absence of educational qualifications, the proportion of time spent unemployed, working-class origins, and whether the household head considers that the household in which she/he grew up experienced great difficulty in making ends meet compared with other families. This set of variables produces a model chi-square of 915.7 with 16 degrees of freedom and a McFadden pseudo R^2 of 0.388, a level of explanatory power similar to that for income poverty.

In making comparisons between the households produced by the two different approaches to measuring poverty, it is necessary to keep in mind that the two sets overlap substantially: as we saw, about 60 per cent of the households below the 50 per cent income line are also below the 60 per cent line and experiencing basic deprivation. In order to focus on the differences between the two, it is helpful to look at the contrast between the 40 per cent of households in each group that are not common to the other. When we move from a 50 per cent income line to the 60 per cent income-plus-basic deprivation criteria, households below the 50 per cent income line but not reporting basic deprivation are excluded from 'the poor'; those between the 50 and 60 per cent income lines and experiencing enforced basic deprivation, on the other hand, are brought in.

What factors distinguish these two groups? Confining the analysis to the 13 per cent of the sample who are in one or other of these groups, we carry out a logistic regression predicting the likelihood of being in the second rather than the first. Table 6.8 shows that the likelihood of being between the 50 and 60 per cent lines and experiencing basic deprivation rather than

[6] The McFadden pseudo R^2 measure is calculated as $D^* = [G^2(0) - G^2(M)]/G^2(0)$ where $G^2(0)$ is the goodness of fit statistic for the model with intercept only and $G^2(M)$ is that for the full model.

Table 6.8   Logistic regression of factors differentiating households experiencing enforced basic deprivation and between the 50% and 60% income lines from those below the 50% income line but not reporting basic deprivation

Labour force status	
Farmer	−2.03***
Other self-employed	−2.06***
Unemployed	−2.05***
Retired	−1.57***
Upper working class origins	0.93**
Lower working class origins	1.65***
Household experienced extreme difficulty in making ends meet when respondent was growing up	0.70**
Proportion of time unemployed	3.66*
Widow	1.14**
Urban centre	1.14**
Constant	−0.77
Model chi-square	150.7
McFadden pseudo-R^2	0.284

*$p < 0.1$ **$p < 0.01$ ***$p < 0.001$

below the 50 per cent line and not experiencing deprivation is reduced by the household head being a farmer, in other self-employment, unemployed, or retired, and increased by household head being in an urban centre, a widow, spending a high proportion of time unemployed, and of working-class origins, in particular lower working-class origins. This set of factors results in a model chi-square of 150.7 with 10 degrees of freedom and a McFadden R^2 of 0.284. Households that are drawn into 'the poor' by the combined 60 per cent income-and-basic deprivation criteria are thus distinguished from those excluded by the adoption of this criterion primarily by a set of factors relating to long-term influences on the accumulation and erosion of resources.

6.5   Understanding Consistency and Inconsistency in those Identified as Poor

So far we have concentrated on what distinguishes the households that will be identified as poor under one versus the other definition. However, from a broader perspective we are interested in exploring not only why some households on relatively low incomes do not appear to be experiencing enforced basic deprivation, but also why some of those on relatively high incomes do report such deprivation. Unless we can understand how this comes about, confidence in our ability to identify those deprived because of a lack of resources via combining deprivation indicators and income will necessarily be undermined. If for example the relationship between income and deprivation is rather weak mostly because either or both are seriously mismeasured, then how confident can we be in the results of combining the two? In fact, combining two mismeasured variables would itself be expected to improve precision. More fundamentally, though, the analysis of the factors influencing basic deprivation scores (and the other indices) in Chapter 5 showed that there are good reasons why its relationship with current income is not stronger, and that deprivation is predictable to quite a high degree when other household characteristics and long-term experiences as well as current income are taken into account. To explore further what the application of joint income–deprivation criteria achieves in the light of these relationships, we now distinguish between four different types of households:

1. households that are above the 60 per cent income threshold and are not experiencing basic deprivation—which we will call consistently non-poor;
2. households that are above this income line but still report enforced basic deprivation, which we call the deprivation-poor only;
3. households that are below the income line but do not report basic deprivation—which we will call the income poor only;
4. households that are below the income threshold and are also experiencing primary deprivation—which we will call the consistently poor.

We first look at the characteristics of the households concerned. Table 6.9 presents a profile of each group of households. Comparing consistently poor and consistently non-poor groups, which account for 16 and 55 per cent of the sample respectively, we can see that these are very sharply differentiated in terms of a range of characteristics. Almost 90 per cent of poor households are from the working class compared with 50 per cent non-poor households, and 30 per cent of poor households compared with only 9 per cent of non-poor are from the lower working class. Furthermore, over 80 per cent of poor households have been intergenerationally stable in the working class—that is, their parents were also in that class—compared with 40 per cent for non-poor households. Not surprisingly, educational qualifications follow a similar pattern, with 75 per cent of the heads of poor households having only primary education compared with 40 per cent of heads of non-poor households.

The consistently poor versus consistently non-poor households are even more sharply differentiated in terms of labour force status. Only 20 per cent of poor households were headed by someone at work or retired compared with over 80 per cent of non-poor households. Poor households are eleven

Table 6.9   Head of household and household characteristics by poverty category

	Non-poor	Life-style-poor only	Income-poor only	Poor	Overall
% working class	50.6	70.4	70.5	88.1	62.6
% lower working class	9.2	16.8	18.7	29.1	14.9
% intergenerationally stable in the working class	40.5	58.7	57.0	80.5	52.0
% at work or retired (non-agricultural)	77.6	62.6	37.0	19.4	60.5
% employees	51.0	44.6	17.2	11.7	39.2
% farmers	10.1	9.5	25.1	12.4	12.3
% home duties	4.7	11.9	9.5	14.8	8.2
% spouses at work	22.4	16.8	12.5	6.0	17.6
% separated/ divorced women	0.5	3.6	2.8	4.9	2.0
% in urban centres	39.4	40.7	14.7	30.1	35.0
% of time unemployed	0.02	0.05	0.05	0.15	0.05
% with more than 2 children	28.8	33.5	32.3	48.1	33.3
Savings (IR£)	£3,149	£782	£1,251	£270	£2,087
Net house values (IR£)	£26,224	£15,752	£21,161	£11,038	£21,376
% major illness or disability	13.8	19.2	18.6	28.4	17.7
% family had extreme difficulty making ends meet when head was growing up	17.6	30.9	27.2	39.2	24.6
% in full-time home-duties	5.9	16.7	12.6	15.0	9.9
% with no educational qualifications	41.3	56.7	67.6	71.8	52.2
Overall in category (%)	54.6	16.4	12.6	16.5	100.0

times more likely to be headed by a separated or divorced women. Heads of poor households have spent far more of their careers in unemployment on average than their non-poor counterparts. Twice as many poor households have what might be considered 'large' families, that is more than two children. Poor households are slightly less likely than non-poor to be located in an urban centre. Non-poor households have assets in the form of housing worth more than twice those of poor households on average. The difference in average savings between the two groups are dramatic: the non-poor have savings that are twelve times higher than the poor, who have very little on average to fall back on. Finally, almost 40 per cent of the heads of poor households were reared in households that experienced extreme difficulty in making ends meet, compared with 18 per cent of the non-poor.

Applying income and deprivation criteria together has therefore certainly allowed us to identify as poor and non-poor two groups of households that are sharply differentiated. Most importantly, they are differentiated in a manner that is entirely consistent with one's expectations: the poor are much more likely than the non-poor to be from the lower social classes, to be detached from the labour market, to have little or no education, to have large families, to have little or no savings, and to be from a disadvantaged background. The only feature that might surprise at first sight is that poor households are not more heavily concentrated in urban areas, given the headlines that urban 'ghettos' attract. The existence of such black spots with very high poverty rates does not however mean that most poor people live in those areas, as we discuss in detail in the next chapter, and an income poverty line would produce even less concentration of the poor in urban areas. So households that are on low income and experiencing basic deprivation have the characteristics one would expect of poor households; the results in that sense have what sociologists term face validity.

Crucially for the justification of our approach, this is less true when an income line alone is used. Table 6.9 also shows the characteristics of households that are income-poor-only; they are below half average income but are excluded from 'the poor' by our approach because they do not report enforced basic deprivation. Although there are substantial differences between this group and the non-poor, these are rather less pronounced than was the case for the consistently poor. The income-poor-only are somewhat less likely than the consistently poor to be from the working class (particularly the lower working class), to have little or no education, and to not be at work or retired. About one-quarter of the income-poor-only are farmers, compared with about 12 per cent of the consistently poor. The income-poor-only have substantially higher savings and housing assets on average than the consistently poor, and have spent less time in unemployment.

What of the households reporting enforced basic deprivation but not below the 60 per cent income line? Table 6.9 shows that, like the income-poor-only, these have characteristics which place them in between the consistently poor and the consistently non-poor. In terms of class, class background, family size, and unemployment experience, they look quite like the income-poor-only, but differ in current labour force status. About 45 per cent of deprivation-poor-only households are headed by an employee, more than twice the figure for the income-poor-only and not much lower than the consistently non-poor. Interestingly, though, the deprivation-poor have levels of savings and housing assets which are much lower than the income-poor (though higher than the consistently poor). The fact that this group reported enforced basic deprivation cannot therefore be simply dismissed as either random or attributable to tastes or to relatively high expectations. Their background and labour force experiences, and particularly the extent to which they have been able to build up savings, distinguish them from the non-poor, and yet they also differ from the consistently poor.

To investigate more formally and fully the ways in which these four groups are differentiated, we again apply logistic regression using the full set of independent variables described earlier. Since we now wish to distinguish four groups rather than two, multinomial logistic regression is employed. The consistently non-poor are used as the reference category, and the analysis in effect looks at the characteristics that distinguish each of the other groups from this reference group. Table 6.10 presents the results, which comprise in column (1) the equation predicting the likelihood of being consistently poor rather than consistently non-poor, in column (2) the equation for the likelihood of being income-poor rather than non-poor, and in column (3) the equation for the likelihood of being deprivation-poor rather than non-poor. (While these could be estimated as three separate logistic regressions, this would fail to take into account the fact that they are not independent of one another: the multinomial procedure overcomes this problem by estimating them jointly.) By comparing results across the equations, we can then see how the three groups other than the reference one differ from each other. (To be clear about how this relates to the regression results seen earlier in this chapter, those in Table 6.7 compared the consistently poor with all others, and those below half average income (whether experiencing basic deprivation or not) with all others, and those in Table 6.8 compared the income-poor with those between the 50 and 60 per cent lines and reporting basic deprivation; here by contrast the entire sample is being broken down into four non-overlapping categories.) The model has a chi-square of 1,172.4 with 63 degrees of freedom and a McFadden R^2 of 0.288, representing a satisfactory degree of explanatory power, and is rather more successful in predicting the consistent than the inconsistent groups.

Looking first at the contrast between the consistently poor and the consistently non-poor, almost all the explanatory variables in the equation are significant in distinguishing these two groups. The omitted labour force category is employee, and having a head in any of the other categories increases the probability of being poor rather than non-poor. This effect is most modest for the self-employed and retired, rising progressively through those in home duties, away from work because of illness/disability, and being a farmer, and reaching its peak where the head is unemployed. Where the spouse of the head is at work or retired, the likelihood of being poor is reduced. The odds of being poor rise with the number of children in the household, but this effect is accentuated for those in the working class (as reflected in the significant interaction term). Households headed by a sep-

arated or divorced woman have a heightened risk of poverty, but the
opposite is the case for those headed by a man in that position. Chronic
illness or disability increase the likelihood of poverty, but being in an urban
area in itself reduces that probability when one controls for all the other
characteristics measured.

Most interestingly, over and above current labour market participation
and family circumstances, a further set of factors likely to have affected the
ability of the household to accumulate resources over time also proves
significant in distinguishing the consistently poor from the non-poor. The

Table 6.10   Multinomial logistic regression of poverty category

	(i) Odds on life-style poverty v. absence of poverty	(ii) Odds on income poverty v. absence of poverty	(iii) Odds on poverty v. absence of poverty
Farmer	0.25	1.96***	2.77**
Self-employed	0.14	0.84**	1.06**
Unemployed	0.35	2.66**	3.15**
Ill/disabled	0.16	2.15***	2.52**
Retired	−0.30	0.66**	1.20**
In home duties	0.33	1.58***	2.13**
Working class	0.41*	−0.23	−0.04
Number of children	0.18*	−0.02	0.29**
Working class number of children	−0.15	0.33**	0.31**
Working-class origins	−0.30	0.11	0.53*
Male	−0.15	0.07	−0.19
Separated/divorced	1.79***	1.91***	2.43*
Male + separated/divorced	−1.05	−2.68***	−2.54*
Absence of Educational qualifications	0.31*	0.47*	0.39*
Chronic illness	0.31*	−0.22	0.41*
Childhood economic circumstances	0.52***	0.20	0.49**
Urban centre	0.38**	−0.91***	−0.33*
Spouse at work	−0.12	−0.80***	−1.32*
Proportion of time unemployed	1.78*	−0.46	2.68*
Log of deposits	−0.19***	−0.15**	−0.35*
Log net house valuation	−0.15***	−0.08*	−0.29
Constant	−0.37	−1.27	0.16

*$p < 0.1$ **$p < 0.01$ ***$p < 0.001$
Model chi-square 117.24 with 63 degrees of freedom; McFadden pseudo R^2 0.288.

level of savings and the net value of house property are highly significant and negatively associated with the likelihood of being poor. The likelihood of poverty increases with the proportion of time the household head spent unemployed in his/her career. This effect is even more pronounced if one omits the savings and house value variables from the equation: the coefficient on time unemployed then doubles, reflecting the extent to which the effect of previous unemployment experience on current poverty operates through its impact on the ability to accumulate resources. Other variables which would be expected to affect long-term accumulation, such as absence of educational qualifications, working-class origins, and experience of financial hardship in childhood, are also significant.

Turning now to the estimated equation predicting the likelihood of being income-poor–only, in column (2) current labour force status of the head has effects which are very similar to but less pronounced than those we have just seen for the consistently poor. Compared with being an employee, all the other categories increase the likelihood of being income-poor rather than non-poor, with the same pattern across the categories but smaller coefficients than for the consistently poor. Both spouse of the head at work and being in an urban area once again reduce the likelihood of being income-poor, while being headed by a separated or divorced woman adds substantially to that likelihood. What sharply distinguishes these results from those for the consistently poor is that the impact of savings and housing assets is much more muted, and the proportion of time spent unemployed by the head, chronic illness/disability, class origin, and childhood financial circumstances are all insignificant. Thus, the factors likely to have influenced long-term accumulation and erosion of resources do not influence the probability of being income poor to anything like the extent that they affect the odds of being consistently poor.

Focusing finally on the probability of being deprivation-poor-only, the pattern in column (3) is quite different. It is the current labour force status of the head and spouse that are now insignificant: the deprivation-poor do not differ from the non-poor in terms of current participation in the labour force, unlike both the income-poor and the consistently poor. Where the household head is a separated or divorced woman this does add to the likelihood of being deprivation-poor, but being in an urban area increases rather than reduces that probability. In sharp contrast to the income-poor-only, the variables affecting or reflecting long-term accumulation of resources are now very important—savings and house value, time spent unemployed, absence of educational qualifications, chronic illness/disability, and a financially very difficult family background all add significantly to the probability of being deprivation-poor rather than non-poor.

Overall, then, the regression results throw up an extremely interesting pattern of differences between the four groups distinguished by our income and basic deprivation criteria. The consistently non-poor differ from the consistently poor across virtually the full range of explanatory variables, which measure current labour force participation, household composition and other factors affecting the demands on income, wider resources, and a variety of factors likely to have affected the capacity to accumulate such resources. Those who are income-poor but not reporting enforced basic deprivation are distinguished from the non-poor primarily by current labour force participation, although being headed by a woman who is separated/divorced is still relevant. Long-term factors are much less important than they were for those who are on low incomes and also experiencing basic deprivation. On the other hand, it is precisely those longer-term factors that serve to distinguish those who report deprivation but are not on low incomes from the consistently non-poor, while current labour force participation in that case has no discriminatory power.

6.6 Validating the Categorization

Overall, the regression results show that the income and basic deprivation criteria clearly distinguish consistently poor and consistently non-poor groups, and go a considerable way towards identifying the characteristics that produce the 'inconsistent' groups. At this point we wish to confront the issue of whether the emergence of such groups is likely to be simply a consequence of inadequacies in the manner in which we have measured income and deprivation. In order to test this, we look at information in the sample on some other features which we would expect *a priori* to be correlated with poverty, which has not been used in producing our categorization. Two variables which are particularly useful in this regard are the self-reported degree of economic strain and the levels of psychological distress of the household head. Table 6.11 shows how these vary across the four categories emerging from our approach.

Self-assessments of the degree of economic strain were measured in the survey through the question 'Is the household able to make ends meet?' with the prompted response categories 'with great difficulty', 'with some difficulty', 'with a little difficulty', 'fairly easily', 'easily', or 'very easily'. We concentrate on the percentage responding 'with great difficulty', which for the sample as a whole was 31 per cent. We see from Table 6.11 that almost three-quarters (73 per cent) of the consistently poor households gave that response, compared with only 12.5 per cent of non-poor households. In income-poor-only households 37 per cent , only half the figure for consistently poor households, said they were having great difficulty. The figure for deprivation-poor-only households, at 46 per cent , was four times that of the non-poor households, though still a good deal lower than for the consistently poor.

Psychological distress has been shown by a substantial literature to be

Table 6.11   Percentages of households experiencing difficulty in making ends meet and above the General Health Questionnaire Psychological Distress Threshold, by poverty category

	% experiencing difficulty in making ends meet	% above the GHQ Threshold
Consistently poor	72.7	41.2
Deprivation poor only	45.3	20.2
Income poor only	36.7	13.7
Consistently non-poor	13.3	9.7
Overall	31.6	17.3

strongly associated with poverty and unemployment, and therefore serves as a valuable independent check on our categorization of households. The measure employed in the survey was the widely used General Health Questionnaire, initially designed by Goldberg (1972). Twelve questions of the following type were put to adults in the survey:

Have you recently
  been feeling unhappy and depressed?
  felt capable of making decisions about things?
  felt you couldn't overcome your difficulties?
  been feeling reasonably happy all things considered?

Responses to these questions were on a four-point scale of the form 'more so than usual', 'same as usual', 'less than usual', 'much less than usual' (with variants for some of the other questions). Full details on the questions and the way in which the response have been scored to produce the GHQ scale are given in Whelan *et al.* (1991) and Whelan (1994a). The results are reported here in terms of the percentage scoring above the GHQ threshold of 2, where it has been found that the probability of being classified as a non-psychotic psychiatric case exceeds 0.5. Table 6.11 shows that 41 per cent of the heads of consistently poor households are above that threshold, while for the consistently non-poor the figure is as low as 10 per cent. For income-poor-only households the risk is 14 per cent, less than one-third of that in poor households. Correspondingly, for those heading deprivation-poor-only households the risk of being above the psychological threshold is 20 per cent, twice that of the non-poor category but only half that of the consistently poor.

Thus, economic strain and psychological distress show variations across the four groups which are entirely consistent with the pattern we saw in the previous section for the level of savings and housing assets: the poor and non-poor are dramatically different, the income-poor-only and deprivation-poor-only are in an intermediate position, with the former less favourably situated than the latter. The deprivation-poor-only group are seen to be experiencing fairly severe economic stress and associated psychological consequences, which lends support to the notion that their reported deprivation is reflecting real economic pressures. Further support for the validity of the categorization produced by our income and basic deprivation criteria will be provided by the housing and secondary items when we come to those shortly, but before doing so it is useful to look in more detail at the current income and broader resources available to the two inconsistent groups.

6.8   Resources of the Inconsistent Groups

Looking at the income-poor-only, how do these households with low reported current incomes manage to avoid basic deprivation? First, we consider current income and the way it is measured. We saw in Chapter 3 that, as is usual in such surveys, the current income measure relates to that received last week (or fortnight/month) for employee income and social welfare transfers, and the average amount received over the previous year for the self-employed (including farmers). Income is subject to (intended or unintended) reporting errors, with self-employment income being particularly difficult to measure adequately, and the year in question was a remarkably bad one for farm incomes, so income as measured in the survey may be an especially poor guide to longer-term income from these sources. For those currently in employment or on social welfare, current income may not always reflect income over the previous year. We do find that annual income significantly higher than current income contributes towards a relatively high level of savings and other resources for some of these low-income households. The importance of this factor should not be overestimated, though: substituting the annual income estimates described in Chapter 3 for the current income ones employed here would result in reclassification of only about 10 per cent of income-poor households as non-poor.

What the regression results highlight is the importance of broader resources and long-term experiences in distinguishing this group from the consistently poor. We have seen that these households are most often not headed by someone who is currently an employee, but that the longer-term experiences of such heads have generally not been nearly as adverse as those on low incomes and experiencing basic deprivation. The resulting differences in wealth holdings between the income-poor and the consistently poor are worth fleshing out. Table 6.12 shows the average level of reported household savings in the form of deposits in banks or buildings societies, and the average value of house property net of outstanding mortgage, for households below the 60 per cent income threshold and experiencing/not experiencing enforced basic deprivation. We see that those not reporting enforced basic deprivation have housing values almost twice as high as those reporting such deprivation, and savings levels six times as

Table 6.12 Households below 60% income line experiencing/not experiencing basic deprivation by labour force status of head: deposits and house property

Labour force status	Mean deposits (IR£)		Mean net house value (IR£)	
	Experiencing basic deprivation	Not experiencing basic deprivation	Experiencing basic deprivation	Not experiencing basic deprivation
Employee	204	1,342	9,398	14,655
Farmer	790	2,208	19,677	27,060
Self-employed	397	2,681	22,537	29,284
Unemployed	45	442	5,335	16,460
Sick/disabled	360	1,741	12,481	19,222
Retired	832	3,052	11,034	22,364
Home duties	27	1,200	14,719	18,047
All	260	1,720	10,974	20,990

high. The table also makes clear, however, that those on low incomes and not experiencing basic deprivation do not constitute a homogeneous group in terms of resources. Within that group, substantially higher levels of resources are available to the households headed by a farmer, other self-employed, or retired person than to those headed by an employee, someone in home duties, the sick/ill, or particularly an unemployed person. This is reflected in the fact that a relatively high percentage of the unemployed reporting difficulty making ends meet, compared with heads of other income-poor-only households. Although not currently experiencing enforced basic deprivation, then, those households under the 60 per cent line with an unemployed head are clearly under greater financial strain than other households reporting similar current income levels.

We now turn to the group of households not on low current incomes but apparently experiencing what they regard as enforced basic deprivation. We have seen that half of those reporting enforced basic deprivation—representing 15 per cent of the sample—are above the 60 per cent income threshold. Once again, we focus first on their current incomes, then on broader resources. The households concerned are not mostly on incomes just above the cut-offs: as we saw in Chapter 5, they are distributed over the (equivalent) income distribution, with an average income well above the thresholds. Why then are these households with current incomes close to or above average none the less reporting basic deprivation? Differences between current and annual income could contribute if these households were on much lower incomes for much of the year—someone who is now an employee may have spent much of the previous year away from work, for example. While this is in fact the case for some of the households concerned, it applies only to a small minority. Other households that have experienced a sharp fall in income could also find it difficult to meet their financial commitments, even if the current level is not particularly low relative to other households: again, this appears to apply only to a minority.

Table 6.13 Mean savings and house property for employee-headed households above the 60% income line by decile and experiencing/not experiencing basic deprivation

Equivalent income decile	Mean deposits (IR£)		Mean net house value (IR£)	
	Experiencing basic deprivation	Not experiencing basic deprivation	Experiencing basic deprivation	Not experiencing basic deprivation
4	833	1,160	15,494	18,383
5	428	1,101	11,414	18,924
6	542	1,024	15,759	20,999
7	599	1,529	14,265	24,097
8	110	1,839	15,994	25,659
9	831	2,847	21,464	25,484
Top	1,713	5,434	15,995	24,120
All	666	2,461	15,442	23,428

Relatively high expenditure on housing, leaving less for other goods and services, also appears to be a factor for some of these households, but once again it is not prevalent.

The importance of longer-term factors for this group, brought out in the regression results, is reflected in the differences in the level of savings and other assets reported by the households above the income thresholds and experiencing deprivation and other households at similar income levels. Controlling for equivalent income decile, Table 6.13 shows that for households headed by an employee—the dominant group—those experiencing basic deprivation have much lower levels of savings and own much less valuable houses on average than corresponding households not experiencing basic deprivation. Our analysis has thus indicated that restricted resources over a prolonged period have a role in explaining the current living patterns of the deprivation-poor-only, and this is also suggested by the fact that over two-thirds of these households come from the upper or lower working classes. (It is also worth mentioning that they are not clustered on a particular item or couple of basic items: the percentages lacking each item are not very different from the households below that income line and experiencing basic deprivation, so they are not showing up as deprived simply because of a 'rogue' item in the basic index.) An unravelling of factors that contribute to their current situation would require a great deal more information than we possess and would probably be fully implemented only with panel data. What appears clear, though, is that this group constitutes not so much a problem for our measurement procedures as a group of substantial interest in their own right and deserving much more in-depth study.

While the long-term dynamics of income and labour force participation probably go a long way towards explaining the current situation of the 'inconsistent' groups, it is not to be expected that resources would fully explain differences in living patterns. As far as the deprivation-poor are concerned, it may be necessary to accept that some households that are doing without what most people regard as necessities themselves consider this to be due to lack of resources, while by societal norms they have relatively substantial resources. Conversely, among those with quite limited resources there will be some who, one way or another, manage to avoid basic deprivation.[7] To what extent is this a 'puzzle' or a problem for the researcher? As Mack and Lansley (1985) put it, any study on poverty and deprivation depends on generalizations about people's needs and circumstances which will not fit every individual. Poverty is not simply deprivation, and such diversity highlights the importance of employing income as well as deprivation criteria in measuring what will generally be seen as exclusion arising from lack of resources.

Could the fact that substantial numbers on low incomes avoid basic deprivation be captured by a purely resources-based poverty measure but one that incorporates both current income and assets? Rather than simply applying an income poverty line, then, one would in effect identify those on low incomes and with little or no other financial resources as poor, without having to measure deprivation directly. This would be particularly appealing in that the issues of how to cope with choices and tastes which loom large in measuring deprivation could apparently be skirted: one is seeking to measure command over resources rather than their use, but taking the limitations of current income into account. It is therefore interesting to compare the results of applying such a resource-based measure to our sample with our income–basic deprivation poverty measure. A crude but illuminating application of a broader resources criterion is to look at the numbers below the 60 per cent relative income line who also report having no more than £250 in savings (on deposit in financial institutions) to fall back on. This is the case for about two-thirds of the households below that income threshold, and so these joint income–savings criteria would identify 22 per cent of all households as 'poor'. These can be compared with the 16 per cent who are below the 60 per cent line and experiencing enforced basic deprivation. About 87 per cent of the latter group also have no more than £250 in savings—most report none—and so would also be identified as poor by the income/assets criteria. However, over one-third of those meeting the income/assets criteria—representing almost 8 per cent of the entire sample—are not experiencing enforced deprivation.

One's concern about the income/savings approach to identifying the poor

[7] Ability to manage one's resources may be a factor, although it is not currently 'politically correct' to advert to it—see Piachaud's (1987) discussion of the importance of budgeting practices, noting the tendency among social scientists to treat this as taboo.

would not therefore be that it misses many of those excluded because of a lack of resources, but that it would count among the poor a substantial number who do not appear to be so excluded. That the income–basic deprivation criteria are indeed more effective in identifying those under greatest economic pressure is indicated by the fact that the levels of financial strain reported by those who meet the income/assets criteria but are not experiencing enforced basic deprivation are considerably lower than those who are experiencing such deprivation. Over two-thirds of those below the 60 per cent income line, with deposits of no more than £250 and reporting enforced basic deprivation, said they were having great difficulty making ends meet. For those below the income line and the deposits cut-off but not reporting basic deprivation, on the other hand, the corresponding figure was only 34 per cent. This suggests that—together with income—the basic deprivation criterion is more effective than the assets criterion in identifying those excluded owing to lack of resources. Mismeasurement of savings could of course contribute to these findings, but a great deal of effort was put into this topic in our survey and the quality of data on that topic may be very difficult to improve. Even if one had confidence that savings could be reliably measured, this would not in our view provide a substitute for direct measures of deprivation.

6.8   The Housing and Secondary Dimensions

We now bring back into the discussion the two other deprivation dimensions identified in Chapter 5, the housing and secondary dimensions. We first compare mean scores on the housing and secondary enforced lack indices across the four categories distinguished by the 60 per cent income line and the basic deprivation criteria. From Table 6.14 we see that the consistently poor again look very different from the consistently non-poor—the mean scores for the poor on the two indices are three to four times those for the non-poor. The income-poor-only and the deprivation-poor-only are yet again in an intermediate position, but with the depri-

Table 6.14   Mean scores on housing and secondary enforced lack indices for consistently poor, income-poor-only, deprivation-poor-only, and consistently non-poor

Category	Mean score on:	
	Housing index	Secondary index
Consistently poor	0.89	4.40
Deprivation-poor only	0.77	3.58
Income-poor only	0.50	2.63
Consistently non-poor	0.22	1.44

vation-poor appearing less well positioned than the income-poor. The mean scores for the income-poor are substantially higher than those for the non-poor, but still not much more than half those for the consistently poor. The deprivation-poor, however, have mean scores that are below but much closer to those for the consistently poor. So this is entirely consistent with the pattern shown by the level of savings, and by the extent of self-assessed financial strain and psychological distress, across the four groups.

This provides another source of support for the validity of our categor-ization. The fact that the deprivation-poor-only are reporting such a sub-stantial degree of enforced absence of the other items reinforces our belief that their reported basic deprivation is not an artefact of the measurement process, and that their position merits and will require in-depth study. In terms of poverty measurement, however, it is the importance of distinguish-ing between the consistently poor and the income-poor-only that stands out. The income-poor have been shown to be much better placed than the consistently poor in terms of levels of savings, self-assessed economic strain, psychological distress, and now the housing and secondary index scores that a poverty measure that fails to distinguish between them—as an income line will do—can only be seen as seriously inadequate.

While the pattern of mean scores on the housing and secondary indices is consistent with the categorization produced by the income-plus-basic depri-vation criteria, this does not mean that these items should or could have been incorporated into the deprivation criterion in identifying the poor in the first place. We have already emphasized that most of the secondary items would not be appropriate for that purpose since they are not over-whelmingly regarded as necessities, even ignoring the results of the factor analysis. The housing and housing-related items are indeed almost all re-garded as a necessity and possessed by most households, but what the factor analysis shows is that housing and basic deprivation are quite frequently experienced by different households. About 58 per cent of the households lacking one or more of the housing items also experience basic deprivation, 44 per cent are below the 60 per cent income threshold, and only 30 per cent are both below the 60 per cent income threshold and have basic deprivation scores of 1 or more. While those we identify as poor using the income–basic deprivation criteria also have relatively high levels of housing deprivation, the latter would therefore not be a good 'marker' for the former.

Looking at the characteristics of the households experiencing enforced lack of one or more of the housing items but not both below the 60 per cent income threshold *and* reporting enforced basic deprivation, what is striking is their distinctive demographic and geographic profile. Almost 60 per cent live in rural rather than urban areas, 50 per cent are headed by either a single person or a widow(er), and 80 per cent are either headed by such an individual or in a rural area. About one-third are elderly single or widowed persons. Quality of housing and housing-related durables for many of these households are probably determined by the combination of relatively low resources over a prolonged period and their marital status and location. These households report significantly lower current levels of financial strain than households below the income threshold and experiencing basic deprivation, and they also have substantially higher levels of savings.

As emphasized by Donnison (1988), housing is the sector in which welfare states have found it easiest to break the links between economic status and living standards. This may mean that in many countries, taken alone or even together with low current income, measures of housing conditions are not particularly reliable indicators of generalized exclusion arising from lack of resources. (As mentioned earlier, this undermines Ringen's illustrative results, which rely heavily on housing-related indicators in showing the weakness of the relationship between income and deprivation, as did McGregor and Borooah (1992) in comparing the living standards of households below income and expenditure poverty lines.) Both the processes producing poor housing conditions and the consequences of such deprivation may be distinctive. Once again, this is an area for further investigation. The general point which it serves to illustrate, though, is that appropriate measures of deprivation will change over time and vary across countries if the objective is to reflect exclusion, and thus what is not included is in a sense as significant as what is included.

A final point about the items not in the basic index is that some of the households below the income cut-off and experiencing enforced basic deprivation do possess items that are not overwhelmingly regarded as necessities. Some might argue that this invalidates the contention that their deprivation is enforced (as reflected in the anecdotal 'they all have video recorders so they cannot be poor' reaction). Mack and Lansley paid particular attention to this issue, and it is worth addressing here. We focus on two items that tend to be highlighted in this context, namely a car and a telephone. About 21 per cent of the households below the 60 per cent relative income threshold and experiencing basic deprivation own a car, 36 per cent have a telephone, and 12 per cent have both. Breaking down the households involved by some relevant characteristics, Table 6.15 shows that those owing a car are predominantly rural, middle-aged, and/or have children. Those having a telephone, by contrast, are more likely to be elderly and/or widow(er)s. It would not be difficult to argue that, for many of the households involved, a car or a telephone could reasonably be regarded as a necessity—and many of the households say they regard them as such. Excluding all households who possess a car would make poverty largely an urban matter, and would certainly mean that almost no rural households with married, middle-aged heads could be classified as poor. Similarly, excluding those with telephones would mean that a considerably smaller number of elderly people would be so classified. Households have to make difficult choices about spending priorities, and it would not in our view be

Table 6.15   Characteristics of households below 60%
income line and experiencing basic deprivation but
having car or telephone

Characteristics of household head	% of households below 60% line and experiencing basic deprivation having:	
	Car	Telephone
Age		
Under 35	25.3	18.8
35–54	49.4	38.3
55 or over	25.3	42.9
Married	87.4	71.7
Widowed	7.4	23.8
Single	5.2	4.5
Female	6.9	25.2
Rural	64.9	53.7

reasonable to regard the decision to give a car or a telephone priority over
one of our basic items as evidence that absence of the latter would not be
seen by most people as enforced by lack of resources.

6.9   Conclusions

This chapter has looked at the implications of taking both current income
and measured deprivation into account in measuring poverty. It has argued,
following Ringen, that both elements are required if the poverty measure is
to be consistent with the widely accepted definition put forward by
Townsend, which relates to exclusion from ordinary living standards arising
from lack of resources. Our aim is to identify those who are unable to have
socially defined necessities because of a lack of resources. In using direct
indicators of deprivation to apply this approach, we have taken into account
that simply adding together indicators of deprivation which may relate to
different aspects or dimensions into a summary index is not satisfactory.
The factor analysis presented in Chapter 5 provides the basis for concentrating on a limited set of items referring to basic deprivation, which are
most likely to reflect the underlying latent variable of generalized deprivation in which we are interested. Rather than seeking to locate an income
threshold, we have examined households both experiencing what they regard as enforced basic deprivation and below relative income thresholds, so
that the sensitivity of the results to the income cut-off employed can be
seen.

The income and basic deprivation criteria allowed us to distinguish four groups: those who are on low incomes and experiencing basic deprivation, those on low incomes and not experiencing basic deprivation, those on higher incomes but experiencing basic deprivation, and those above the income cut-off and not experiencing basic deprivation. About half the households below income poverty lines were experiencing enforced basic deprivation, while substantial numbers above those lines reported such deprivation. Distinguishing households as poor using both income and basic deprivation produces a poverty profile that differs significantly from the results of simply applying the current income lines, most obviously in terms of current labour force status: households headed by a farmer, other self-employed, or retired person are less important, and those headed by an ill or disabled person or someone in home duties more important, among the poor, while those with an unemployed head continue to be the most substantial group. The role of labour force experience and resources over a prolonged period, rather than simply the current status of these, in determining the risk of current poverty was shown by the results of regression analysis.

Information external to that used in implementing the four-way categorization of sample households provided support for the validity of the results. Those identified as consistently poor, on low income, and experiencing basic deprivation were seen to have much higher levels of self-assessed financial strain and of psychological distress, and much higher levels of deprivation in terms of items not included in the basic index, than those on low incomes but not reporting basic deprivation. The importance of distinguishing between these groups is a central message of this chapter and indeed of the volume as a whole. It was also demonstrated that measuring those on low current incomes and reporting little or no financial savings, though more effective in identifying those experiencing deprivation than an income cut-off alone, was not an adequate substitute for direct indicators of deprivation.

Many questions are raised but not fully resolved by the results. The households above the income thresholds but reporting basic deprivation clearly require more consideration. The relationship between housing/durables and resources, and its implications both for assessing the position of households experiencing housing deprivation and for policy, need to be examined further. Similarly, analysis of the satisfaction of educational or health needs, which are largely organized outside the market in many countries, would complement the study of exclusion from marketable goods and services. Moving from a point in time to the analysis of changes in poverty over time would raise a further host of questions about the way in which the deprivation and income criteria would reflect changes in the general standard of living. These and other issues that arise within the framework of applying combined deprivation-plus-resources criteria to measuring poverty will be considered briefly in our concluding chapter.

More fundamentally, though, following through this measurement approach serves to highlight features of the definition itself. Households are to be categorized as poor only if they are both at low incomes—however defined—*and* experiencing deprivation and exclusion—again, however defined. We have seen that a considerable number of households with current low incomes are not experiencing basic deprivation. Leaving aside the precise way in which deprivation is defined and measured, as well as the problems of measuring income accurately, it is clear that some households have current incomes which would *not* be adequate to avoid exclusion and deprivation, but manage to do so by running down accumulated resources and by borrowing and/or relying on help.[8] Others may be able to avoid deprivation only by being particularly good managers of their limited resources. Harking back to Atkinson's (1985) distinction between poverty as deprivation in terms of minimum standard of living and poverty as concerned with *minimum rights to resources*, mentioned in Chapter 2, falling below a minimum income level may be seen as a violation of rights even if it does not always or immediately result in deprivation. This has obvious policy as well as conceptual and methodological implications. Whether we wish to call such households 'poor' or not, clearly social security policy will be concerned to provide income support to those with inadequate incomes even if they could not (yet) be categorized as 'excluded from ordinary living patterns'. We discuss the conceptual and policy issues raised by our approach and results in Chapters 8 and 9.

Before doing so, we wish to focus in the next chapter on the perspective our approach provides on the relationship between poverty and social class, and what this reveals about the processes that produce poverty. The role of long-term factors affecting the accumulation and erosion of resources as determinants of deprivation is a striking aspect of the results presented in this chapter and the previous one, and is reflected in the strength of the relationship between poverty as we measure it and social class. We have seen that the risk of poverty (measured by the joint income–basic deprivation criteria) rises inexorably as one moves down the class hierarchy, from 2 per cent for the professional and managerial class up to 30–35 per cent for the lower working class. Our findings on the extent to which poverty varies by class origins and childhood economic circumstances provide a salutary reminder of just how far back we may need to go in tracing the causal path that produces this pattern. It comes as no surprise to find that the major part of the effect of class origins on poverty operates indi-

---

[8] An analysis of panel data on US households by Ruggles and Williams (1989) showed that about one-third of those entering poverty—falling below the official poverty line—had sufficient savings to allow them to maintain their standard of living above that line through their full poverty spell, by running down savings to supplement income support.

rectly through such factors as education and labour market experience—analyses in terms of class, human capital, and the labour market are, from our perspective, complementary rather than competing. However, rather than arguing for the declining relevance of class, as some have done, in relation to poverty in Ireland, it seems more plausible to argue that social class has become more rather than less important, with poverty increasingly associated with long-term labour market difficulties which in turn are disproportionately borne by households in particular social classes and from a similar class background. In the next chapter, we take up the issue of the relevance of class, and particularly of the notion of an 'underclass', for understanding poverty.

Class, Underclass, and Poverty

7.1 The Concept of an 'Underclass'

The concept of 'the underclass', or, as it is most frequently applied, the 'urban underclass', has generated the most vigorous debate on the nature of poverty in the USA since the 1960s. It is a term, as Peterson (1991) notes, that can appeal to conservatives, liberals, and radicals alike. Conservatives can focus on dependency culture and rational behaviour. Radicals can identify a group shaped and dominated by macroeconomic and political forces but denied a productive role. Liberals can direct their attention to the contrast between mainstream America and marginalized groups. Analyses of the urban underclass have had a major influence on the debate on 'visions of poverty' and the appropriate vocabulary of poverty. Perhaps the most influential contribution has been Charles Murray's (1984) *Losing Ground*. Murray's book formed part of the onslaught of the radical right. For Murray the underclass is a consequence of the perverse interventions of the welfare state and, in particular, of policies that seduce in the short term but have the long-term consequence of creating a dependency culture. While Murray's explanation has a clear cultural component, it must be distinguished from the culture-of-poverty explanations of anthropologists. In the USA such explanations can lead to a focus on the roots of the black underclass in the rural south (Marks 1991: 451).

For Murray, the welfare system is crucial. The underclass is not bound by an unchangeable cultural milieu but is in fact behaving quite rationally in response to the inadvertent creation of a new set of incentives for marginal members of American society. Murray (1990) has also been happy to extend his conclusions to the UK. He seeks to direct attention to the manner in which well-intentioned reforms exacerbate the problems they sought to solve by contributing to a moral stance which removes the will to effort and contributes to the creation of a vicious circle of poverty. The argument that collective provision has actually had the consequence of undermining individual capacities has been central to the neo-liberal emphasis on 'active citizenship and the duties of citizens as opposed to the rights of individuals to particular forms of collective provision' (Crompton 1993: 142).

Murray's thesis has been subjected to relentless criticism. Thus, reviews of the disincentive effects of welfare systems provide no evidence of effects on the scale implied by his line of reasoning. The available evidence for the

USA and the UK suggests that such effects as do exist are of a modest nature (Atkinson 1992; Dilnot 1992; Moffit 1992). Authors such as Dilnot (1992) have highlighted the fact that, on the basis of the available evidence, the scale of the cuts required in unemployment benefit for it to have a dramatic effect on the level of unemployment would create a regime so different from the regime under which the estimate of elasticities was derived that their predictive usefulness would be at least doubtful. Similarly, Duncan and Hoffman (1991) argue that, although the shift from work to welfare among black women exhibiting 'bad' teenage behaviour accounts for much of their increased poverty, it does not conform to any simple explanation based on trends in incentives.

Paradoxically, Peterson concludes that:

The most powerful force contributing to the formation of the urban underclass . . . may be the changing values of mainstream American society in which the virtues of family stability, mutual support and religiously based commitment to the marriage vow no longer command the deference they did. (Peterson 1991: 19)

Murray, who is untroubled by such concerns, suggests scrapping the entire US federal welfare system for working-aged persons (Murray 1986). In fact, his attitude towards the significance of empirical evidence is even more cavalier than the foregoing suggests:

How big is the British underclass? It all depends on how one defines its membership; trying to take a head count is a waste of time. The size of the underclass can be made to look huge or insignificant depending on what one wants the answer to be. (Murray 1990: 23)

As employed by Murray, the concept is hopelessly imprecise empirically. It can, as Dean (1991) observes, be as extensive as one's concerns with what does or does not constitute deviant behaviour. Indeed, for Murray the habitual criminal is the classic member of the underclass. More generally, as Dean (1991) stresses, the underclass is defined in terms of criteria of productive work and/or family life from which its members are excluded. The language of the underclass, Lister (1991) emphasizes, is not only imprecise, it is the language of disease and contamination. Liberal attempts to homogenize the poor are rejected, while at the same time all able-bodied poverty comes to be understood in terms of behavioural poverty.

An accumulating body of evidence has tended to undermine the notion that phenomena such as unemployment, crime, single motherhood and poor education are all causally related in a way that requires one overarching explanation rather than reference to a diversity of structural processes (Dilnot 1992; Duncan and Hoffman 1991; Jencks 1991; Morris and Irwin 1992; Peterson 1991). A good deal of the recent literature on the 'underclass' concept in its conservative form has focused on establishing its long and undistinguished pedigree which re-emerges in various guises and at various times, with its echoes of notions of 'deserving' and 'undeserving' poor (Dean 1991; Lister 1991; Macnicol 1987). It is tempting, therefore, to conclude, following Gans (1990), that 'underclass' should be dispensed with as a value-laden pejorative term. There is, however, as Wilson (1991) argues, a need to take into account that, if there is a danger in the use of such terms, equally there is risk that, in attempting to avoid the charge of blaming the victim, social scientists may inhibit the kind of research that is necessary in order to develop an understanding of the processes of marginalization and exclusion. He notes how, in the aftermath of the Moynihan Report (Moynihan 1965) on the black family and the acrimonious debate over the existence and nature of the culture of poverty, scholarly studies of the inner-city ghetto ground to a halt with the void being filled by journalists. Similarly, in the UK social policy analysts have steered clear of 'researching cultural or behavioral aspects of social division for fear of offering hostages to right wing opinions' (Jordan and Redley 1994: 156).

The use of the term 'underclass' on both the left and the right appears to have been associated more with the adoption of positions on the issues of blame and responsibility rather than with systematic empirical inquiry. If we accept Piachaud's (1987) argument, that the term 'poverty' carries with it the implication of moral imperative that something should be done about it and that the study of poverty is only ultimately justifiable if it influences individual and social attitudes and actions, then it becomes impossible for 'academic' treatments of poverty to avoid these issues. What can be done is to situate such debate in the context of a precise specification of empirical issues and a careful elaboration of theoretical arguments. From this perspective, the controversy over the underclass can be seen to have productive as well as confusing consequences, and, as Wilson (1991) argues, 'any crusade to abandon the concept could result in a premature closure of debate'.

While there is no generally shared view of what is implied by the concept of 'an underclass' at a very general level, definitions tend to share three common features:

first an underclass is a social stratum that suffers from prolonged labour market marginality; second it experiences greater deprivation than even the manual working class and third it possesses its own distinctive sub-culture. (Gallie 1994: 737)

One of the difficulties, however, with the underclass literature is that research frequently fails to encompass the distinct elements, with a consequent blurring of the distinction between these types of analysis. The most common occurrence involves an attempt to draw conclusions regarding individuals and households from aggregate data:

What tends to happen . . . even in the most sophisticated analysis, is a subtle form of the ecological fallacy: the attributes of a shared space are believed to imply shared attributes among individuals occupying that space. (Hughes 1989: 190)

Thus, as Hughes emphasizes, to go from an identification of areas with particular characteristics, such as female-headed households, welfare recipients, male unemployment, and the fact that such groups share the physical attribute of residence in a particular area, to assumptions regarding shared values and behaviour involves 'a heroic inference'. Furthermore, as the rates of such characteristics are intended to *explain* the underclass, they can hardly at the same time *define* it.

Following Katz (1993), we identify the central issues in the underclass debate as relating to the balance between individual agency and structural factors in the creation of poverty and the role of cultural factors in perpetuating poverty and disadvantage. However, unlike authors such as Aponte (1990), we see no point in replacing a 'behavioural' or cultural conception of the underclass with one defined solely in terms of deprivation. It is, however, possible to assign primary causal significance to structural factors while still allowing a potential role for sub-cultural factors which would justify the use of the term 'underclass'.

Our concern in this chapter is with such a conception and, in particular, with the hypotheses generated by Wilson (1987, 1991). The term 'underclass', he notes, was coined by Myrdal to describe those who had been driven to extreme economic marginality because of changes in what is now called post-industrial society. This development of the concept points to an interpretation which stresses that certain sectors of the population are prone to unemployment and poverty as a consequence of economic changes. While accepting the accuracy of anthropological descriptions of the urban underclass, Wilson provides an explanation which focuses on the unintended social consequences of the uneven impact of economic change. His central propositions are as follows (see also e.g. Peterson 1991):

1. Economic change leads to a demand for different forms of labour and is associated with significant institutional change in labour market arrangements.
2. These changes have a disproportionate effect on particular groups.
3. The major change involves a weakening of attachment to the labour market among such groups, with a dramatic decline in the proportion in stable, reasonably well paid jobs.
4. These effects are aggravated by outward migration.
5. The effects of economic change are compounded by social isolation. Marginalization has differential consequences in terms of the risks of persistent poverty depending on location.

The issue is not simply that the underclass or 'ghetto poor' have a marginal position in the labour market similar to that of other disadvantaged groups, it is also that their economic position is uniquely reinforced by their milieu. (Wilson 1991: 12)

6. Joblessness, especially prolonged joblessness, is likely to be associated with, or to produce feelings of, low perceived self-efficacy. People

come to seriously doubt that they can accomplish what is expected of them, or, even where this is not true, they may give up trying because they consider that their efforts will be futile given the environmental constraints within which they operate. It is hypothesized, furthermore, that such feelings of low self-efficacy are reinforced by the feelings and values of others operating in the same social context, producing what Bandura (1982) termed 'lower collective efficacy'. The psychological self-efficacy theory must be considered in the context of the structural problem of labour force attachment and the role played by cultural factors in the transmission of self and collective beliefs. A particular pattern of behaviour is explained by a combination of constraints, opportunities, and social psychology. Wilson rejects one social psychology—that implied in the culture-of-poverty thesis—in favour of a more situational psychology which provides the indispensable link between structure and action (see Zelditch 1993: 101–2).

In its most general form, Wilson's model involves exogenous factors such as changes in the economy, exogenous determinants consequent on those exogenous factors, distribution of employment and income, migration, size of pool of marriageable men, and, finally, endogenous determinants including social isolation unique to the underclass, such as neighbourhood resources and role models and cultural isolation from mainstream networks.

The structural emphasis in Wilson's work is particularly important. Elwood (1989) has identified three approaches to the issue of dependency, i.e. rational choice, expectancy, and culture, which he sees as corresponding roughly to the disciplines of economics, social psychology, and anthropology. He acknowledges, however, the difficulties he experienced in incorporating a sociological emphasis on major differences by class. Wilson's formulation provides at least the possibility of moving beyond the situation where economists are seen to study how people make choices while sociologists study how people have no choices to make (Prosser 1991: 14). It is also consistent with the rejection of Elwood's insistence on separating out 'pure models' of choice and culture and his adherence to the notion that culture itself contains a significant element of rational choice (Sullivan 1989). Wilson stresses that his conceptual framework can be applied not only to all ethnic and racial groups but also to other societies. What is crucial is a combination of weak labour force attachment and social isolation which may exist without the same level of concentration inherent in the American ghetto. Drawing out the implications of Wilson's model, we would wish to restrict the application of the term 'underclass' to those situations where evidence exists of effects of a kind which, through their impact on factors such as feelings of self-efficacy, contribute to 'vicious circle' processes in terms of detachment from the labour market (Ultee *et al.* 1988). This position may be contrasted with that adopted by Runciman

(1990) and Smith (1992), who reject a culturally based definition of the 'underclass' in favour of one based solely on ineffective participation or non-participation in the labour market.

7.2   Class and Underclass Perspectives

At this point it is our intention to provide an assessment of the relative value of class and underclass perspectives using the Republic of Ireland as a test case, drawing on the results of our analysis of deprivation and poverty in previous chapters. The single most important feature of the Irish situation in this context, which makes it a particularly interesting and useful test case, is the level of long-term unemployment. Between 1980 and 1987 the total at work fell by 76,000, and despite high levels of emigration the numbers unemployed soared to 232,000 or almost 18 per cent of the workforce. The dramatic increase in the level of unemployment between 1980 and 1987 was accompanied by a steady increase in the proportion who were long-term unemployed. Statistics on the registered unemployed show that in April 1980 35 per cent of those on the Live Register had been registered continuously for over a year; by April 1987 this figure had reached 44 per cent. While the overall unemployment rate was well above average for those aged under 25, most of the long-term unemployed were aged over 25 or over and 80 per cent were men. The increasing importance of long-term unemployment was accompanied by a shift in the pattern of social welfare support. Whereas in 1980 47 per cent of those on the Live Register were in receipt of insurance-based unemployment benefit (UB), and 48 per cent received the means-tested unemployment assistance (UA), by 1987 only 37 per cent were on UB and the percentage on UA had risen to 58 per cent (O'Connell and Sexton 1994).

This level of long-term unemployment makes Ireland quite distinctive among OECD countries. By 1992, 44 per cent of the registered long-term unemployed had been unemployed for over three years. The depth of the problem is further illustrated by data on unemployment survival rates. Persons unemployed for under a year have a probability of 0.3 of being unemployed a year later; for those who have been unemployed for between one to two years the probability is 0.61, and for those who have been unemployed for over two years the figure rises to 0.74. Furthermore, the relationship between length of unemployment and exit probability became more pronounced as the level of unemployment increased. This finding is consistent with the application of a ranking rule whereby employers prefer to employ the applicant with the shortest current spell of unemployment. The implication of such a ranking procedure is that those who are currently employed have little to fear from unemployment, even when aggregate unemployment is high. This hypothesis is supported by evidence that, while the initial rise in unemployment during the early 1980s had a significant restraining effect on wages, this effect declined as the incidence of long-term unemployment increased, and the total negative effective of unemployment on wage inflation is back at levels prevailing prior to the explosion of unemployment (K. Whelan 1994). Against this background, it is hardly surprising that references to an 'underclass' have come to be increasingly frequent in discussions of unemployment and poverty. Explanations of the inherent persistence of long-term unemployment make reference to processes of de-skilling and de-motivation and to the consequence that the long-term unemployed may come to be regarded by employers as not 'employable' and, in a sense, may cease to be part of the labour market (NESF 1994).

The central issue that we seek to address is whether the Irish situation can be most fruitfully approached through a search for an underclass, and a focus on a category of the population that is nominally separated from other groups, or, alternatively, through concentration on processes that affect all classes (as Fainstein 1993 puts it). In pursuing this issue, it will become clear that it is necessary to keep in mind that the swiftness and unevenness of the pattern of class transformation sets Ireland apart. Ireland in the 1950s was still very much a sub-region of the UK labour market. The broad stability of the class structure was largely attributable to emigration. For those remaining, the unemployment rate was relatively low. In 1961, the number of males employed in non-skilled manual occupations was still three-and-a-half times greater than the number unemployed. Over the 1960s and 1970s, as the Irish economy became an almost textbook example of a small open economy, the position of most families in the new class structure was established. Upper middle-class employment for men increased from 7.6 to 16.1 per cent of all jobs between 1961 and 1981, while at the same time non-skilled positions declined from 21 to 14 per cent. The new positions were largely beyond the reach of those whose positions in indigenous industry had been undermined (Breen et al. 1990).

In a situation where there was a continuing high natural increase in the Irish labour force, together with a rapid exodus from agricultural employment, the relative competitive ability of the lower working class declined in important respects. Structural change was accompanied by a remarkable stability in class mobility chances at the extremes of the class hierarchy. At the same time, those from lower working-class backgrounds lost out in competition for both service class and skilled manual positions to the children of the petit bourgeoisie and small farmers (Hannan and Commins 1992; Whelan et al. 1992). While the number leaving school without educational qualifications has declined dramatically, such failure has become increasingly concentrated among those from lower working-class origins, and the consequences of educational failure have become more serious. By 1990 the total number of males employed in non-skilled manual work was only 70 per cent of the number of unemployed males (O'Connell and Sexton 1994). If one holds the view that distinctive ethnic or racial characteristics are a *sine qua non* of an underclass, the application of the term to the Irish case must be ruled out; otherwise the possibility holds that the Irish case might provide particularly fertile ground for the application of a model such as Wilson's. Wilson's (1978) early contribution, which argued that blacks were increasingly being stratified and differentiated by class, was entitled 'The Declining Significance of Race'. While his thesis has been challenged, this does not invalidate the argument we have presented relating to the range of applicability of the model (Fainstein 1993).

In applying this model, we will seek to take the following steps:

1. Identify a marginalized working class in terms of labour market experiences.
2. Consider whether it is necessary to distinguish different forms of working-class marginalization.
3. Evaluate whether the consequences of marginalization are such as to produce a level of deprivation significantly different from the manual working class.
4. Assess the extent to which those in the marginalized working class are socially isolated from the remainder of the working class.
5. In the light of the evidence relating to the incidence and risk of working-class marginalization, and the manner in which this varies by type of marginalization, develop the argument that the nature of working-class marginalization in Ireland must be understood in the context of the rapid and uneven nature of the transformation of the class structure.
6. Evaluate the evidence for the existence of an interaction effect between working-class marginalization and milieu which in terms of its consequence for level of fatalism is consistent with Wilson's thesis.

The approach adapted here in seeking to test for milieu effects is, necessarily, indirect, given that our analysis is based on a national sample of households. It takes advantage of the fact that we have information available not only on the labour market experience of households but also on the location and types of housing tenure. The evidence from analysis employing these data will be supplemented by the results deriving from 'small-area' census data relating to the extent to which unemployment is concentrated in particular areas.

Our analysis takes its starting-point from the understanding that the substantive significance of the milieu effects which we seek to explore depends both on the strength of the statistical effect and on the degree of geographical concentration of the marginalized working class in such locations. Consequently, our first step in dealing with the issue of social isolation is to examine the extent to which the marginalized working class is concentrated in urban areas or, more particularly, in public-sector housing in such areas, and the degree to which the observed level of concentration is consistent with the potential emergence of an underclass. Since we recognize that the term 'underclass' would not necessarily be expected to apply to all marginalized working-class households in urban public-sector housing, we extend our attempt to identify the socially isolated component of the class by focusing on urban public-sector tenants, and by distinguishing between different types of marginalization.

Within Wilson's framework, class and underclass perspectives are complementary rather than mutually exclusive. The impact of economic change has a disproportionate effect on particular classes, and the particular form that the working out of such change takes in a specific milieu is what leads to the creation of an underclass. Again, this position can be distinguished from that adopted by Runciman (1990), where the long-term unemployed, being among those 'whose roles place them more or less permanently at the economic level where benefits are paid by the state to those unable to participate in the labour market', are placed in a residual category. With this definition, as with Smith's (1992), the underclass fall *outside* the class schema.

The competing approaches are based on differing responses to the challenge raised for class analysis by large-scale and long-term employment. Morris and Irwin (1992) note that Runciman and Smith's definitions 'fail to engage with conventional class analysis' and with the fact that vulnerability to employment, and in particular long-term employment, is a feature of location in the working class (p. 402). Approaches that obscure this connection undermine our ability to understand the dynamics of labour market experience (Morris 1993). Thus, as Marshall *et al.* (forthcoming) argue, critiques of the treatment of the unemployed in class analysis frequently involve the tendency to think of class in static rather than dynamic terms, or as structure rather than process. The fact that people are not in employment at a particular point in time does not imply they have dropped out of the class structure or that their previous class experiences have become irrelevant.

In what follows, each household included in our analysis will be allocated a class position employing an aggregated version of the CASMIN class schema. As Gallie (1994: 739) notes, conceptions of the 'underclass' differ in terms of whether they treat the individual or the household as the unit of analysis. Given the variety of issues raised by those employing the term, there appears to be little point in adopting a dogmatic stance on this issue. Within the framework we have adopted, the crucial issue, in class terms, is whether there is a class that, as a consequence of weak labour force attachment, extreme deprivation, social isolation, and distinctive sub-cultural characteristics, cannot be identified simply as an element of the working class. The need to establish the connection between detachment from the labour market and deprivation provides a basis for focusing on the household as the unit of strategic action in terms of consumption and production. The choice of the household as the unit of analysis enables us to explore the consequences of the labour market detachment of, in particular, the person considered by the household members to be the 'head of household' for 'experiences of affluence or hardship, of economic security of insecurity, of prospects of continuing material advance, or of unyielding material constraints' (Erikson and Goldthorpe 1992: 236). Although in the case of married couples we take into account the labour market situation of both parties, we have chosen not to pursue the 'dominance' approach in this case, because of the likelihood that the relative probabilities of the husband or wife being currently the one with the 'dominant' relationship to the labour market may reflect the scale of detachment from the labour market (Erikson 1984).

7.3 Working-Class Marginalization

Detachment from the labour market is the first step in the hypothesized causal sequence leading to the emergence of an underclass. Smith's definition of the underclass as those 'family units having no stable relationship with legitimate gainful employment' conveys a clear sense of such marginalization, while leaving the whole question of operationalization open (Smith 1992: 5). However, taken together with a frame of reference which seeks to establish whether there is a class that needs to be thought of as other than a fraction of the working class, this approach allows for the identification of a *marginalized working class* defined solely in terms of current class situation and labour market experience. The consequences of such marginalization, in terms of deprivation, remain an empirical question, as does the extent of geographical concentration, or the existence of contextual effects.

In pursuing a definition of the marginalized working class, we exclude both households with a head aged 65 or over and farm households. This leaves us with a sample of 2,153 households. Our focus is, as Buck (1992: 11) puts it, on the 'stable absence of relationship to employment, on the one hand, and unstable relationship with employment on the other'. Arriving at a definition of the marginalized working class involves taking a number of criteria into account. Varying the cut-off points on any of these criteria will affect our estimates of the size of the group. However, rather than examining in detail a variety of cut-off points, our analysis proceeds in terms of the preferred options while directing attention to some of the most important consequences of such options.

The first criterion relates to stability of membership of the unemployed; here two years' unemployment is chosen as the cut-off point. With regard to stable relationship to employment, use is made of a measure of proportion of potential labour market time spent unemployed. The denominator excludes time spent ill or disabled or in retirement. Any cut-off point is bound to be arbitrary. The option chosen is one of 20 per cent of potential labour market time, with the additional condition that the individual must have been at least five years in the labour market. The choice has been made because the notion of marginalization implies severe problems in establishing a connection with the labour market. Varying the cut-off point does not have a dramatic effect on our results, and such differences as do exist are further moderated by the requirement that the household satisfy other criteria.

Thus, where the household head is currently in employment, and has not experienced a spell of unemployment in the previous twelve months, the household is excluded from the marginalized working class. Furthermore, since concern is with family units having no stable relationship with legitimate gainful employment, those households in which the spouse is in employment are excluded. Finally, it is necessary for the household head to be a member of the working class. The definition of 'the working class' is crucial in determining the final outcome of our procedures. There would appear to be no virtue in restricting attention to the lower working class because *a priori* we would expect that at least some significant section of the upper working class would have been exposed to consequences of the structural change that we see as the major factor contributing to the potential emergence of a marginalized working class. This view is supported by the results set out in Table 7.1, in which the labour market experience of heads of household is broken down by social class. (Except as a class of origin, farmers do not figure in this analysis.)

From the table, the scale of the labour market difficulties that have been experienced by lower working-class households becomes clear. More than four out of ten are currently unemployed. They have been unemployed for,

Table 7.1 Labour market experience of head of household, by social class

	% unemployed	No. of weeks unemployed in previous 12 mos.	Career unemployment: no. of years unemployed	Career unemployment: proportion of potential labour market time unemployed	Number of cases
Salariat	0.8	0.81	0.21	0.01	450
Intermediate non-manual	5.7	2.49	0.66	0.03	361
Upper working class	21.1	9.28	1.51	0.07	999
Lower working class	41.6	19.33	4.00	0.16	268
Total	16.7	7.57	1.40	0.06	2,078

on average, for nineteen weeks in the previous twelve months, for four years in their 'careers', and for 16 per cent of their potential time in the labour market. The situation of the upper working class, while a good deal more favourable, still provides a picture of substantial unemployment problems. Over one in five were unemployed. They have been unemployed for, on average, more than nine weeks in the previous year; for one-and-a-half years throughout their careers, and for 7 per cent of their potential labour market time. The situation of those outside the working class is substantially more favourable.

On the basis of these findings, in our analysis of marginalization, 'working class' is defined as including both the upper and lower working class. The working definition of the marginalized working class is as follows:

1. The head of household is in the working class, *and*
2. the head of household has been unemployed for two years or more or has spent 20 per cent or more of his/her potential labour market time since leaving full-time education unemployed and has been in the labour market for at least five years, *and*
3. the spouse of the head of household is not in employment.

In addition,

4. Where the head of household is currently employed and has not experienced a spell of unemployment in the previous twelve months, the household is excluded.

Such households constitute 11 per cent of non-farm households where the head is under 65. Adopting a criterion of 15 per cent of potential labour market time as a cut-off point, the figure rises to 12 per cent.

We also wish to allow for the possibility that the consequences of relatively persistent labour market difficulties throughout one's time in the labour force may be rather different from those arising from a limited number of spells of long-term unemployment. A further distinction has therefore been introduced between what we term *pervasive* and *restricted* working-class marginalization. The former refers to a situation where the household head has been unemployed for at least 20 per cent of his/her potential labour market time, while the latter relates to the situation where this does *not* hold but the conditions for marginalization are still fulfilled. The pervasively marginalized working class contains 7.9 per cent of non-agricultural households where the head is aged less than 65, with 3.2 per cent falling into the restricted marginalization category. The experience of the former group would appear to approximate most closely the situation envisaged by Wilson. We will, therefore, pay particular attention to this group.

Having established the existence of a sizeable marginalized working class and drawn attention to a degree of differentiation within this group, we now proceed to an examination of the second element of Gallie's definition of the underclass. This involves attempting to establish whether this group experiences a degree of deprivation greater than even the manual working class.

7.4   Working-Class Marginalization and Deprivation

Since working-class marginalization refers to a process occurring over a considerable period of time, we might expect that the distinction we have made throughout the previous chapters, relating to current income and longer-term resource accumulation and their implications for different dimensions of life-style deprivation, will prove particularly salient in this case. In exploring the extent of deprivation associated with working-class marginalization, it is necessary to go beyond current levels of income and take into account differential accumulation of resources. The full range of measures of resources and deprivation that we report is as follows:

1. income in terms of mean decile position in the equivalent income distribution;
2. mean level of savings in the form of deposits in banks or building societies;
3. percentage of households owning their house;
4. mean score on the enforced basic deprivation index;
5. mean score on the enforced secondary deprivation index;
6. mean score on the enforced housing deprivation index;
7. percentage of households falling below 60 per cent of average income and reporting enforced basic deprivation;
8. percentage of households experiencing extreme difficulty in making ends meet.

The breakdown of these variables by class situation is set out in Table 7.2. In subsequent analysis, in order to focus on key comparisons, the upper and middle classes have been combined. The threefold distinction between the middle class, the working class, and the marginalized working class will be referred to as the 'class situation'. In order to provide an adequate test of the hypothesis that those in the marginalized working class experience a degree of deprivation that is distinctive, we have also provided details of further differentiation of households by labour market status within the non-marginalized working class.

From Table 7.2 we can see that household income varies systematically across the categories of the class situation variable. The decile score for income declines from 7.59 for the middle class to 5.49 for the non-marginalized working class, finally reaching 2.65 for the marginalized working class. Even among those not in employment in the non-marginalized

Table 7.2 Resources and deprivation, by class situation

Class situation	Mean income decile	Mean savings (IR£)	% owning house	Mean index score			% poor	% experiencing economic strain
				Basic deprivation	Secondary deprivation	Housing deprivation		
Middle class	7.59	2,925	86.4	0.33	1.36	0.13	3.7	17.1
Non-marginalized working class in employment etc.	5.49	1,491	74.8	0.79	2.91	0.38	17.5	36.0
unemployed	5.98	1,660	75.6	0.70	2.67	0.33	12.9	31.6
head 50–64 and retired or ill and disabled	3.94	474	66.4	1.04	3.75	0.37	30.7	49.8
Marginalized working class	3.74	1,497	80.1	1.10	3.63	0.74	30.9	51.5
Restricted marginalization	2.65	292	39.2	2.71	4.83	0.77	66.7	75.1
Pervasive marginalization	2.80	791	58.3	1.75	4.52	0.63	50.1	58.5
	2.59	74	31.3	3.12	4.96	0.83	73.8	82.4

working class, income levels are significantly higher than for those in the marginalized group. There is relatively little variation within the marginalized working class. The situation in relation to savings is rather different. While the savings level of the non-marginalized working class is at approximately half the level of middle-class households, it is over five times greater than that reported by the marginalized group. In this case, however, it is necessary to take into account significant variation between the segments of the working class. The groups reporting the lowest levels of savings are those households within the non-marginalized working class with unemployed heads of households and those experiencing pervasive marginalization: their respective deposit levels are £474 and £74. In the non-marginalized households where the head is in employment this rises to £1,660; and for the marginalized who have not experienced persistent unemployment it reaches £791. The pervasively marginalized households are also distinguished by a particularly low level of house ownership, with less than 33 per cent owning their homes. For the restricted marginalized group the figure comes closer to 60 per cent, and it is not too far distant from that for non-marginalized working-class households where the head is unemployed. Pervasively marginalized households are distinctive in the extent to which they are characterized not only by a shortfall in current income but also by the erosion of, or failure to accumulate, longer-term resources.

The impact of class situation varies depending upon the type of life-style deprivation on which one focuses. Although those households in the marginalized working class display the highest level of housing deprivation, the extent of variation across class situation is relatively modest. This appears to reflect the extent to which the availability of the rather basic housing facilities included in this index is affected by factors other than labour market situation. Secondary deprivation is more strongly related to class situation. In this instance the gap between the middle class and the non-marginalized working class is of a similar order to that between the two segments of the working class. Relatively little variation is observed within the marginalized working class. It is in relation to basic deprivation that the most dramatic consequences are observed. While the average difference in scores between the middle class and non-marginalized working class is 0.46, it rises to 1.98 between the sections of the working class. It is the extent of enforced absence of basic items relating to food, clothing, and heat that most sharply differentiates the marginalized working class from all other households. For those households experiencing pervasive marginalization the basic deprivation score reaches 3.12, which is almost twice that of restricted marginalization group, four times that of the non-marginalized working class, and, indeed, three times that of those not in employment in the non-marginalized group.

As the penultimate column makes clear, what is most distinctive about the marginalized working class, and particularly the pervasive marginalization group, is the extent to which they are exposed to poverty. Less than 4 per cent of middle-class households are below the 60 per cent income line and experiencing enforced basic deprivation. This figure rises to over 17 per cent of the non-marginalized working class, although among those not employed it is as high as 31 per cent. For the marginalized working class as a whole, however, the level of risk reaches 67 per cent, with the respective figures for restricted and pervasive marginalization reaching 50 and 74 per cent, respectively.

Furthermore, the subjective experience of the pervasively marginalized also sets them apart from all other groups. Thus, the percentage of households indicating that they are experiencing extreme difficulty in making ends meet rises from just over 17 per cent of the middle class to almost 50 per cent of the unemployed working class, but the pervasively marginalized group, where the figures exceed 80 per cent, once again occupies a distinctive position.

Our analysis clearly demonstrates that Gallie's second condition is met. Labour market marginality is associated with a level of deprivation significantly greater than that experienced by the remainder of the manual working class including those where the household head is not in employment. Furthermore, the pervasively marginalized working-class households experience a degree of erosion of resources and a resultant level of deprivation and economic strain that sets them apart from all other households.

7.5 Marginalization and Social Isolation

The distinctive underclass sub-cultural characteristics identified by Wilson are seen to arise from the combination of labour market detachment and social isolation. The substantive importance of a contextual effect depends both on the strength of the effect and on the degree to which marginalization is concentrated in particular locations. For this reason, our initial focus is on the incidence of marginalization, i.e. the percentage of all those marginalized who are to be found in particular categories.

In Table 7.3 we show the distribution of the incidence of marginalization by location and housing tenure. In terms of location, we distinguish between those living in the main urban centres and those residing elsewhere. These centres range in size from Dublin with a population of over one million to Waterford with just over 90,000 inhabitants. The major distinction in relation to tenure is between public- and private-sector housing; we distinguish further, however, within the public sector between tenants and those purchasing their houses from the local authority.

There is no evidence of concentration of marginalization in the main urban centres, despite a tendency to presume so in previous discussions (Breen *et al.* 1990). Over 65 per cent of the group are located outside these

Table 7.3 Incidence of working-class marginalization, by housing tenure and location in a main urban centre (%)

	Marginalization			Distribution of the non-marginalized working class
	Overall	Restricted	Pervasive	
Urban centres				
All households	34.5	34.3	34.6	35.3
Public housing	23.9	20.9	25.2	16.4
Purchase scheme	3.5	4.5	3.2	6.7
Tenant	20.4	16.4	22.0	9.7
Private housing	10.6	13.4	9.4	18.9
Outside urban centres				
All households	65.5	65.7	65.4	64.7
Public housing	37.6	22.4	44.0	17.0
Purchase scheme	5.8	4.5	5.7	6.5
Tenant	31.8	17.9	38.3	10.5
Private housing	27.9	43.3	21.4	47.7

urban centres, compared with just under 60 per cent of all non-farm households with a head aged under 65. Restricting attention to Dublin strengthens this conclusion: one in five marginalized working-class households are located in Dublin compared with almost one in three non-farm households. Furthermore, the urban–rural breakdown is almost identical for pervasive and restricted marginalization.

It is housing tenure rather than location that emerges as the crucial factor in relation to concentration. Location in rented public-sector housing is the key factor. The contrast that emerges, however, is between the pervasively marginalized working class and all others, rather than between the marginalized and the non-marginalized. Six out of ten pervasively marginalized households are found in such housing compared with one in three restricted marginalization households and one in five of the non-marginalized. The most plausible hypothesis relating to social isolation would involve households in urban rented public-sector housing being comprised predominantly of pervasively marginalized households. This possibility is explored in Table 7.4, where the class composition of rented public-sector housing in urban and rural areas is revealed.

Despite the high probability of the pervasively marginalized working-class households in urban centres being found in rented public-sector housing, they constitute only 21 per cent of such households; in rural areas it rises to 31 per cent. In neither case do the figures suggest social isolation. In urban centres 73 per cent of households are drawn from outside both sections of the marginalized working class; in rural areas the corresponding figures is 64 per cent. If the case for social isolation of a substantial segment

Table 7.4 Class composition of rented public-sector housing, by urban–rural location (%)

	Urban	Rural
Middle class	14.4	7.5
Working class		
Non-marginalized	58.4	56.5
Restricted marginalized	6.5	5.9
Pervasive marginalized	20.7	31.1
Total	100.0	100.0
Number of cases	170	196

of the pervasively marginalized working class is to be sustained, some further powerful differentiating factors within the rented public sector will need to be identified.

The conclusions we have reached are consistent with analysis based on the most spatially disaggregated 1986 Population Census unit, namely the district electoral divisions (DEDs). While 3 per cent of DEDs had unemployment rates over twice the national average, in order to cover a majority of the unemployed, it would be necessary to widen the focus to incorporate the 30 per cent of DEDs with the highest unemployment rates, within which almost 40 per cent of the population are contained. The DED analysis confirms that substantial variation in the risk of unemployment across areas is consistent with a distribution of the unemployed which confirms that unemployment is a spatially pervasive phenomenon (Nolan *et al.* 1994; Williams 1994).

7.6 Cohort Experience and Working-Class Marginalization

The process of working-class marginalization in Ireland must be understood not in terms of the location of particular classes, but rather in terms of the rapid and uneven nature of the transformation of the class structure and the variable consequences of such transformation for different cohorts and class origins. While marginalization is not concentrated in urban centres, its incidence is strongly related to age. This is not the case, however, in regard to overall marginalization, because the impact of age operates in opposite directions for restricted and pervasive marginalization. The pattern of results is set out in Table 7.5. Pervasive marginalization is concentrated among those households where the head is under 40. Over 70 per cent of the group fall into this category, and 60 per cent of the household heads are aged between 25 and 40. The situation in relation to restricted marginalization is just the opposite, with 75 per cent being over 40; indeed, more than 50 per cent are over 50. The risk figures show that for pervasive

Table 7.5 Incidence of working-class marginalization, by age group (%)

Age of head	Marginalization			Size of age group
	Overall	Pervasive	Restricted	
18–29	19.2	25.4	4.6	14.4
30–39	38.8	46.9	19.9	33.7
40–49	13.0	9.3	21.9	21.9
50–64	28.9	18.4	53.7	30.0

marginalization the sharpest contrast is between those under 40 and all others. Differences between age groups on either side of this divide are relatively modest. In the case of restricted marginalization, the risk rises gradually by age group.

An age effect is to some extent built into our definition of the different types of marginalization. Only where the head has ten or more years in the labour force can he or she, at the same time, be two or more years unemployed and have spent less than 20 per cent of potential labour market time unemployed, thereby fulfilling a condition of membership of the restricted marginalization group. However, given the requirement of having been in the labour market for at least five years, only 4 per cent of working class households are, in principle, capable of fulfilling the conditions for pervasive marginalization but not those for restricted marginalization.

The main issue that it is necessary to consider is whether the effect observed is predominantly an age or a cohort one. What is the probability that the observed labour market experiences of the younger cohorts simply represent the early stages of a path that will with advancing years come near to that observed for the older cohorts? Alternatively, we may ask to what extent the earlier experience of the older cohorts may have resembled that of the younger ones, but this is obscured by our dependence on summary measures of labour market experience rather than detailed labour market histories. The balance of evidence, we argue, is decisively in favour of a cohort rather than an age explanation. The observed variation reflects substantial differences in the early labour market experiences of the younger and older cohorts, and there is little reason to think that their experiences will converge over time. The differences between the cohorts must be understood in the context of the pattern of class transformation outlined earlier in this chapter. The younger working-class groups have been exposed to a high risk of unemployment for a relatively higher proportion of their labour market careers. The older group, on the other hand, spent a great deal of their working lives in the labour market at a time when the absence of employment opportunities was reflected in large-scale emigration rather than long-term unemployment and a potential marginalized working class was thereby exported. Declining opportunities outside

Ireland for those without skills and qualifications, coupled with a reduction of the gap in social welfare benefits, has reduced the attractiveness of emigration for the kinds of household making up the pervasively marginalized working class (O'Connell and Rottman 1992).

7.7 Marginalization, Location, and Fatalism: a Test of the Milieu Effect Hypothesis

The evidence from both our household survey and the Census small-area data indicates that working-class marginalization and, indeed, unemployment are spatially pervasive phenomena. It remains a legitimate question, however, whether marginalization is experienced in a qualitatively different manner in some locations as opposed to others. In the context of the underclass debate, the comparison that is of most interest is that between the pervasively marginalized working class located in rented urban public-sector housing and other pervasively marginalized households. In the analysis that follows, we explore the relationship between pervasive working-class marginalization, location in urban rented public-sector housing, and fatalism. In statistical terms, the 'underclass' hypothesis implies that the impact of location in urban public-sector rented housing on fatalism is greater for the pervasively marginalized working class than for other households. It is this interaction that appears to be crucial, rather than any outcome that could arise simply from the additive effects of marginalization and location. In fact, an adequate test of the 'underclass' hypothesis requires that we control for characteristics of households other than pervasive marginalization, which are correlated with location in rented public-sector housing. This is necessary because additional variables, such as poverty, which are strongly related to fatalism, display greater variation by location *outside* the pervasively marginalized working class. This pattern of variation might be expected to produce an interaction effect with the opposite sign to that suggested by the underclass hypothesis.

The pervasively marginalized working-class households in rented urban public-sector housing appear to be the prime candidate for the designation 'underclass'. However, the evidence we have presented suggests that the class composition of such housing is sufficiently heterogeneous to make unlikely the type of social isolation that would characterize an underclass. It remains possible that the pervasively marginalized urban working-class households are socially isolated from other households *within* the rented public sector. However, a significant interaction of the kind implied by the underclass hypothesis would provide support for the existence of some such process of social segregation.

It could be argued that the distinction between the pervasively marginalized working class in urban rented public-sector housing and all other households involves the wrong contrast, or operates at too aggregated a level. In the USA a number of studies have provided evidence that, whatever the consequences of poverty, there is little evidence that the poor are more isolated than they have been in the past. Wilson (1991) has responded by arguing that evidence relating to a concentration of poverty in standard metropolitan areas is not relevant to his thesis because it does not identify ghetto neighbourhoods. Peterson (1991) notes that Wilson strengthens his theory by narrowing his focus to those neighbourhoods that are characterized by extreme economic marginality and extreme isolation, but at the expense of narrowing its explanatory focus.

In Ireland, the pervasively marginalized working class in urban rented public-sector housing constitute 1.6 per cent of all households where the head is aged less than 65, 15 per cent of marginalized working-class households; and 9 per cent of all households meeting our combined income–basic deprivation poverty criteria where the head is aged less than 65. If this class cannot be accurately characterized as an urban 'underclass', then it appears that an Irish 'underclass' when identified either would look very different from what might have been expected on theoretical grounds, or would constitute a sub-set of such households sufficiently small that they would constitute a relatively trivial component of poor or marginalized working-class households.

The issue of the relationship between social class/socio-economic status and feelings of *fatalism* is one to which a great deal of attention has been devoted (Mirowsky and Ross 1990; Whelan 1992*a*). In measuring fatalism, we have drawn on a set of items that have been fairly widely used in the literature (Pearlin *et al.* 1981):

1. I can do just about anything I set my mind to.
2. I have little control over the things that happen to me.
3. What happens to me in the future depends on me.
4. I often feel helpless in dealing with the problem of life.
5. Sometimes I feel I am being pushed around in life.
6. There is a lot I can do to change my life if I want to.
7. There is really no way I can solve some of the problems I have.

Respondents were asked to react to each of the items on a four-point scale running from 'strongly agree' to 'strongly disagree'. Scoring on the items has been carried out so as to take into account the direction of the items. The final scale has a very satisfactory level of reliability, with Cronbach's alpha reaching a value of 0.73, and has a potential range of scores running from 4, indicating the highest possible level of fatalism, to 1, indicating the lowest possible level.

The concept of fatalism is itself far from being unproblematic. As Marshall *et al.* (forthcoming) note, its potential range of meanings varies from the strict sense of a system of beliefs, which holds that everything has an appointed outcome which can not be altered by effort or foreknowledge, to a sense of resignation based on the realities of a difficult life-situation, to a more imprecise set of connotations covering cynicism towards established values of work and order. The operationalization we have chosen focuses on the intermediate sense of resignation which is the level most appropriate to Wilson's hypothesis. The attitudes involved are ones which on an *a priori* basis we would expect to be related to the extent of job search. In order to provide a reference point for our results relating to fatalism, we have reported alongside them the corresponding level of psychological distress. The latter was measured using a twelve-item version of the Goldberg General Health Questionnaire and the GHQ scoring procedure (Whelan 1994a). The items included in the measure are designed to give information about the respondent's current state. It is neither a measure of long-standing personality attitudes nor an assessment of the likelihood of falling ill in the future.

We find that marginalization does have an effect on the level of fatalism, which contrasts with the evidence deriving from studies dealing with somewhat more diffuse conceptions of fatalism (Marshall *et al.* forthcoming). The results set out in Table 7.6 show that, to some extent, fatalism is a feature of working-class life. The fatalism score for the non-marginalized working class is significantly higher than that for the middle class. However, the impact of marginalization is shown by the fact there is an identical gap between the former and the pervasively marginalized group. Within the marginalized working class, variation is extremely modest. Fatalism is a variable that appears responsive to the influence of both long-term class experiences and more recent labour market experience. The findings relating to the marginalized groups are consistent with the evidence of declining

Table 7.6 Incidence of fatalism, by class situation

Class situation	Mean scores (for household heads)	
	Fatalism	GHQ
Middle class	2.18	0.74
Working class		
Non-marginalized	2.39	1.22
Restricted marginalized	2.56	1.93
Pervasive marginalized	2.60	2.52
Total	2.33	1.15
N	2,073	2,077
Proportion of variance explained by class situation	0.093	0.049

exit rates by length of unemployment and the likelihood that reduced search behaviour is a contributory factor. It is interesting, however, to note that, unlike the situation in relation to poverty and economic strain, the pervasively marginalized are not distinguishable from the restricted marginalized in terms of fatalism. This is of particular interest because such sharp differentiation does emerge once again in relation to psychological distress. The items that are included in the GHQ measure, because of their capacity to discriminate between those experiencing minor psychiatric disturbance and all others, are not, as one would expect on *a priori* grounds, those referring to traditional phenomena of illness such as psychosomatic symptoms. The items that best define such illness are 'inextricably connected with the patient's perceiving himself to be unable to cope with his problems and to deal with his social difficulties' (Goldberg 1972: 91). The pervasively marginalized appear to be psychologically distinctive not in terms of sub-culturally induced levels of fatalism, but in terms of the level of psychological distress arising from being denied access to the sources of self-esteem arising from employment and the constant need to engage in economic brinkmanship.

For the purpose of testing the underclass milieu hypothesis, it is not the difference in the extent of fatalism by marginalization that is crucial, but evidence of the interaction beween such fatalism and the life-situation. In Table 7.7 we show the impact of pervasive marginalization and location in

Table 7.7 Multiple regression of the impact of pervasive working-class marginalization and location in urban rented public-sector housing on fatalism scores of head of household

	(i)	(ii)
Pervasive working-class marginalization	0.35***	0.08*
Urban rented public-sector housing	0.26***	0.03
Pervasive working-class marginalization × urban rented public-sector housing	−0.35***	−0.18*
Poor (below 60% line experiencing basic deprivation)		0.13***
Male		0.05*
Age		0.004***
Education		
Some secondary		0.00
Completed secondary		−0.04*
Third level		−0.18***
Secondary deprivation		0.06***
Physical illness or disability		0.14***
Constant	2.29	1.91
R^2	0.057	0.286
N	1,987	1,987

*$p < 0.1$ **$p < 0.01$ ***$p < 0.001$

urban rented public-sector housing, and the interaction of such variables on fatalism. In the first equation, focusing solely on these variables, the crucial interaction term is statistically significant but negative in sign rather than positive, as required by the 'underclass' milieu hypothesis. The pattern of results reflected in the coefficient of −0.35 is one whereby, within the pervasively marginalized group, the fatalism score for those in urban rented public-sector housing is 0.09 less than for those located elsewhere, while for all others it is 0.26 higher. In equation (ii), as discussed earlier, we introduce a set of controls, to allow for the possibility that a significant context effect is being concealed by greater variation in household characteristics by housing tenure among those households outside the pervasively marginalized class. The introduction of the set of controls has the effect of reducing the coefficient for the housing variable among this group from 0.26 to 0.03, which is not statistically significant. The value of the interaction coefficient is almost halved and declines from −0.35 to −0.18, although it remains statistically significant.

Among the pervasively marginalized group, the mean fatalism scores of those in rented public-sector housing is −0.15 lower than for those located elsewhere, even when we have taken a range of control variables into account. Whatever advantages are associated with location outside of rented public-sector housing for the heads of household of the pervasively marginalized working class, they do not include increased feelings of self-efficacy.

7.8 Fatalism and Agency

Finally, it is necessary to stress that an emphasis on structural factors and a rejection of vicious-circle-type arguments of an underclass nature does not require a neglect of issues of agency. The findings we have presented are entirely consistent with the evidence that those at the bottom of the class hierarchy are socialized to be more fatalistic in their current perceptions, with a consequent undermining of persistence and effort when confronted with problems. A belief that one is, at least to some extent, master of one's own fate leads one to search the environment for potentially distressing conditions, to take preventive steps, and to accumulate resources or develope skills or habits that will reduce the impact of the unavoidable. In contrast, fatalism—the belief that important events in one's life are predetermined by external circumstances—leads one to ignore problems until they actually happen, and will in the long run be more pervasively harmful. In consequence, there is a magnification of differences, with the fatalists suffering an increasing number of problems, which reinforces a feeling of lack of control. This in turn produces passivity in the face of subsequent difficulties. Lower-class people may then carry a triple burden. They have more problems to deal with; their personal histories are likely to have left them with a deep sense of powerlessness; and that sense of powerlessness discourages them from marshalling whatever energy and resources they have in order to try to solve their problems. The result for many is a multiplication of despair (Wheaton 1983).

Of course, it is possible to argue that for many deprived respondents feelings of fatalism are simply an accurate reflection of their environment. They might even be taken as simply reflecting an accurate understanding that their deprivation arises from wider structural factors over which they have no control. Fortunately, a number of items in the Irish survey dealt with perceptions of the causes of poverty. Respondents were asked to indicate the extent of their agreement or disagreement with the following statements:

1. When people are poor it is usually their own fault.
2. By and large, the reason people are poor is that society does not give them a chance.
3. Lack of ambition is the root cause of poverty.
4. Only by completely changing the way the country is run can we reduce the number of people in poverty.

Our analysis shows that there is no significant relationship between fatalism and perceptions of the causes of poverty. This finding suggests that it is possible to facilitate people to develop feelings of personal efficacy without encouraging the tendency to make scapegoats of the deprived, or to deny the importance of structural factors. While it is important not to neglect the capacity for autonomous action of the poor entirely, it is not necessary to link such capacity to arguments that it is the peculiar nature of the poor's capacity for action that explains their material circumstances (Crompton 1993: 162).

Going beyond fatalism *per se* to the issue of political engagement, we find that, while there is substantial evidence demonstrating the degree of hurt, pain, and anger associated with marginalization, the evidence in relation to political alienation is less clear-cut. Heath (1992) in Britain, using a household labour market experience type definition of the underclass, found that, once education had been controlled for, there was no evidence that people so classified were more likely to be non-participants in the political process or that they had a lower level of political efficacy. Hardiman and Whelan (1994), in their analysis of the Irish data in the European Values Survey, found that the following features applied to the unemployed:

They were relatively uninvolved in the political process but no more so than others of comparable class and background.

Their propensity to participate in conventional forms of protest is less than that displayed by employees but the difference appears unlikely to be a consequence of unemployment *per se*; they are less likely than employees or indeed the overall young of lower working class groups to rule out unconventional forms of protest.

In terms of left-wing values, what distinguishes them from all others is their commitment to left-wing economic values which stress egalitarianism and collective responsibility.

They did not display a distinctive profile in terms of religious, moral or family values.

Comparative analysis of a range of European countries confirms the absence of a values profile peculiar to the unemployed. In this context, it seems more appropriate theoretically and politically to emphasize what the working class have in common rather than what divides them, and to argue the case for improved participative structures in the context of such an understanding.

Neo-liberals should not be allowed to monopolize the notion of active citizenship. Those who have been concerned to avoid 'blaming the victim' have often been reluctant to discuss motivational factors. The battle lines have been drawn, so that restricted opportunities or attitudes and values have been seen as competing rather than complementary explanations. It is possible, however, to view motivation as the outcome of a complex set of interactions in which restricted opportunity plays a central role. Psychological theory predicts that, when faced with uncontrollable circumstances, people ultimately respond with learnt helplessness. Any motivational defect observed among the poor need not be understood in terms of an immutable pathology. At the same time, individuals who have become conditioned to a lack of control will not necessarily grasp opportunities for control when they are offered.

7.9 Class and Underclass Perspectives Reconsidered

The starting-point of our analysis in this chapter was the issue of whether, given the scale of long-term unemployment in Ireland, the concept of an 'underclass' might be fruitfully applied in this case. Following Gallie (1994), we have taken labour market marginality, extreme deprivation, and a distinctive sub-culture as the crucial elements constituting an underclass. Our focus has been on the 'radical' conception, and in particular on Wilson's formulation which directs attention to the combination of weak labour force attachment and social isolation and identifies a particularly interesting form of vicious circle process. We have adhered to the view that, in the absence of evidence for such patterns of causation, the underclass framework is redundant, and it is sufficient to refer to the extent of marginalization and deprivation.

Our analysis of the Irish situation has identified a significant marginalized working class, members of which experience a degree of deprivation that is distinctive even by reference to the remainder of the working class. However, a crucial distinction is necessary between what we have termed 'restricted' and 'pervasive' marginalization. This distinction is made necessary by the uneven nature of the process of class transformation in Ireland whereby the labour market experiences of the young cohorts have come to have a qualitatively different character from those of their predecessors. Members of the pervasive marginalization group are not concentrated in urban centres although they do have a very high probability of being in rented public-sector housing. It is among the pervasively marginalized working class in rented urban public-sector housing that we might most plausibly expect to find the 'underclass'. However, the class composition of such housing is sufficiently heterogeneous as to make social isolation unlikely. If, though, some process is operating to produce a segregation of the pervasively marginalized working class within that housing sector, then it could be reflected in evidence of a significant interaction between marginalization and location in their impact on the level of fatalism. However, no evidence was found for such an effect.

The Irish situation provides a good example of a case where the search for an underclass, and a focus on a category of the population that is nominally separated from other groups, proves less fruitful than a concentration on the larger-scale processes affecting all class groups. Ultimately, the evidence relating to the social and psychological consequences of a high level of long-term unemployment in Ireland, rather than pointing to the value of an underclass perspective, provides support for Goldthorpe and Marshall's (1992) argument for the 'promising future of class analysis'. What we are confronted with in Ireland is the outcome, in a situation involving a substantial surplus of labour, of the competition between classes for secure positions, and the means of access to such positions, in circumstances where the traditional solution of exporting the marginalized is no longer a feasible option. To the extent that those in the marginalized working class 'cease to be a part of the labour market', it is not simply a consequence of their particular characteristics, or indeed their location, but of the working out of a complex set of relationships between social classes.

It is clear from the Irish case that widespread long-term unemployment, the concentration of the unemployed in public-sector housing, and the existence of significant pockets of concentrated deprivation do not, of themselves, generate the cultural distinctiveness that characterizes an underclass. It is possible, of course, that, in circumstances of racial or ethnic segregation of a kind that is entirely absent in Ireland, the outcome might be quite different. In that case, however, the general applicability of the terms must be questioned and the possibility faced that underclass terminology simply 'offers a way of speaking about race in a language of class that implicitly rejects the importance of race' (Fainstein 1993: 385).

8

Implications for Conceptualizing and Measuring Poverty

8.1 Introduction

In this chapter we explore the implications of the analysis and results that have been set out in previous chapters for the way poverty is conceptualized and measured, focusing particularly on how they throw a good deal of light on current debates. We begin by reiterating our understanding of the key concepts of deprivation and poverty, and setting out the central message of our own empirical approach and results. We then structure the discussion around a set of distinct but related concerns of the recent literature: the influential capability approach put forward by Sen, debates about defining and measuring deprivation and the implications of its multidimensionality, the relationship between poverty and social exclusion, the rights approach to poverty and minimum income, and poverty and the underclass.

8.2 Conceptualization and Measurement: the Central Message

Since the discussion will be dealing with related and often loosely defined concepts, it may be helpful to reiterate at the outset our own understanding of the core concepts of poverty and deprivation. 'Deprivation' we take to mean inability to obtain the types of diet, clothing, housing, household facilities, and environmental, educational, working, and social conditions generally regarded as acceptable in the community in question. Deprivation refers to conditions covering both material and social aspects of life, and is by definition multidimensional. In measuring deprivation, different aspects will of necessity be distinguished—for example inadequate diet, over-crowded or health-damaging housing conditions, failure to participate in different family, social, or community activities. One can then talk of a state of generalized or multiple deprivation, where deprivation across a range of dimensions or aspects of life is being experienced. We discussed at some length in Chapter 4 how this differs in two crucial respects from Townsend's own definition of deprivation, which refers to the lack of the types of food, clothing, housing, environment, and so on that are customary, or at least widely encouraged or approved, in the society. The first difference is that we take *views* in the society about what constitutes necessities as the touchstone, rather than what most people have or do. The second is that, to constitute deprivation, lack of the item or failure to participate in the activity must reflect what most people would regard as inability to participate—because of a lack of resources, ill-health, discrimination, or whatever—rather than simply choice.

'Poverty', defined in terms of inability to participate owing to lack of resources, occurs when the reason people lack these items or are unable to participate in society is because they do not have the income and other financial resources to do so. It is implicit in this definition that poverty refers to enforced and generalized deprivation, rather than either multiple deprivation attributable to factors other than lack of resources, or deprivation that is enforced but only in an isolated area of life. Those experiencing isolated or even multiple deprivation are not necessarily poor, but under this definition of poverty, to be considered poor one must not only have inadequate resources but must also be experiencing generalized deprivation. This is not the only way in which poverty has been or could be defined, but in our view it is the most logical and consistent interpretation of Townsend's widely accepted definition, which involves both lack of participation and enforcement by constrained resources.

Our central theme has been that, although Townsend's definition of poverty is widely quoted and apparently accepted, it does not in fact underpin most poverty measures and its implications have not been fully recognized and properly addressed at conceptual or empirical levels. Currently, most poverty studies take Townsend's definition as point of departure, but identify the poor on the basis of a resources constraint. Townsend's own empirical work, though seeking to locate the appropriate resources cut-off via non-monetary indicators of deprivation, follows conventional practice in identifying all those below that cut-off as poor. This practice would be an acceptable implementation of the definition if almost all of those meeting the inadequate resources criterion were in fact experiencing generalized deprivation. This cannot be taken for granted: the evidence we have presented supports the contention that income alone is not a reliable indicator of enforced generalized deprivation. Ringen's critique of the inconsistency between conventional definition and measurement is therefore valid and important. This has serious implications for conceptualization and measurement. To have consistency between concept and measure, one is in effect faced with the choice of rethinking the concept, or coming up with better ways of identifying those experiencing enforced generalized deprivation. One could redefine poverty as low income (or broader resources), which is one direction in which the 'rights' approach for example could lead. Alternatively, development of the general approach to using non-monetary deprivation indicators together with resources in identifying the poor, which we have set out, offers a way of implementing the definition now in general use. Even if one were happy to redefine poverty as low income, it would remain of interest to be able to identify what would then be the sub-set of the poor who were experiencing generalized deprivation, so such an approach would still have its place.

In developing this approach to using both resources and deprivation indicators, much can be done to improve the measures of each element, as will be discussed later in the chapter. Our results have shown the importance of financial resources going beyond current weekly or annual income in influencing living patterns, and it may be possible to broaden the measure of income to take other financial resources into account. In measuring deprivation, the set of indicators available to us was limited in coverage, and a good deal of thought needs to be given to developing the range and type of indicators employed. However, as we will discuss below, there is a danger that the object of the exercise will be lost sight of in attempting to encompass various aspects of living conditions. The aim, in the context of poverty measurement, is not to capture in a multidimensional manner the level of adequacy or participation in each and every aspect of life: it is rather to identify those who are experiencing generalized deprivation. Some of the deprivation indicators employed in other studies appear unsuitable to us for that purpose, and there also appears to be a good deal of confusion about what is to be achieved by distinguishing different life-style or deprivation dimensions. These points will be developed as we relate our findings to current conceptual and methodological debates in the remainder of this chapter.

8.3 Sen's Capability Approach to Living Standards and Poverty

At a conceptual level, Sen's proposed 'capability' approach to assessing living standards has also been an important feature of recent debates on poverty measurement, though it has not so far had much impact on empirical practice. It may therefore be useful to try to tease out what bearing, if any, our findings have for the value of a capability perspective. In setting out what that approach involves, Sen defines *functionings* as the various things a person manages to do or be in leading a life. Examples of functionings mentioned include very elementary ones such as being adequately nourished and being in good health, and more complex ones such as having self-respect and being socially integrated. The *capability* of a person then reflects the alternative combination of functionings that person can achieve, and from which he or she can choose one collection (see e.g. Sen 1993: 31). Functionings thus represent achievements, whereas capabilities represent the freedom to enjoy different possible combinations of achievements (see Sen 1980, 1983, 1987, 1992, 1993).

The implications of the capability perspective for poverty measurement have for the most part been discussed at a conceptual rather than empirical level. Much of that discussion has related to Sen's argument that a capability approach helps to clarify the absolute versus relative poverty debate: 'poverty is an absolute notion in the space of capabilities but very often it will take a relative form in the space of commodities or characteristics' (1983: 161). In a rich country, more income may be needed to buy enough commodities to achieve the same social functioning, such as 'appearing in public without shame'. Sen thus argues that there is no conflict between the irreducible absolutist element which he sees in the notion of poverty and thoroughgoing relativity in terms of commodities and resources: 'When Townsend estimates the resources required for being able to "participate in the activities of the community", he is in fact estimating the varying resource requirements of fulfilling the same absolute need' (1983: 161).

As Sen himself acknowledges, the debate provoked by this claim has been heated and not invariably enlightening (Sen 1992: 116, n. 39).[1] Framing the discussion in terms of activities and the goods that are inputs to pursuing those activities, Atkinson (1985: 16) has described Sen's claim as misleading, since there is a clear difference, at least in principle, between those who would hold constant the set of activities incorporated in a poverty standard (although the goods associated with them might change) and those who would be influenced in the specification of activities by the prevailing customs and expectations of the society. This might not be the case if 'activities' are defined at a sufficient level of generality, like Sen's functionings, such as 'avoiding shame' or 'participating in the life of the community'. However, in our view there is then substance in Piachaud's criticism that 'Sen's absolute goals, save that of physical survival, are too vague to be of any theoretical or practical use' (Piachaud 1987: 148). What we take this to mean is not that these goals are unhelpful as starting-points in thinking about poverty, but that regarding them as representing an 'absolutist core' does not advance matters.

The capability perspective could none the less be a productive way to conceptualize poverty, but assessment of its value is hindered by the fact that little effort has been made to apply it empirically, certainly as far as developed countries are concerned. This may be attributable in large part to the fact that capability and functionings as discussed by Sen are at a level of generality that makes empirical implementation difficult. In a developed country context Sen mentions the Scandinavian level of living surveys, described for example in Erikson and Aberg (1987) and Erikson (1993) as 'having done much to demonstrate and clarify the empirical possibility of examining diverse functionings as the basis of quality of life' (Sen 1992: 39, n. 2). These surveys sought to measure not only household resources including income and wealth, but also health and access to health care, employ-

---

[1] For the debate itself see particularly Townsend (1985) and the response by Sen (1985).

ment and working conditions, education and skills, family and social integration, housing, exposure to crime, leisure pursuits, and political participation. Without going into detail about the concepts and measures involved, they are not of direct assistance here because the aim was to measure *inequality* in the distribution of the individual's overall command over resources 'through which he can control and consciously direct his living conditions' (Erikson 1993: 72–3), not poverty. Indeed, Erikson sees it as a desirable feature that 'the intellectually rather empty discussion of whether the poverty line should be drawn here or there has been avoided' (1993: 80).[2] Sen does also mentions Mack and Lansley's work in this general context, but without spelling out how it can be related to a capability approach.

Sen sees poverty as the failure of basic capabilities to reach certain minimally acceptable standards; and non-monetary indicators of deprivation such as those to be employed by Mack and Lansley, and in particular those included in our own basic deprivation index, can be seen as direct, if crude, measures of success or failure in achieving particular concrete aspects of the broader functionings entailed. The capability approach emphasizes that a poverty analysis concentrating only on incomes can be quite remote from the main motivation with our concern with poverty (viz. the limitation of the *lives* that some people are forced to live), and may fail to provide empirical guidance regarding the genesis and prevalence of deprivation (Sen 1992: 116). Our poverty measure includes direct measures of the limited lives that people are actually leading, and our findings regarding the extent of poverty and the processes generating it do differ from those produced by a focus on income poverty lines alone. However, it remains to be shown that the capabilities approach of distinguishing different 'functionings' makes any easier the selection of indicators of success or failure to achieve participation in society.

Ysander (1993) points out, in commenting on the Swedish level of living indicators in this context, that, although the underlying concept in mind was close to Sen's capability, in an overwhelming number of cases the investigators had to make do with particular achievements. In saying that this shows that 'capabilities are often rather elusive things to catch', he could not be accused of exaggeration. The crucial step is linking failure to achieve specific functionings with resource (or other) constraints. In our analysis, taking income as well as deprivation indicators into account first of all allows those on low incomes who are not experiencing basic deprivation to be distinguished. Since despite low current income they are not failing to achieve the activities included in the basic index, counting these people as

---

[2] Discussing this emphasis on inequality rather than poverty in Swedish welfare research, in contrast to many other Western nations, Erikson sees it as natural that poverty should become the central socio-political issue where social liberalism dominates, whereas inequality becomes the main problem of welfare where social democracy is dominant.

non-poor appears entirely consistent with Sen's approach. Incorporating both income and deprivation also provides some basis for distinguishing those whose failure to achieve is attributable to lack of resources from those who, though apparently failing to achieve the basic functionings, are not on low current resources. It therefore goes some way towards incorporating opportunity sets rather than simply achieved states, though it is clearly limited in its coverage of resources. The capability approach has served a valuable function in highlighting the importance of the freedom or ability to achieve rather than simply of outcomes, but it has not made clear how that can be taken into account in measurement going beyond income.

In addition to emphasizing freedom to achieve, the capability approach stresses the point that the conversion of income into capabilities may vary a great deal not only across communities but also across individuals, so that 'an interpersonally invariant "poverty line" income may be very misleading in the identification and evaluation of poverty' (Sen 1993: 41). The examples given of variation across individuals usually refer to health or age: someone with a disability may need a much higher income to be able to do various things than someone without that disability. As Sen acknowledges, one response would be to adjust the income poverty line to take these differences into account, so that those with disabilities for example are attributed a higher 'need' for income. Such an adjustment could be readily incorporated within our measurement approach. How would the appropriate adjustment be derived? This is clearly closely related to the problem of adjusting income for differences in household size and composition conventionally tackled via equivalence scales, so one approach is to rely on analysis of expenditure patterns to produce scales that also take disability into account (see Jones and O'Donnell 1995 for an empirical example). An alternative would be to use non-monetary indicators of the type employed in this study to see how much more pronounced the risk of deprivation is for someone with a disability at particular income levels.

Our indicators did show that, where the household head had a long-term illness or disability, the risk of basic deprivation was increased, even having controlled for income, assets, long-term labour market experience and other characteristics. This suggests that, in the specific case of disability, variation across individuals in 'needs', or in the ability to convert income into capabilities, however one wishes to put it, has to be taken into account in poverty measurement. Going beyond disability, however, it is not clear that interpersonal variation is so pronounced as to pose a major problem. Indeed, our analysis of the characteristics of those who were experiencing basic deprivation but not below the income thresholds showed that, for the most part, they were not distinctive in terms of personal or household characteristics that might affect 'needs'. Instead, their distinguishing feature was experience of long-term labour market problems and disadvantaged social and educational background. In contrast to Sen's emphasis on cross-sectional interpersonal variation in ability to convert income into capabilities, our results thus highlight the role of long-term dynamics in producing differences in current living standards and ability to avoid deprivation among those on similar income levels.

The capability approach has clearly influenced how researchers think about poverty in developed countries, and its emphasis on the ability to avoid deprivation is of major importance, but the gap between concept and application remains wide. So far, although it has been widely discussed for over a decade, the approach has had little or no impact on empirical studies which seek to measure and understand poverty, and proponents may need to ask themselves why. If it is to have an impact, those advocating the approach need to show how it should be implemented and to demonstrate the 'value added'. This could involve teasing out how it relates in practice to, for example, measuring poverty through a broader resources measure than current income, one that also takes special needs into account, or through a combination of income and non-monetary indicators of deprivation along the lines developed in this study.

8.4   Welfare and Deprivation

Another question prompted by the ambitious scope of the capability approach is how wide the coverage of potential areas of deprivation should be in measuring poverty. In discussing that approach, it was noted that the Scandinavian level of living surveys measured living conditions across nine different areas or components of life: economic resources, health and access to health care, employment and working conditions, education and skills, family and social integration, housing, exposure to crime, leisure pursuits, and political participation. The indicators used included ability to walk 100 metres, unemployment experiences, physical demands of work, years of education, marital status, and voting in elections. This has to be seen in the light of the breadth of the aim of the exercise, which was to assess welfare or well-being, but a similarly broad range of indicators has been seen by some as relevant in measuring deprivation. For example, Townsend and Gordon (1989), in seeking to measure deprivation in the 1985–6 Greater London Survey, considerably expanded from Townsend's earlier work the areas of deprivation on which information was sought. A distinction was drawn between material and social deprivation, a division into thirteen specific types of deprivation across these two was made, and a total of seventy-seven indicators or groups of indicators were selected. The indicators used covered not only deprivation in terms of food, clothing, housing and home facilities, and family and recreational activities, but also local environment, working conditions, employment experience and rights, participation in social institutions, and education attained. Items counting as indicators of deprivation include air pollution in the locality, working 'unsocial' hours, experiencing unemployment of two weeks or more in the previous twelve months, not voting at the last election, experiencing racial harassment, and having fewer than ten years' education. One has to ask whether some of these are best seen as aspects of deprivation, correlates of deprivation, or causes of deprivation—or in some cases whether they are likely to represent deprivation at all.

Even if one simply sees deprivation as the obverse or flip side of welfare so that it is desirable to cover the full range of activities and possessions one would wish to encompass in a measure of welfare, simply measuring non-achievement or non-participation is not satisfactory: as we have argued earlier, it is an *inability* to participate rather than non-participation that represents what most people would regard as deprivation. One response to the difficulty of assessing opportunity sets rather than outcomes is to employ as deprivation indicators only those items/activities that we could reasonably expect most people to wish to avoid if possible. Indeed, Eriksom (1993) describes the Scandinavian level of living surveys themselves as taking exactly this tack, measuring 'evil conditions' rather than welfare itself because it is much easier to order such states in ways that most people would accept. In a similar vein, in discussing the concept of deprivation Townsend (1988) talks *inter alia* of people who lead restricted or stunted social lives, who do not or cannot enter into ordinary forms of family or other social relationships (p. 128). He also quotes Brown and Madge:

Deprivations are loosely regarded as unsatisfactory and undesirable circumstances whether material, emotional, physical or behavioural, as recognised by a fair degree of societal consensus. (Brown and Madge 1982: 39)

When one casts the net that wide, identifying 'evil conditions' cannot but become contentious. Some of the indicators used both in the level of living surveys and in Townsend and Gordon's measurement of deprivation do not appear to be inherently 'evil conditions'. Not voting, for example, is a basic right in some (though not all) democratic countries, and not socializing with one's family does not appear necessarily either unsatisfactory or undesirable. Without becoming preoccupied with specific items, there is a significant danger that the activities and possessions included will be influenced by what the investigator, or the socio-political élite or whoever, sees as appropriate behaviour. The measurement of deprivation can then have a substantial prescriptive element, falling into precisely the trap for which poverty research in the past has been so heavily criticized.

Further, even conditions that would be seen by most people as inherently painful or unpleasant may be traded off against other goals. For example unpleasant working conditions are sometimes associated—as neoclassical economic theory would lead us to expect—with compensation in the form of higher earnings. Working on an oil rig means being away from home and family and in some danger, but earnings are correspondingly higher than from similar work on shore. Rather than any specific item or activity, then, it is the relationships across potential deprivation indicators that are of central importance. It is those items that can be demonstrated to be usually associated with other 'bads', and thus serve as reliable indicators of a more generalized state of deprivation, that are of primary interest. Obviously these can be established only by a wide-ranging investigation of potential candidates, but in doing so the object of the exercise must be kept to the forefront.

When the aim is to identify those excluded from society because of a lack of resources, we are still using deprivation indicators to pick up an underlying latent variable, the experience of generalized deprivation; we combine this with a measure of resources in an attempt to hone in on those experiencing generalized deprivation arising from inadequate resources. It seems to make sense, in that context, to also keep enforcement by resource constraints in mind when selecting deprivation indicators in the first place. In other words, we will not want to include indicators where failure to participate is as likely to be due to choice or to some non-resource constraint as to inadequate resources, and is not very likely to be associated with other aspects of deprivation. On that basis, we would doubt whether—to give some examples—not voting, not participating in local community associations, and not meeting family members regularly would be satisfactory deprivation indicators for our purpose. It could be argued that this decision should be left to the empirical analysis, following our own general procedure: if 'not voting' does not cluster with other aspects of deprivation, it would not be included among the 'basic' indicators. However, in selecting items for inclusion in the first place, it seems sensible to give priority in allocating scarce survey questionnaire space to those we have reason to expect—from other studies or on *a priori* grounds—to be related to resources and generalized deprivation.

It also seems important to distinguish in so far as possible processes and outcomes in the measurement of poverty. Unemployment we would see as a predominant cause of material and social deprivation and poverty, but is it helpful in that context to include it as a form of deprivation? Racial discrimination and harassment will in some instances lead to poverty, but will also be experienced by many people who are not poor without pushing them into poverty: is it helpful to include it as an indicator of deprivation? In the same way, ill-health often leads to generalized deprivation and poverty, but many physically or mentally ill people are not poor. It seems particularly important to us to preserve what is distinctive about the concept of poverty, rather than to see it encompassed in a very broad measure of welfare or deprivation across all aspects of life. Poverty is not inability to participate owing to unemployment, it is not inability to participate owing to racial discrimination, it is not inability to participate owing to ill-health:

it is inability to participate owing to lack of resources, which each of these factors may but does not necessarily produce. While incorporation of a resources criterion into the measurement procedure does ensure that central element is not lost, we would argue that it should also be kept to the forefront in selecting items to test as indicators of generalized deprivation.

8.5   Poverty versus Social Exclusion

Discussion of the breadth of coverage of deprivation indicators for measuring poverty leads on to the related issue of the relationship between poverty and social exclusion. As noted in Chapter 2, the term 'social exclusion' has been increasingly widely employed in the European Union, and by the mid-1990s has come to dominate official EU terminology. This has happened for a variety of reasons, but so far one result has been a good deal of confusion: no coherent picture has emerged as to the implications of focusing the attention of researchers and policy-makers on social exclusion rather than poverty. Here our main concern is to see what light our own conceptual and analytic approach may throw on the distinction, and vice versa: does our approach help to clarify the relationship between poverty and social exclusion, and does that distinction provide a valuable perspective on our results?

The widespread use of the term 'social exclusion' is new, and is a result of a deliberate shift in usage away from 'poverty' by the EU in the late 1980s and early 1990s. Towards the end of the Second Poverty Programme, which ran from 1985 to 1989, the term 'social exclusion' began to appear in official documents, and from 1989 it has systematically appeared in various official documents. The Council Decision of July 1989, on which the third Poverty Programme was based, was for a medium-term programme concerning the 'economic and social integration of the least privileged groups in society'.[3] In September 1989 the Council of Ministers adopted a Resolution on 'combating social exclusion'.[4] The preamble to the Social Charter, to which all the member states except the UK agreed in 1989, stated that 'in the spirit of solidarity it is important to combat social exclusion'. In implementing the 1989 Resolution, the Commission set up in 1990 an 'Observatory of independent experts' to report regularly on national policies 'to combat social exclusion' (see Room et al. 1992). Article 1 of the Agreement on Social Policy between all the member states except the UK at the time of the Maastricht Treaty in 1992 includes among the objectives of the Community 'the combating of exclusion' (see Council and Commission of the European Communities 1992: 197). In proposing a successor to the Poverty-3 Programme in 1993, the Commission set out the objective as being to 'combat

---

[3] Official Journal No. L224, 2 Aug. 1989.   [4] Ibid. No. C277, 3 Oct. 1989.

exclusion and promote solidarity' (Commission of the European Communities 1993). Similarly, the Commission research initiative under the aegis of the Fourth Framework Programme for Research and Technological Development launched in 1995 includes research under the title 'Social Integration and Social Exclusion in Europe'.

We quoted earlier Room's (1994) remark 'How far these shifts reflected any more than the hostility of some governments to the language of poverty, and the enthusiasm of others to use the language of social exclusion, is a matter for debate' (p. 6). Berghman (1994) certainly sees the original reason for the systematic shift towards 'social exclusion' by the Commission as political, being a 'less accusing' expression than 'poverty'. None the less, substantive claims have been made for the merits of conceptualizing the issue in terms of social exclusion rather than poverty, and it is worth trying to tease out the issues and arguments. This is far from being straightforward or unproblematic, because social exclusion is often used in a loosely defined way, without spelling out what is meant, and even where an attempt is made to define it, clarity does not invariably result. It makes sense to start with the official justification by the Commission, which has set out in the final report on Third Poverty Programme the reasons for 'the increasing use of the concept of social exclusion which, in the majority of the Member States and at Community level, is gradually replacing the concept of poverty' (Commission of the European Communities 1993: 43, paras. 1.1, 1.2).

This, it explains, is because the nature of poverty has changed and so has public opinion and debate over the previous fifteen years. Urban crises, the resurgence of homelessness, interracial tension, the increase in long-term unemployment, the marginalization of young people who have not been able to gain employment, the persistence of poverty in certain rural areas, and the slide into poverty of households in debt are 'new phenomena which are more visible and numerous than in the past and have contributed to this transformation of the debate on poverty and social exclusion'. Poverty can no longer be regarded as a residual state of affairs, and can no longer be regarded as merely an absence or insufficiency of financial resources affecting individuals:

On the contrary, we must acknowledge the structural character of poverty and the mechanisms which lead to it and the multidimensional nature of the processes by which persons, groups and sometimes urban or rural areas are excluded from the social exchanges, practices and rights which are an intrinsic part of social and economic integration. (Commission of the European Communities 1993: 43)

Talking of social exclusion rather than poverty highlights the gap between those who are active members of society and those who are forced to the fringes, the increasing risks of social disintegration, and the fact that, for the persons concerned and for society, this is a process of change and not a set of fixed and static situations. A large percentage of the population is exposed to social exclusion resulting from changes in employment and family and social structures. Rather than one group living in permanent poverty and exclusion, there is a variety of—increasingly large—groups whose economic and social integration is insecure, who experience periods of sporadic or recurrent poverty and who are threatened by the loss of social ties that accompanies the process of social exclusion.

This reveals a good deal about why this shift towards 'social exclusion' has taken place, and at the same time conveys how amorphous the concept is. Apart from the political objections of certain member states to the use of the term 'poverty', internal EU politics have made 'social exclusion' a more useful term in that it could be directly related to concerns about the impact of the move towards closer economic integration between the member states from the Single European Act. It is more palatable, and perhaps more effective in terms of the dynamic of EU decision-making, to talk in terms of the need to accompany integration of economies with measures to promote social integration and combat social exclusion than to highlight the possibility that economic integration could result in poverty for some vulnerable people and areas. The Commission discussion mentions the key elements on which others have also focused in discussing the distinction between poverty and social exclusion: poverty is seen as static, social exclusion dynamic and related especially to structural change; poverty is seen as about situations, social exclusion about processes; poverty refers 'only' to financial resources, social exclusion is multidimensional. (The last of these was foreshadowed in the *Final Report by the Commission on the Second European Poverty Programme* (1991), where it states that 'poverty is not only about money'.) But although these contrasts are pointed up, there is still no attempt to define social exclusion directly. As a result, it is not clear whether social exclusion describes a process, an outcome, or both. Nor is it clear whether poverty and exclusion go together or what would represent poverty without exclusion or vice versa. In one sense social exclusion is clearly intended to be much broader than poverty because many are seen as vulnerable to it; but it is not clear that all those poor at a point in time would necessarily be experiencing social exclusion.

The Observatory of independent experts set up by the Commission to report on national policies 'to combat social exclusion', faced with the problem of empirical application of the term, had to begin with an attempt to define it. The *First Annual Report* of the Observatory defines social exclusion 'first and foremost in relation to the social rights of citizens', so it can be analysed in terms of the denial or non-realization of social rights (Room *et al.* 1992: 5). Commonly acknowledged social rights include the right to a certain basic standard of living, and one aim of the Observatory is stated to be assessing whether governments are effectively implementing the minima set out in their own income maintenance schemes. Explicit reference is made to Marshall's (1950) discussion of citizenship and social class. While citizenship consists of political and civil as well as social rights, the former are covered by the Observatory only to the extent that they are linked with the analysis of social exclusion: by implication, then, political and civil rights are considered to be in general outside the realm covered by social exclusion *per se*.[5] In practice, the Observatory investigates what social rights the citizen has to, for example, employment, housing, and health care; how effectively national policies enable citizens to secure those rights; and the barriers and processes by which people are excluded from these rights. They then go on to study the evidence that, where citizens are unable to secure their social rights, they will tend to suffer processes of generalized and persisting disadvantage and an undermining of their social and occupational participation. They therefore look at patterns and processes of generalized disadvantage in terms of education, training, employment, housing, financial resources, etc., and attempt to determine whether those who suffer such disadvantages have substantially lower chances than the rest of the population of gaining access to the major social institutions.

The problem with taking social rights as the point of reference in defining social exclusion is that these are themselves difficult to characterize: the whole question of what constitute widely accepted social rights is a highly contested one. However, on the basis of these and other treatments of social exclusion versus poverty (such as Robbins 1991, Berghman 1994), it appears that three central distinctive features are claimed for the concept of social exclusion. It is presented as relating to dynamics and processes, to multidimensional disadvantage, and to inadequate social participation; whereas poverty is presented as static and descriptive, unidimensional, and narrowly financial. Taking each of these in turn, we will argue that our own analysis of poverty illustrates how this contrast is based to a significant degree on a caricature of the concept of poverty; further, that, where there are in fact substantive differences between the concepts, in our view what 'poverty' loses in terms of breadth may for many purposes be offset by the fact that it is less diffuse and more in tune with popular notions of social goals.

Although empirical poverty research may often have been guilty of adopting a static perspective, concentrating much of its effort on description of those identified as poor at a point in time, there is absolutely nothing in the way poverty is generally conceptualized which has such a static or descriptive connotation. Indeed, US experience demonstrates clearly that poverty can accommodate a dynamic perspective: 'social exclusion' is a term rarely used there, but poverty research, driven by the availability of panel data, has led the way internationally in highlighting income dynamics,

---

[5] Berghman approvingly comments on the more encompassing approach suggested by Commins (1993), the Irish contributors to the Observatory, who included what they termed civic, economic, social, and interpersonal integration; however, this was clearly a somewhat broader compass than the Observatory itself was happy to adopt.

movements into and out of poverty, the duration of poverty spells. Even without such data, many studies of poverty from Rowntree on have taken the description of those identified as poor as the starting-point for an analysis of what leads them into that situation, the processes involved. This is clearly seen as far back as Rowntree's own emphasis on the movement into and out of poverty as families progressed through the different stages of the life cycle—hardly a static perspective. While the processes at work may now be somewhat different, that does not in itself seem a good argument for changing the terminology employed. By applying combined income and deprivation criteria to identifying the poor at a point in time, what our own analysis has served to highlight is precisely the importance of the dynamics of income and labour force participation, the accumulation and erosion of resources, in producing poverty. The increasing availability of longitudinal data makes it all the more likely that analysis of these dynamic processes will move centre-stage in poverty research throughout the developed countries. We therefore see little merit in the argument that replacing poverty with social exclusion is necessary or has advantages in order to focus attention on processes rather than descriptive static account.

As Berghman 1994 points out, defining poverty as the outcome and social exclusion as the process that produces it, though that is sometimes the way the terms are used, only confuses matters further. Berghman himself suggests seeing social exclusion as a process leading to the outcome deprivation, and pauperization as a process leading to the outcome poverty. (One runs into unavoidable linguistic difficulties here, in that the term 'pauper' would seem to be the outcome of the process of pauperization in normal English usage, and would not be exactly equivalent in meaning to 'poor': 'impoverishment' might be a better general term to describe the various processes that lead people into poverty.) He uses Dutch data to show that the overlap between deprivation and poverty as measured by an income poverty line is far from perfect, and on that basis argues that 'different realities' are being referred to when one talks of poverty versus deprivation/social exclusion. However, this in fact brings us right back to the central theme of this book, which is that the conventional definition of poverty involves both deprivation and a resource constraint. The fact that a significant proportion of those on low incomes are not deprived, as our own results demonstrated in considerable detail, in our view raises the question of how best to measure poverty as generally understood, and whether income alone is adequate for that purpose. Tackling this directly seems far preferable to changing terminology so that poverty *means* low income.

The second claim made for social exclusion is that it is more comprehensive than poverty, relating to multidimensional disadvantage. Here again, the argument is based more on the contrast with the way poverty is most often measured—via income—than with the way it is conceptualized. Poverty is indeed centrally about lack of financial resources, but Townsend's definition makes clear that the importance of inadequate resources is that it manifests itself in inability to participate across a wide spectrum of activities and possessions. Poverty is not simply lack of money, it is what lack of money leads to—and, as Berghman (1994) emphasizes, in a market economy the access to a certain standard of living depends upon the resources available to attain such a standard. Our own results show that focusing entirely on current income does not fully capture command over resources, but our conclusion once again is that current income will not then be an entirely reliable indicator of poverty. Even in a predominantly market economy, of course, some areas of consumption will be outside the market—most often this is the case, to a greater or lesser extent, for health care, education, and housing. Referring once again to our own results, this is precisely why we argue that housing-related indicators of deprivation were not suitable as indicators of generalized deprivation in our data: poor housing was not highly correlated with other aspects of deprivation, because of the impact of public provision of housing.

We return to our emphasis on the definition of poverty as generalized deprivation resulting from lack of resources. While one could extend the notion of poverty to encompass non-market activities, it is in our view preferable for conceptual and empirical clarity to confine it to those areas of life where consumption or participation are determined primarily by command over financial resources. It is clearly valuable to complement results on the extent and nature of poverty defined in this way with an assessment of aspects of living standards determined via other processes, such as (in many countries) publicly provided housing or health care. This is a major challenge for researchers, since variations in institutional structures and public provision mean that the scope of the market differs across countries. So far, in our view, although going some way in that direction, 'social exclusion' has not been defined and operationalized in a way that allows it to serve this useful function. The danger in a wholesale shift to a more comprehensive concept is that the core notion of poverty will be lost sight of.

The third strand of the social exclusion literature is that poverty is about 'distributional' issues whereas social exclusion is about 'relational' ones; poverty is about financial resources and commodities, social exclusion is about family and social relations. Thus, although Townsend is concerned with the ability to participate in society, his focus is on the resources that individuals need to have at their command in order to do this. Room (1994) sees this as reflecting an Anglo-Saxon intellectual tradition and a liberal and individualistic vision of society. Notions of social exclusion, he argues, are more in keeping with a continental European tradition of social analysis, which sees society as consisting of a status hierarchy rooted in some broader moral order, with social exclusion the process of becoming detached from this moral order (see for example Castel 1990). From this perspective, the interest in social exclusion has close links with the upsurge of concern about the emergence of an 'underclass' detached from society and its values, which was discussed in Chapter 7 and to which we return shortly in this chapter. Without encroaching on that discussion, what this illustrates about the way the term 'social exclusion' is being used is just how poorly defined it is. The one thing on which the underclass literature is agreed is that only a sub-set of the poor could be considered to constitute an underclass, however defined and empirically operationalized. Rather than being the much broader and more encompassing concept than poverty that some regard it, if social exclusion refers to those detached from the prevailing moral order, it is in fact a good deal narrower.

In our view, the importance of the extent of popular usage and understanding of the concept of poverty should not to be undervalued. Poverty is a notion for which people have an intuitive grasp. Some see this as the greatest problem with using the term 'poverty', arguing that it arouses strong feelings but a great deal of confusion because to different people it means different things, both within a particular society and across societies. In contrast, we see the fact that most people do have a—sometimes not very well thought out—notion of what poverty means as its greatest strength. The key assumption is that within a society there is a broad consensus, across income groups and social classes, about what it means to be poor. Our reading of the evidence, from our own results and those of Mack and Lansley and Dutch and Danish studies,[6] is that there is indeed such a consensus about what constitutes a societal minimum acceptable way of life in many developed countries. The researcher's first task, in seeking to measure poverty in a particular society, is to assess whether there is such a consensus and, if there is, to identify the elements that go to make up that minimum. Measuring the extent of deprivation that is due to lack of resources then taps into a widely understood concept. 'Social exclusion', in sharp contrast, is a term that has little or no place in popular usage—indeed, in many countries it has only recently been introduced into academic and policy-making discourse, and there as we have seen it is generally used in an ill-defined way, apparently meaning quite different things to different people. As Mack and Lansley and Veit-Wilson emphasize, trying to keep experts in their place has been a recent feature of poverty research, and retaining a central focus on poverty seems more likely than a wholesale shift to 'social exclusion' to keep the role of experts in perspective.

It is not therefore simply a matter of semantics, that it does not matter whether one employs the term 'poverty' or 'social exclusion' as long as we define it clearly enough. As Sen (1992) comments with respect to poverty, while such 'nominalism' does make some sense, the fact remains that poverty is a major evaluative concern in most societies, with some clear associ-

---

[6] See Muffels (1993) on the Netherlands, and the Danish results quoted in Mack and Lansley (1985: 84).

ations that constrain the nature of the concept (p. 107). Moving from 'poverty' to 'social exclusion' may help to sensitize researchers and policy-makers to dynamics, processes, multiple disadvantage, but at a cost. That cost is the spark that 'poverty' ignites because of its everyday usage and evaluative content. This is clearly one of the factors behind the preference of some EU governments for the term 'social exclusion'. Despite that, the shift to 'social exclusion' could turn out to be have strategic advantages. To be optimistic, one could see it as analogous to the emphasis by Scandinavian social scientists on inequality rather than poverty as the core concept: arguably, policies directed to reducing inequalities in those countries were also particularly effective in tackling poverty, at least until recently. Policies promoted under the umbrella of a drive to promote an 'inclusive society' could stand a greater chance of adoption and/or be more effective than those presented simply as anti-poverty. Much depends on how the term comes to be used, and the agendas that come to dominate its use: there social scientists could have a significant impact as they seek to dispel the confusion currently surrounding it.

8.6   The Rights Approach to Minimum Income

Our discussion of poverty throughout this volume has relied for the most part on the formulation set out by Townsend, in terms of inability to participate in the life of society because of a lack of resources. However, as pointed out in Chapter 2, an important distinction has been made between notions of poverty arising out of concern with living standards, and those based on minimum rights to resources. Atkinson, in setting out this distinction, describes the former as a concern that people attain a specified level of consumption, whereas

On the rights approach, people are entitled, as citizens, to a minimum income, the disposal of which is a matter for them. The reference to citizenship is deliberate. Entitlement to a minimum is seen both as a reward for citizenship and as a pre-requisite for participation in society. (Atkinson 1985: 4)

To illustrate the distinction, he notes that from a standard-of-living perspective one could see differing nutritional requirements leading to a differential between men and women in the poverty line or income support rates, whereas that would be very hard to defend on a minimum rights approach. Another example mentioned is that on a rights approach it might be argued that the minimum entitlement to support for a couple should be twice that for a single person, whereas benefit systems generally pay significantly less than that because they allow for economies of scale in living together.

The notion of a right to a minimum income arises from Marshall's concept of social rights, to which we have already referred in discussing social exclusion. Social rights for Marshall refer to 'The whole range from the right to a modicum of economic welfare and security to the right to share to the full in the social heritage and the life of a civilised being according to the standards prevailing in society' (Marshall 1950: 11). Recent developments in that tradition have emphasized that full participation in the life of society, including the exercise of civil and political rights, requires a minimum command over resources, and that citizens therefore have an entitlement to such a minimum. Here we will not attempt to explore the basis in political philosophy for such a claim and the debates associated with it (on which see for example Plant 1988). However, our analysis of poverty, resources, and deprivation raises some important questions for this approach, which may be helpful in developing it further. As we have argued, the Townsend-type definition of poverty incorporates both living standards and resources, and our own approach to implementing it empirically means that only someone who is experiencing both deprivation and a low income will be counted as poor. From a rights perspective, the assumption seems to be generally made that all those below a minimum income entitlement are to be counted as poor. While that is consistent with Townsend's own measurement procedure, we have seen that (in our sample) it entails including among the poor a substantial number of people who do not appear to be experiencing basic deprivation. Two questions then arise for the rights approach: are people below the minimum income necessarily being deprived of an entitlement, regardless of other circumstances? And even if they are, does it help to call all those below that minimum 'poor'?

Although the idea of income support as of right is central to the modern welfare state, that right has in practice been conditional rather than absolute. Under social insurance, contributions earn entitlement, while under social assistance, support is given on the basis of means-testing. While some of those writing from a rights perspective would argue in favour of a universal, non-means-tested payment to all—a basic or citizen's income, which we discuss in detail in Chapter 9—that is not an unavoidable implication of a rights approach, and the right to such a universal payment has clearly not so far been recognized in practice. Instead, even where the right to support is linked to contributory payments, there are generally limitations. For the unemployed, for example, insurance benefit cannot be received indefinitely, and other conditions such as availability for work and job search activity are imposed. For those relying on social assistance, the requirement is to prove that support is 'needed'. Marshall linked the right to a certain standard of civilization as absolute, 'conditional only on the discharge of the general duties of citizenship' (1950: 94). However, as Morris (1994) points out, it could be argued that the duties of citizenship include, for the unemployed, being available for and actively seeking work. Indeed, one could also debate whether means-testing *per se*, or only certain stigmatizing and degrading forms of means testing, is necessarily inconsistent with providing support as an entitlement. This is not intended to reflect on the merits of universal versus insurance-based versus means-tested support, to which we return in the next chapter: rather, it is simply to make the point that the right to support has always been conditional, the central issue being the nature of that conditionality.

This is directly relevant to the first question we posed, which is whether people below the minimum income are necessarily being deprived of an entitlement, regardless of other circumstances. Some examples may help to illustrate. Person A is living alone and is unwilling to take up paid employment when offered, in what would generally be seen as a reasonably well-paid and otherwise suitable (in terms of for example location) job, because she wants to write poetry. Person B is similarly unwilling to take up paid employment because she is caring for children, but her spouse is earning. Person C is self-employed and currently making a loss, but has very substantial assets including some which can be readily liquidated to finance current consumption. All three of these people are currently equally below an established minimum income level. We would expect to find quite a divergence of views about whether each of these individuals has a right to support from the rest of the community. We would not expect many people to feel that person C has an entitlement to support, since he or she is clearly not going to experience a substantial fall in living standards, much less basic deprivation, without that support. More varied views about A and B would probably be found. To simply postulate an absolute right to a minimum income and regard everyone below it as 'poor' would thus appear to entirely miss the subtleties that underpin attitudes both to rights and to poverty.

This means that we need to know *how* some of those on low incomes are avoiding basic deprivation before we can properly assess their situation, and see how others would regard it. This has been identified by our research as a priority for further exploration. In doing so, however, we would again argue for the merits of preserving what is distinctive in the concept of poverty, rather than necessarily seeing it as coterminous with a violation of social rights—here, the right to a minimum income. For example, suppose that there was general agreement that individuals should have a right to a minimum income on an independent basis, without having to rely on a spouse for support because that was seen as placing them in a dependent position. Suppose further that many women did not in fact have access to that independent income, but within most middle and upper-income families resources were shared so that the spouses had similar living standards. One could regard that as a violation of the rights of the individual to a minimum income, but one need not conclude that all the women involved were poor. The violation of rights to a minimum income could then be— and might best be—regarded as serious gender-structured inequality, without being called poverty. Indeed, calling it poverty runs the risk of obscuring the plight of those women in middle-income families who, owing to very unequal distribution of resources within the household, *are* actually experiencing deprivation.

This is not to argue that the term poverty must or can only be applied to those experiencing deprivation because of a lack of resources: although our interpretation is that the Townsend-type definition necessarily involves 'inability to participate', one response may be to frame a definition of poverty more broadly. Some of those on low income may be avoiding deprivation only by recourse to expedients that are widely regarded as unacceptable—for example, having to rely on occasional help from neighbours or extended family or from charities.[7] However, a definition of poverty based entirely on command over resources, rather than on standard of living or a combination of the two, clearly need not extend all the way to a rights-based focus on individual current income. It could instead seek to distinguish circumstances in which low income is generally regarded as unacceptable, even if basic deprivation is being avoided for the time being, from circumstances in which it would not be so regarded. Such an approach faces formidable obstacles both in formulation and implementation, but is clearly worth investigation.

In a final comment on the rights approach, the relationship between the right to a minimum income and standard of living appears to us to merit more attention than it has received. While the two have tended to be seen as distinct concerns, as Sen emphasizes repeatedly, income is not an end in itself but rather a means to an end, allowing freedom to function and participate. It is clear from Marshall that he conceived the right to resources as enabling people to attain an acceptable standard of living and participate fully in their society. We quoted earlier Atkinson's example that it is argued from a rights perspective that the minimum entitlement to support for a couple should be twice that for a single person, although economies of scale in living together mean that they will attain a higher standard of living than an individual living alone. Need these economies be ignored from a rights approach, or could the central message of that approach not be that each member of the couple should be entitled to the same payment, which could be lower than that going to the single individual?

8.7 Poverty and the Underclass

The concept of an underclass has played a major role in recent debates about poverty and anti-poverty policy, and has been one of the mostly hotly contested features of those debates. Despite the fact that it has received so

[7] It is worth nothing that regular cash transfers from outside the household from any of these sources would in general be included in the income of the household as measured in comprehensive surveys.

much attention, there is no consensus about how the term 'underclass' is best employed, so people have been using the term to mean different things and talking past each other. However, as we saw in Chapter 7, three features dominate definitions of the underclass: prolonged labour market marginality, greater deprivation than even the manual working class, and a distinctive sub-culture. Some have concentrated exclusively on one or other element, adopting for example a culturally based definition or one based solely on ineffective or non-participation in the labour market, but Wilson's influential formulation in a US context incorporated all three. In applying the concept here, we therefore felt it was productive first to identify a marginalized working class in terms of labour market experience, then to assess whether their levels of deprivation were significantly higher than those of the manual working class, and finally to examine whether the levels of fatalism found among that group were consistent with the effects that Wilson hypothesized labour force marginalization and social isolation to have on attitudes and behaviour.

The results of that analysis were instructive on the possible relevance of the concept of an underclass for developed countries experiencing prolonged high levels of unemployment, and were also revealing about the relationship between poverty and the underclass. Those identified on the basis of labour force histories as marginalized were found to have much higher levels of deprivation than the non-marginalized working class, even where the latter were currently unemployed. This was particularly pronounced for the indicators of basic deprivation. Measuring poverty in terms of our combined income and basic deprivation criteria, poverty rates for the marginalized working class were similarly much higher than for the non-marginalized working class. Simply distinguishing those who are marginalized in that sense therefore serves to focus attention both on their particular needs, and on the processes at work in producing labour market detachment as the crucial point for intervention.

Calling this group an underclass, however, most often carries with it the connotation of what are loosely called sub-cultural effects. A great deal of confusion can arise in discussing such effects, because they are not always clearly distinguished, in conceptual discussions or empirical assessments, from the impact that prolonged unemployment itself is likely to have on motivation and behaviour. The distinctive underclass sub-cultural characteristics identified by Wilson are seen to arise from the combination of labour market detachment and social isolation, that isolation being a result of spatial segregation and concentration. We therefore focus attention on those who are marginalized in labour force terms and living in rented public housing in large urban centres, who could most plausibly be hypothesized to face such social isolation. Importantly, these in fact make up a relatively small proportion of the marginalized. This is consistent with evidence on spatial segregation of the poor in the USA, so the explanatory focus of the underclass concept is on a relatively small sub-set of the poor. In any case, the results of our analysis failed to show a significantly higher level of fatalism for the marginalized in these urban public housing estates than elsewhere, having controlled for other relevant personal and household characteristics.

8.8   Conclusions

In this chapter we have attempted to draw out the implications of our approach and results for some recent preoccupations of the literature on poverty. Since the evidence presented in previous chapters supports the contention that income alone is not a reliable indicator of enforced generalized deprivation, to have consistency between concept and measure one is faced with the choice of rethinking the concept, or coming up with better ways of identifying those experiencing enforced generalized deprivation. Applying both income and deprivation criteria, as we have done, seems the best route to follow, though undoubtedly the measures of each element could be improved—it may be possible to broaden the measure of resources to take other financial resources into account, and the set of indicators available to us was limited in coverage.

Sen's capability approach, much discussed in the literature, has served a valuable function in highlighting the importance of freedom or ability to achieve rather than simply outcomes, but has not been particularly helpful in advancing ways of achieving that aim empirically. Our own use of both income and deprivation goes some way towards incorporating opportunity sets rather than simply achieved states in the poverty measure. The capability approach also stresses that the conversion of income into capabilities may vary a great deal not only across communities but also across individuals: apart from disability, however, it is not clear from our results that such interpersonal variation is so pronounced as to pose a major problem.

In measuring generalized deprivation, the danger of casting the net too wide was noted. There is also the risk that in trying to identify items or activities that most people would do without only if they have to, a prescriptive element can creep in. Further, even conditions that would be seen by most people as inherently painful or unpleasant may be traded off against other goals. Rather than any specific item or activity, it is those items that can be demonstrated to be usually associated with other 'bads', and thus serve as reliable indicators of a more generalized state of deprivation, that are of primary interest. It also seems more productive to see factors that can cause deprivation and poverty—such as unemployment or racial discrimination—as processes rather than to use them as deprivation indicators *per se*.

'Social exclusion' has replaced 'poverty' in official European Union ter-

CONCEPTUALIZING AND MEASURING POVERTY

minology, partly because it can be directly related to concerns about the impact of the move towards closer economic integration. Social exclusion is presented as relating to dynamics and processes, to multidimensional disadvantage, and to inadequate social participation, whereas poverty is presented as static and descriptive, unidimensional, and narrowly financial. Our own analysis illustrates how this contrast is based to a significant degree on a caricature of the concept of poverty; further, where there are in fact substantive differences between the concepts, in our view what 'poverty' loses in terms of breadth may for many purposes be offset by the fact that it is less diffuse and more in tune with popular notions of social goals. Moving from poverty to social exclusion may help to sensitize researchers and policy-makers to dynamics, processes, and multiple disadvantage, but at a cost.

Much has been made of the distinction between notions of poverty arising out of concern with living standards and those based on minimum rights to resources to permit full participation in the life of society. We have seen that a substantial proportion of those below an income line are likely not to be experiencing basic deprivation: are people below the minimum income necessarily being deprived of an entitlement, regardless of other circumstances, and even if they are does it help to call all those below that minimum 'poor'? We noted that the right to income support from the state has always been conditional: we need to know *how* some of those on low incomes are avoiding basic deprivation before we can properly assess their situation, and see how others would regard it. If the Townsend-type definition of poverty necessarily involves 'inability to participate', one response may be to frame a broader definition. Some of those on low income may be avoiding deprivation only by recourse to expedients that are widely regarded as unacceptable, which would focus attention on distinguishing circumstances in which low income is generally regarded as unacceptable from those in which it is not.

We also argued that distinguishing those who are marginalized in terms of labour force participation serves to focus attention on their particular needs and on the processes at work in producing labour market detachment. Calling this group an underclass, however, most often carries with it the connotation of what are loosely called sub-cultural effects. We saw in the previous chapter that the marginalized in labour force terms who live in public housing in large urban centres make up a relatively small proportion of the marginalized, and do not show a significantly higher level of fatalism, so adopting the 'underclass' terminology may do more harm than good.

9

Implications for Tackling Poverty

9.1 Introduction

Having discussed the implications of our work for the conceptualization and measurement of poverty in economically advanced countries, we now turn to consider what can be learnt from our approach and findings about how poverty is to be tackled in those countries. We look first at their relevance to assessment of the adequacy of the levels of support provided by the social security system, which is of central importance in effectively alleviating poverty. In the light of what we have found to be the key processes that make and keep some people poor, we then concentrate on the lessons for social security and for the role of social security versus other policies in combating poverty.

9.2 Assessing the Adequacy of Social Security Support

In Chapter 2 we referred to the need to be clear about the purpose of the poverty measurement exercise, and to Veit-Wilson's (1989) distinction between aiming to *count* the numbers defined as poor, *explain* why people are poor, and *prescribe*, *report*, or *discover* an income poverty line. We have viewed identifying and counting those who are excluded owing to lack of resources primarily as a crucial step in explaining the processes that lead to people being in that situation. Given what we have seen to be the complex nature of the relationship between income and deprivation, we do not regard this as providing a basis on which to report or discover an income threshold below which most people are 'excluded'. However, it may allow some conclusions to be drawn about the extent to which the social security system's support rates provide recipients with the minimum resources necessary to avoid such exclusion. Our approach can thus help in addressing one of the most critical and yet problematic issues in framing income support strategies: are social security support levels 'adequate', and if not what would be an adequate level?

This is an extremely difficult question to tackle head-on. Social security rates are most often set without an explicit justification in terms of the standard of living they are intended to provide. Even where rates were based initially on calculations of the cost of a specified consumption basket, they have tended to evolve over time without being directly linked to such calculations. In the UK, for example, the rates of support recommended by the Beveridge Report were influenced by the cost estimates in Rowntree's poverty studies (though the precise relationship between the two remains a matter of debate[1]). When the Beveridge proposals were implemented, the rates set for National Insurance benefits were below those recommended, recipients with no other income being expected to fall back on National Assistance, but whether the assistance rates themselves matched those proposed by Beveridge when inflation was taken into account is also a matter of controversy. In any case, rates have subsequently been up-rated from one year to the next with reference to prices or earnings, rather than comparing either budget studies or studies of the standards of living attained by those relying on social security with those of the rest of the population. While official statements are made from time to time about the adequacy of the rates provided, these are not backed up by direct evidence—a pattern common to most though not all developed countries.

In those countries that do have regular official assessments of the adequacy of social security rates, budget studies provide an important input (for example in Norway and, until recently, in Germany). This is also the approach widely used by 'unofficial' researchers elsewhere in examining adequacy, and has been most recently applied in the UK by Bradshaw and colleagues at the University of York's Family Budget Unit (see e.g. Bradshaw 1993).[2] Comparison of social security rates with the cost of purchasing a specified basket of goods, intended to represent the minimum necessary standard of living, demonstrates the extent to which those rates permit recipients to attain that minimum. The budget standard methodology as a way of deriving a poverty line was discussed in detail in Chapter 2, and the central problems identified there also apply when it is used to assess the adequacy of social security rates. Most important are the essentially prescriptive nature of the exercise and the extent to which the results are determined by the judgements and sometimes necessarily arbitrary choices of the investigators. As Veit-Wilson (1994) puts it, going back to Rowntree, this approach in essence sets out to prescribe the minimum income on which people ought to be able to live a social life and just avoid deprivation if they spend their money as suggested—'a kind of prescriptive poverty line' (p. 29). More recent implementations do go to considerable lengths to take into account how people actually spend their money, and what the public thinks about standards of need and adequacy, but the

---

[1] It is not clear whether the Beveridge recommendations were intended to reflect Rowntree's 'subsistence' scale or his more generous 'human needs' scale, with differing interpretations of what Beveridge himself intended—see Veit-Wilson (1989), Atkinson (1990).

[2] Piachaud (1979) applied the same methodology to assess the adequacy of UK income support for children, an exercise recently carried out for Ireland by Carney et al. (1994).

nature of the exercise is fundamentally unchanged. This means that the results can be effective in demonstrating what *cannot* be afforded on a particular income level, even with what would generally be seen as stringent budgeting practices. At root, though, the components of the specified minimum level of living are based on prescriptive judgements about what goes into the basket of goods, and in what qualities and quantities.

An alternative—or complementary—approach is to examine empirically the living standards actually attained by people at different income levels, especially those relying on social security, and the extent to which they fail to attain socially defined needs. Survey-based poverty studies investigating the extent of deprivation have always been valued in part because of the light they throw on the adequacy of social security. Townsend's development of deprivation indicators brought a new dimension to such studies, and he placed a great deal of emphasis on the gap between social security rates and the income threshold he identified below which deprivation 'escalated disproportionately'. Indeed, one of the reasons why identifying a threshold was so important was precisely because it allowed him to make that comparison. While the existence of such a threshold itself has been hotly debated, as we have discussed at a number of points, deprivation indicators continue to be seen as having great potential in assessing the adequacy of social security rates. Veit-Wilson, for example, in arguing for the institution of an official Minimum Income Standard in the UK, sees the deprivation indicator method as 'probably the most reliable for giving us a direct picture of the lifestyle which people themselves define as minimally adequate, and also the income level which households need in order to achieve it' (1994: 27). He notes that such an income level is more likely to be a band than a single sum (for a given household type), but he clearly expects that such a band, below which most people are likely to be severely deprived, can be identified. (This would not automatically determine where social security rates should be set, because other factors legitimately come into play, but it would represent the adequacy standard that is a key criterion against which they could be judged.)

Our own analysis of the relationship between income and deprivation indicators shows a more diffuse pattern, with even a range of 'adequate' income being difficult to identify and many of those below such a threshold or range not experiencing basic deprivation, but these indicators can none the less be very useful in reflecting the extent of deprivation experienced by those relying on social security. We demonstrate this by examining the extent to which households in our Irish sample relying on social security for their current income are experiencing basic deprivation. Comparing the position of households relying on different social security schemes gives some indication of the relative effectiveness of these schemes in providing the support required to avoid such deprivation. Our aim here is to illustrate the approach rather than to present an assessment of Irish social security rates, so only the briefest description of the Irish system is necessary as background.[3]

The Irish system is based on an insurance/assistance structure very similar to that of the UK, with insurance-based Old Age, Widow's, and Disability Pensions and Unemployment and Disability Benefits for those who meet the contribution conditions, and means-tested Non-Contributory Pensions, Unemployment Assistance, Disability Payments, and Deserted Wife's and Unmarried Mother's Allowance for those who do not. In addition, there is a safety-net means-tested scheme called Supplementary Welfare Allowance for those who are not in work but do not qualify for any of the insurance or other means-tested schemes, and the Family Income Supplement which—like the UK Family Credit—provides a supplement to those on low earnings with child dependants. The way the rate of support provides varies across schemes is illustrated by the amount paid (in 1987) for a single adult.[4] This was highest for the insurance-based Contributory Old Age Pension, at about £54 per week, then came the contributory Widow's Pension, the Non-Contributory Old Age Pension and Widow's Allowance, and the insurance-based Invalidity Pension, all at between £46 and £48, then Unemployment and Disability Benefit at £41, Unemployment Assistance at £33–£37 depending on duration (with the higher rate paid for the long-term unemployed), and Supplementary Welfare Allowance with the lowest rate of £33. Unmarried Mother's Allowance paid £56 for a single mother with one child. The amount paid to recipients of Family Income Supplement varied depending on income and number of children.

Table 9.1 shows the percentage of households in the sample in receipt of payment from each of the main schemes, which corresponds quite closely with what one would expect from the administrative statistics (as detailed in Appendix 1). The percentage of households in receipt ranges from 13 per cent for Unemployment Assistance, 8–10 per cent for Unemployment Benefit, Contributory Old Age Pension, and Non-Contributory Old Age Pension, 4–5 per cent for Disability Benefit, Invalidity Pension, and Contributory Widow's Pension, and only 1–2 per cent for Disabled Person's Allowance, Supplementary Welfare Allowance, and the Unmarried Mother's Allowance.[5] Given the numbers involved, one can obviously be much more confident in using the sample to analyse the situation of, for example, households receiving Unemployment Assistance than of those receiving Supplementary Welfare Allowance. The numbers receiving Family Income Supplement are even smaller, so it is not included in our analysis.

---

[3] There have in any case been significant changes in the levels of payment under various schemes, and the relationships between them, since 1987 which would need to be taken into account in an up-to-date assessment.

[4] In the case of the assistance schemes this is the maximum amount, i.e. paid to someone with no other income.

[5] This scheme has subsequently been restructured and renamed Lone Parent's Allowance.

Table 9.1 Households relying on social welfare below income poverty lines/experiencing basic deprivation, by scheme

	% of households receiving under scheme	% of recipient households reliant on scheme[a]	% of those reliant on scheme who are:	
			below 50% line	below 60% line and experiencing basic deprivation
Unemployment Benefit	8.0	42.3	25.4	29.3
Unemployment Assistance	13.4	48.1	46.8	44.6
Disability Benefit	4.9	42.1	24.7	26.8
Invalidity Pension	3.5	56.0	10.4	38.5
Old Age Contributory Pension	8.9	70.2	0.9	5.4
Old Age Non-Contributory Pension	10.0	49.0	11.2	10.0
Widow's Contributory Pension	4.3	47.0	3.1	13.3
Widow's Non-Contributory Pension	1.6	39.2	11.2	36.6
Deserted Wife's Allowance	0.4	76.6	30.1	42.8
Unmarried Mother's Allowance	0.9	36.6	20.6	53.2
Supplementary Welfare Allowance	1.0	23.4	38.8	55.5
Disabled Person's Allowance	1.7	27.6	22.2	28.5

[a] i.e. more than half household disposable income is from scheme.

Many of the households in receipt of social welfare support also have incomes from other sources, and some are also receiving payment from more than one scheme. Here we are interested primarily in households relying on the scheme in question, particularly in making comparisons across schemes. It is therefore necessary to focus on those households that are largely reliant on particular social welfare schemes, and for current purposes we take this to be the case where payments from the scheme account for more than 50 per cent of household income. Table 9.1 shows the proportion of households in receipt of each scheme who are in this sense reliant on it, and we see that there is considerable variation across schemes. About half the households receiving Unemployment Assistance, Non-Contributory Old Age Pension, and Contributory Widow's Pension relied on these payments; for Unemployment Benefit and Disability Benefit the figure is 42 per cent, but for Non-Contributory Window's Pension, Unmarried Mother's Allowance, and especially Disabled Person's Allowance the proportion of recipients relying on the scheme is lower. (The percentage of Supplementary Welfare Allowance recipients 'reliant' on that scheme is only 23 per cent, but this is due to the fact that many are in receipt of one-off payments or top-ups rather than the full weekly rate available under that scheme.) By contrast, more than half the recipients of Invalidity Pension, 70 per cent of those receiving Contributory Old Age Pension, and over three-quarters of households receiving Deserted Wife's Allowance were relying on those payments.

Concentrating now on the households relying on the scheme in question, the table then shows the percentage below the 50 per cent income poverty line, and the percentage that is both below the 60 per cent income line *and* experiencing basic deprivation. Looking first at the percentage below the income poverty line, as one would expect, poverty rates on this basis were highest for the schemes that were means-tested and had the lower rates of support, notably Unemployment Assistance. Half the households relying on that scheme were below half average income, compared with about 40 per cent of those on Supplementary Welfare Allowance, one-quarter of those relying on Unemployment Benefit and Disability Benefit, only about 10 per cent of those relying on Non-Contributory Widow's and Old Age pensions, and hardly any of those on Contributory Old Age Pension.

If, instead of measuring poverty using half average income, one uses a higher income line but also incorporates the experience of basic deprivation into the criterion, a somewhat different pattern is shown. Now, over half of those relying on Supplementary Welfare Allowance and Unmarried Mother's Allowance fell below the 60 per cent line and were experiencing basic deprivation. The corresponding figure was between 35 and 45 per cent for Unemployment Assistance, Invalidity Pension, Non-Contributory Widow's Pension, and Deserted Wife's Allowance, and about 25–30 per cent for Unemployment Benefit, Disability Benefit, and Disabled Person's Allowance. It was strikingly lower, at 5–10 per cent, in the case of old age pensions, whether contributory or non-contributory.

These results demonstrate the value of having information on indicators of deprivation in assessing the adequacy of social security rates, and indicate how this adds to what can be learnt from relative income alone. They show clearly that, although a relatively high proportion of the Irish households receiving social security old age pensions in 1987 were relying on these payments for much or most of their income, few of the households relying on these payments were experiencing basic deprivation. The emphasis during the 1970s and early part of the 1980s on improving social security support for the elderly, already mentioned, does appear to have had a major impact on the living standards of that group. Although only about one in six households receiving the insurance-based unemployment and illness schemes met the combined income-plus-deprivation poverty criteria, many were receiving income from other sources. Where Unemployment Benefit or Disability Benefit was the main income coming into the household, a substantial proportion of recipients were experiencing basic deprivation, which suggests that adequacy of the support rates cannot be taken for granted. However, Unemployment Assistance and Invalidity Pensions both had a higher proportion of recipients relying on them and a higher percentage of those below the 60 per cent line *and* experiencing deprivation, even though the former is means-tested and the latter is not, and the rates paid were not much lower than Unemployment or Disability Benefit. What distinguishes these schemes is not means-testing versus insurance or the level of support paid, but the fact that many recipients are dependent on these schemes long-term. This points once again to the importance of the dynamics of income over time, in particular the erosion of assets and the exhaustion of borrowing opportunities for those who are dependent on certain schemes for a prolonged period. For Supplementary Welfare Allowance (SWA) and Unmarried Mother's Allowance, the proportion of recipients reliant on the payment as the main source of household income was relatively low, but for that subgroup the extent of basic deprivation was particularly high. The rates paid under SWA were low compared with other schemes at the time, but it may be at least as important that the special factors or needs that lead households to be relying on that safety-net scheme, and the special needs associated with single parenting, put those relying on these schemes at particular risk.

The fact that about half of those relying on some of the social security schemes were below the 60 per cent income line and experiencing basic deprivation certainly puts a serious question-mark over the adequacy of those rates. Indeed, substantial increases in the lowest rates of support in real terms have subsequently been implemented, reflecting a broad political consensus that they were below a socially acceptable minimum. However, it will be clear from these results and our earlier discussion of the income–

deprivation relationship that this type of analysis is not likely to provide a basis for easy identification of the level of support that *would* be adequate to ensure avoidance of basic deprivation. This is, first, because one does not have a set of control groups with which to compare those currently relying on social welfare, like them in all other respects but at successively higher income levels; even if we did, the regression results presented in previous chapters suggest that the proportion experiencing basic deprivation would decline as income rises, but that even at much higher income levels some proportion would still be experiencing basic deprivation. It is then a matter of judgement as to what proportion is 'low enough' to represent adequacy.

Second and more fundamentally, the central message from our analysis of the relationship between deprivation, income, and broader resources is that current income is only one—though a key—determinant of deprivation, and that how households arrived at that income greatly influences its impact on living standards. Rather than simply emphasizing how much more difficult this makes it to identify a current income level that is adequate to avoid basic deprivation, though, for us this highlights the need for a dynamic perspective in assessing adequacy and framing policy. This involves taking into account the fact that resources and needs may vary for households at similar current income levels, that the point at which intervention takes place is crucial, and that social security can be seen only in the broader context of other policies. These are points that are taken up in the next section, which moves from adequacy to the broader issues of the role and design of social security in the light of the findings of this study.

9.3 The Role of Social Security in Anti-Poverty Strategies

We saw back in Chapter 3 that major changes have taken place over the last quarter-century in the types of household falling below income poverty lines, both in Ireland and in many other developed countries. The elderly now make up a much smaller proportion of the Irish low-income population than heretofore, while families with children account for a much more substantial proportion. Households containing children accounted for 35 per cent of those below half average equivalent income in 1973 but almost 60 per cent of those below that income line in 1987. This reflected changes in the labour force status of the low-income population: in 1973 almost half the households below the 50 per cent income line had a head who was retired or 'in home duties' and only 10 per cent had an unemployed head, but by 1987 the corresponding figures were 20 and over 33 per cent. This was due to the dramatic rise in the numbers unemployed in the population—not to a worsening in the relative position of the unemployed—and to the relatively rapid rise in social welfare support levels for the elderly and widows, as well as wider coverage of occupational pensions. We also saw that an improvement in the income position of the elderly and a deterioration in that of households with children has been seen over that period in many other developed countries including the UK, the USA, Sweden, the Netherlands, and France. While there are differences across countries, the improvement in old age and retirement pensions has been a key common factor for the elderly, while high unemployment or stagnant earnings growth has adversely affected the position of families with children. The increase in the number of single-parent families has also been a factor in increasing the risk of poverty for children in some countries.

Our subsequent analysis employing indicators of deprivation has served to reinforce the conclusion that, in the late 1980s, it was households headed by an unemployed person rather than an elderly or retired one that were the most sizeable element in the Irish poverty population. (In addition, households where the head was in home duties appeared to at greater risk than suggested by income lines alone.) The Irish evidence suggests that the broad compositional change in the low-income population in other countries would also be shown if one were able to measure poverty on the basis of income and experience of deprivation, though of course one would wish to have this confirmed. The changing poverty profile, notably the fact that far more of the poor are now actually or potentially in the labour force, clearly has major implications for the role of social security and its relationship with other policies, and for the design of social security systems. Increases in the levels of social security coverage and support have been central to the improvement in the relative position of the elderly in recent years. The maintenance of this improved situation for the elderly cannot be taken for granted, as growing numbers depending on pensions will put pressure on the levels of support provided. The way in which the gains to pensioners can be eroded quite rapidly is demonstrated by the UK experience (noted in Chapter 3) since pensions were indexed to prices rather than earnings in the early 1980s. One certainly cannot conclude that poverty among the elderly has been 'solved' by social security, but the predominance of other types of household among the poor means that poverty is now much less amenable to a strategy relying primarily on social security.

The dominant role of unemployment in producing poverty means that labour market policy moves centre-stage. Obviously success in job creation is of central importance, but while highlighting that fact, once again our research is not intended to provide insights into issues of macroeconomic or industrial policy. (One's view of the likely success of job creation policies does however affect attitudes to the appropriate structure for income transfers, as we discuss shortly.) It is also now a commonplace that social security and taxation systems have to become more 'job-friendly', though the extent to which current systems in fact act as a disincentive to taking up employment or to job creation by employers remains hotly contested. However, a central message from our results was the importance of the processes whereby resources are accumulated or eroded over time, in particular the way in which long-term or repeated experience of unemployment leaves those affected much less able to avoid deprivation than others on a similar income level, because they often have no other resources on which to draw. It is not simply unemployment, but the marginalization or exclusion from the labour force that sustained unemployment produces, which is critical in producing deprivation; a policy response that concentrates on being job-friendly and maximizing job creation may not help those who need it most.

Our research has highlighted the cumulative disadvantages experienced by the sub-set of the unemployed who were identified in Chapter 7 as marginalized in labour force terms. The individuals involved are mostly lacking in training and often have only the most basic education. Analysis of our sample shows that failure to obtain some second-level educational qualification greatly increases the risk of poverty, of current and long-term unemployment, of lengthy unemployment experience over one's career, and of low pay when employed.[6] In a trend that has also been noted elsewhere, owing to changes in the occupational structure, the consequences of educational failure have become more serious over time, and those without qualifications—drawn mostly from lower working-class backgrounds—have become more and more limited to unskilled manual occupations at a high risk of unemployment. There has been a sharper and sharper polarization between those who leave school early without any qualification and their more successful peers. A key issue for education and training policy is thus how to design and target programmes for those who have already left school with little or no qualifications, and to reduce the numbers leaving school each year in that position.

General training schemes tend to help those most able to take advantage of them, rather than those most in need. For those with few or no qualifications, second-chance education may often be necessary as a prelude to training.[7] As far as reducing the flow of unqualified early leavers from education is concerned, there is a temptation to focus exclusively on schools in disadvantaged areas; but evidence from a number of countries shows that most children who fail badly in education do not live in socially highly disadvantaged areas—though they do come predominantly from poor households. Resources have to be directed towards badly performing schools or children themselves, to provide supplementary remedial teaching and improve links between home and school. Even with second-chance education and targeted training, those currently marginalized in labour force terms find it very difficult to compete effectively for available jobs. A common response internationally has been programmes providing an incentive for employers to increase employment levels and/or to hire the

[6] See Chs. 4 and 6 above, also C. T. Whelan (1994) and Nolan (1993).
[7] See e.g. Sexton and O'Connell's (1993) recent evaluations of the effectiveness of EU structural funds expenditure on 'human resources'.

long-term unemployed—in the Irish case these have included employment subsidies and exemptions/'holidays' on the employer's social insurance contributions. However, generalized subsidies have been found to have a large 'deadweight' element, subsidizing employment that would have occurred anyway, and even targeted employment subsidies generally have great difficulty in overcoming employers' reluctance to hire the long-term unemployed. Where temporary direct employment schemes have been implemented for the long-term unemployed, these have often been at wages little higher than social security, and may do little for future employment prospects of participants.

Such labour market programmes have received a great deal of attention from researchers and policy-makers, with evaluation of their effects generating its own sub-literature,[8] and a great deal of uncertainty persists about what 'works' and what does not. However, highlighting the way in which people can become more and more detached from employment and the impact this has in producing deprivation provides a particular perspective on such evaluations. For example, even if sizeable employment subsidies aimed at the long-term unemployed did not have much impact on overall numbers in employment, a more equitable sharing of the burden of unemployment could have a substantial impact on deprivation. Direct employment of the long-term unemployed by public authorities for a time, at something approaching market wage rates, could also play a role in assisting the renintegration of those who appear unlikely to obtain employment otherwise. Such options will probably cost substantially more than simply continuing to provide income support, but assessments of costs and benefits should take fully into account the impact such targeted programmes could have on current living standards and the long-term prospects of those most exposed to deprivation. (Re-integration of the marginalized could also make wage bargaining more sensitive to the level of unemployment.)

Our findings on the extent and nature of poverty and of labour market marginalization also have implications for the role of area-based strategies, which have featured prominently in the evolution of anti-poverty policy at EU level.[9] Community-based projects can make an important contribution to harnessing the energies of local communities and promoting participation in decision-making by those actually experiencing poverty, but it is important to have realistic expectations about what such projects can achieve. The structural factors producing poverty have to be tackled primarily at national and, for EU member states, EU level: purely local

[8] See e.g. OECD (1991) for a methodological review of this evaluation literature.

[9] The main EC action specifically designed towards combating poverty within member states has been the area-based pilot action projects under the Poverty Programmes. In the Irish case there has also been a great deal of recent emphasis at national level on area-based projects as one response to long-term unemployment.

action can generally be expected to have little impact on unemployment in an area. Further, we have seen that, while unemployment and poverty rates are indeed very high in certain areas or types of area, most of the unemployed and most poor households are not to be found in these areas. This is true even when we focused on the sub-set of the poor or unemployed who are marginalized in labour market terms and experiencing basic deprivation. Those living in 'black spot' areas are particularly likely to be in that position and face especially severe problems for a variety of reasons, and designing policies to meet their particular needs (having first determined what those are) is of great importance. However, such strategies will affect only a minority of the unemployed or the poor. This is relevant not only to policy but also to perceptions of the extent and nature of poverty. The poor are not simply to be identified as those living in particularly disadvantaged urban public authority housing estates with high poverty rates: in Ireland most poor people do not live in such estates, and this is consistent with the evidence on spatial concentration of poverty in, for example, the USA. Strategies targeting the most disadvantaged areas, however necessary and valuable, constitute only one element in a comprehensive response to poverty.

9.4   The Design of Social Security Systems

As well as affecting the role of social security versus other policy responses, the changing nature of poverty has major implications for the design of social security systems and how they interact with taxation. As we have noted, the notion that social security and taxation systems have to become more 'job-friendly' is widely accepted. Indeed, there has been a resurgence of interest in various countries in a radical restructuring of the way income support is provided by the State, with a good deal of discussion and analysis of basic income schemes that break the links between labour market status and entitlement to income support (see e.g. Atkinson 1995; Healy and Reynolds 1992). More generally, the ways in which social security and tax systems affect the labour market have come to be seen as of critical importance, the tax system being relevant because of the way in which it can interact with social security to create serious unemployment and poverty 'traps', where people face very high marginal tax plus benefit withdrawal rates if they take up employment or increase their gross earnings.

Social security structures and levels of support have always been framed with one eye to the labour market and concern about the extent to which the incentive to work is undermined. Despite the wealth of highly sophisticated research on the topic of the incentive effects of income support for the unemployed, much of the debate about support levels has been a rather fruitless dialogue of the deaf between those who argue that rates are not adequate and those who argue that they leave little or no incentive to take up work. Both could of course be true: it is the policy implications drawn that usually distinguish those emphasizing one or the other view. Here it is important to distinguish the possible effects of unemployment 'traps' on the level of unemployment and those on particular types of household: even if a rise in benefits leads to an increase in the duration of unemployment for some people, their 'place' in the queue for jobs may be taken by others with little or no impact on the rate of unemployment.[10] Families with children, now often facing a high risk of poverty, are also most likely to have relatively high replacement rates—the proportion of income when in work received when unemployed—or marginal tax/benefit withdrawal rates. This is because social security generally (though not always) incorporates additional payments where there are child dependants which will be lost on taking up work; means tests for non-cash benefits generally set a higher limit for those with children; and such families are most likely to be receiving assistance with housing costs and programmes that supplement in-work income incorporating high withdrawal rates as earnings increase. Because of these factors, one can see from our 1987 Irish sample that most of those facing high replacement rates[11]—of 60 per cent or more, for example—have dependent children (see Callan *et al.* 1994), and this is consistent with findings elsewhere.

This serves to focus attention on the way child income support is structured, and in particular on the role of universal payments made in respect of all children, irrespective of the means or employment status of their parents. The case for increasing this universal payment in order to assist families with children and improve incentives by reducing the role of means-tested payments has often been advanced, for example in debates about child benefit in the UK. Similar arguments, put forward by one of the present authors among others (Nolan and Farrell 1990; Callan 1991; Callan *et al.* 1994), have had some success in Ireland. Significant increases in child benefit were implemented in 1995, although the rate is still substantially below that paid in the UK, or below the child additions for those depending on social security in Ireland. The payments going to 'non-poor' households are from this perspective *not* simply waste and evidence of bad targeting: not only is some support to such families desirable in itself, but the very fact that the payment is not restricted to the poor is central to its impact on incentives. The fact that the payment is received by the mother—and often may be her only independent source of income—and that its use is generally

---

[10] Blackwell (1991), in reviewing the international evidence for the OECD, emphasizes this point in concluding that, 'On balance, it is unlikely that much of the increase in the long-term rate of unemployment occurring in European countries since the early 1970s could be due to increases in the replacement ratio' (p. 114).

[11] Loosely, the ratio of income when unemployed to income when in work.

under her control means that this could also make a contribution towards promoting gender equality.[12]

Some extend the logic of such an emphasis on universal child benefit to argue for a fundamental transformation of the income maintenance system into a basic income scheme. While there are a number of variants, the central feature of such schemes is that everyone in the population receives a payment (every week or month), regardless of labour market status. The 'pure' version sees these payments as replacing all existing social welfare transfers, to the unemployed, the elderly, the ill, and so on. They would also replace all income tax allowances, so income tax would be payable on all other income. This type of scheme can appeal to those from quite different political or ideological standpoints. The fact that the payment is received whether one is at work or unemployed is seen as the only effective way of overcoming the disincentive effects of the unemployment 'trap' created by means-tested and contingency-based schemes. However, the central obstacle that proponents of such schemes face is that financing this payment to everyone may involve what would be seen as too high a tax burden.

Attempting fully to quantify the costs and benefits of such a scheme poses a variety of complex methodological problems (see Atkinson 1989, 1995). As Atkinson points out, one valuable tool in such an exercise is a tax/benefit model based on a representative sample of households, which allows one to see how different households are immediately affected, who gains and loses, and what tax rates would be required to finance a given level of transfers. Behavioural responses to these changes are not generally taken into account, but the static 'first-round' effects provide a basis on which to begin the assessment. For example, such a model of the Irish income tax and social welfare systems, based on the sample of households obtained in the 1987 survey but updated in line with the tax and benefit structures, shows that a fully fledged basic income scheme providing current income support levels would *ceteris paribus* require an income tax rate well in excess of 60 per cent (Callan *et al.* 1994). In response to this type of finding about the affordability of a full individual basic income replacing social security, various partial basic income schemes have been advanced and analysed in different countries, but none has so far come close to implementation.

Basic income schemes represent one approach to achieving full integration of the income tax and social welfare systems, which could also be brought about through a negative income tax. Much of the discussion about

---

[12] There has also been on-going debate in the UK and Ireland about whether child benefit should be liable for tax, some arguing that making it taxable would help to finance an increase in the rate while at the same time targeting it more towards those on low incomes. The main objections seem to arise from the fact that child benefit is currently paid to the mother while the tax generally affects the father: taxation could therefore give rise to disharmony within the family, and there is often the misperception that the mother herself would be directly liable even if she has no other income.

'integration' of the two systems does not refer to such radical restructuring, and is bedevilled by the fact that what is meant by the term is often unclear. The common underlying theme, though, is a concern about the poverty and unemployment traps created by the way the tax and social welfare systems currently interact. These traps are in essence a product of means-testing, which is often justified on the grounds that it allows resources to be directed towards those most in need. However, means-testing is by no means a *sine qua non* for effective targeting. Once again, Ireland serves to illustrate the general point: a very high proportion of all Irish social security spending, not only of means-tested social assistance payments but also on social insurance, goes to bringing those below income poverty lines up towards those lines (see Callan and Nolan 1989).[13] As Atkinson (1993*a*) argues, 'for all the rhetoric about targeting, means testing has not worked, and a major aim of policy in Britain should be to reduce dependence on means-tested income benefits' (p. 23). He sees improved and modernized social insurance complemented by a partial basic income scheme as the best route to follow to bring this about and provide an effective national minimum. Although not itself providing an adequate income, a partial universal payment conditional on 'participation'—which could include caring for the elderly or children and voluntary work—could substantially reduce the numbers depending on means-tested benefits. While the merits of such a scheme need in-depth investigation in the specific setting involved, the demerits of means-testing do not. Reducing dependency is an aim on which people from either end of the ideological spectrum can agree, and relying on means-testing as a way of bringing that about should by now be discredited.

9.5   Conclusions

In this chapter we have shown how deprivation indicators can be very useful in reflecting the extent of deprivation experienced by those relying on social security, though the nature of the income–deprivation relationship means that they do not provide a basis for easy identification of the 'adequate' level of support. The fact that unemployment is now the dominant cause of poverty in many countries has focused attention on the need for social security and other policies to be more 'job-friendly', but that will not in itself help those who are most marginalized in labour force terms, who have been shown by our results to be most vulnerable to poverty. The long-term unemployed require specially targeted labour market measures, and the anti-poverty effectiveness of such programmes rather than simply the effect on the level of unemployment should be fully taken into account in assessing their benefits. In reforming social security, reducing rather than increas-

---

[13] See Beckerman (1979) for the methodology involved and an application to the UK, and Deleeck *et al.* (1992) for similar results for a number of other EU countries.

ing the role of means-testing is the way to reduce dependency. Improved benefits for children are a particularly effective way to improve incentives; they can be seen by proponents of a basic income as a step in that direction, but have an independent justification in their own right.

10

Conclusions

10.1 The Point of Departure

In this concluding chapter, we set out the central thrust of the argument put forward in this volume, review the key findings, and discuss their implications for poverty measurement, anti-poverty policy, and further research. Despite its importance—or perhaps because of it—there is remarkably little consensus among social scientists on how best to measure poverty. Our aim in this book has been to identify and address key problems with the ways in which poverty has generally been conceptualized and measured in relatively rich countries. We have sought to first demonstrate the extent to which current practice fails satisfactorily to measure poverty as it is now most often defined in these countries. We then proceeded to develop an approach to measurement which is more in accord with that definition, employing both income and direct indicators of deprivation.

Our point of departure has been Townsend's classic definition of poverty in terms of exclusion from the ordinary life of society because of a lack of resources. While this is the definition most often advanced by those setting out to measure poverty, most studies do not attempt to measure exclusion directly. Instead, they rely on income (or less often expenditure) and count all those below a particular income line as poor. We have discussed in some detail the various approaches that are used to select a particular income cut-off as 'the' poverty line, and the problems associated with each. Reflecting the scale of these problems, an increasingly common practice is to apply a number of different income lines rather than a single cut-off, these lines often being derived as proportions of mean or median income. While this allows the sensitivity of the results to the exact location of the poverty line to be assessed, it still assumes that income is a reliable indicator of exclusion owing to lack of resources. In debates on whether expenditure is better for this purpose than income, confusion has been rife between arguments based on the reliability of survey data on income versus expenditure, and those distinguishing resource-based from standard-of-living-based concepts of poverty.

While these debates have raged, the potential of non-monetary indicators in measuring and understanding poverty measurement has so far been under-exploited. In this book we have taken seriously Ringen's critique of reliance on income in measuring poverty, and have reported on the implementation of a research programme which has much in common with that suggested by Donnison (1988) in his response to Ringen. We have developed an approach to identifying the poor which implements Ringen's suggestion that both income and deprivation be incorporated into the measure, and have examined the implications of taking that approach. We have set this in the wider framework of an analysis of the relationships between income, broader resources, and deprivation, and see our central contribution not simply as the development of an approach to measuring exclusion resulting from lack of resources, but as the illumination of those poorly understood relationships.

10.2   The Key Findings

The analysis has been based on information on income, characteristics, experiences, assets, and a range of non-monetary indicators of deprivation for a large representative sample of Irish households from a specially designed survey. While using Irish data, the findings highlight conceptual and methodological issues and causal processes that are of quite general relevance. With these data we first applied relative income poverty lines, following the general approach now often used in making poverty comparisons across countries. The results showed that 20 per cent of the sample were in households below half average equivalent income, and 30 per cent were below an income threshold set at 60 per cent of that average. Using annual rather than current income, or the narrower family rather than the household as income recipient unit, were seen to make little difference to the numbers falling below these lines. A number of the well-known difficulties with the use of income were also discussed, including the time period over which income is measured and the inherent difficulties in measuring income accurately by means of survey techniques. However, the fundamental issue about reliance on income in measuring poverty is not simply one of measurement: it is whether income, properly measured, in fact tells us what we want to know when we set out to measure poverty.

We then turned from income to the measurement of deprivation. Being 'excluded' in this context is generally taken to mean experiencing various forms of what the society in question regards as serious deprivation, and the validity of the common practice of using low income as a 'marker' for exclusion can be assessed only by comparison with direct measures of deprivation. Examination of the limited number of previous poverty studies that have employed indicators of deprivation showed that the key issues were what criteria to apply in selecting suitable indicators, and how best to aggregate across indicators in order to provide a summary measure. Our objective in employing such indicators has not been to provide a comprehensive picture of deprivation in all its aspects, but rather to be able to identify households experiencing generalized deprivation enforced by lack of resources.

Like Mack and Lansley, we set our objective as the measurement of enforced lack of socially defined necessities, since the underlying concept of poverty is itself based on the notion that expectations are culturally conditioned. However, it is not enough that items be regarded as necessities: the relationships between the items themselves also need to be taken into account if they are to be indicative of generalized deprivation. The life-style items on which we have data are drawn largely from previous studies such as Townsend (1979) and Mack and Lansley (1985), but we take into account the fact that deprivation may best be treated as multidimensional rather than unidimensional and that various dimensions may behave rather differently. Factor analysis allowed three different dimensions, three sets of items that cluster together, to be distinguished, which we termed the basic, secondary, and housing dimensions. Separate indices for each of these sets of items were then constructed, the scores showing how many of the items in that set a household lacked and said that was because they could not afford it.

Regression analysis was used to estimate the relationships between these scores and a wide range of independent variables, covering current income, savings and other assets, factors affecting demands on household resources, labour force status, social class and class background, education, and experience of unemployment. The results add considerably to our understanding of the processes at work, and also helped in deciding which indicators were most useful in measuring poverty. Deprivation scores were seen to be strongly related to such variables, in a way that varies across the dimensions, with a substantial proportion of the variance in deprivation scores (by social sciences standards) explained by the equations. While current income is an important influence on deprivation, so are many other aspects of a household's current situation and how they arrived there.

The fact that the income–deprivation relationship is not more pronounced does *not* therefore mean that differences in tastes are dominating life-style, but it does mean that current income should not be taken as the sole indicator of current living standards and/or command over resources in measuring poverty. The results highlighted the role of long-term factors in influencing households' current situations even when one controls for current income level, relating most importantly to the way resources have been accumulated or eroded over time. They reinforce the crucial role of dynamics, but suggest that the focus needs to be longer-term, rather than simply on dynamics from one year to the next. The fact that the various explanatory variables were seen to impact rather differently on the basic, housing, and secondary indices showed how important it can be to distinguish between different dimensions in using deprivation indicators to measure poverty.

We then looked at how one might take both current income and measured deprivation into account in measuring poverty, on the basis that, following Ringen, both elements are required if the poverty measure is to be consistent with the widely accepted definition which relates to exclusion from ordinary living standards owing to lack of resources. Our aim was to identify those unable to have socially defined necessities because of a lack of resources. In using direct indicators of deprivation in applying this approach, we took into account that simply adding together indicators of deprivation, which may relate to different aspects or dimensions, into a summary index is not satisfactory. We concentrated on the set of items referring to basic deprivation that cluster together and are widely regarded as necessities, which we felt were most likely to reflect the underlying latent variable of generalized deprivation. Rather than seeking to locate an income threshold, we examined households that were experiencing what they regarded as enforced basic deprivation and were also below relative income thresholds, so that the sensitivity of the results to the income cut-off point used could be seen.

The income and basic deprivation criteria allowed us to distinguish four groups: those on low incomes and experiencing basic deprivation, those on low incomes and not experiencing basic deprivation, those not on low incomes but experiencing basic deprivation, and those not on low incomes and not experiencing basic deprivation. Only about half the households below income poverty lines were experiencing enforced basic deprivation, but there were also substantial numbers above those lines reporting such deprivation. Distinguishing households as poor using both income and basic deprivation produced a poverty profile which differed significantly from that observed when simply applying the current income lines, most obviously in terms of current labour force status: households headed by a farmer, other self-employed, or retired person were less important, and those headed by an ill-disabled person or someone in home duties more important, among the poor. Households with an unemployed head continued to be the most substantial group.

The role of labour force experience and resources over a prolonged period, rather than simply current status, in determining the risk of current poverty was shown by the results of regression analysis. These results revealed major differences between the four groups distinguished by our income and basic deprivation criteria. The consistently non-poor differed from the consistently poor across virtually the full range of explanatory variables—current labour force participation, household composition and other factors affecting the demands on income, wider resources, and a variety of factors likely to have affected the capacity to accumulate such resources. The income-poor not reporting enforced basic deprivation were distinguished from the non-poor primarily by current labour force participation, with long-term factors much less important than they were for those who were on low incomes and also experiencing basic deprivation. On the other hand, it is precisely those longer-term factors that served to distinguish those reporting deprivation but not on low incomes from the consistently non-poor, while current labour force participation in that case had no discriminatory power.

Information external to that used in implementing the four-way categorization of sample households provided support for the validity of the results. Those identified as consistently poor—on low income and experiencing what they saw as enforced basic deprivation—were seen to have much higher levels of self-assessed financial strain and of psychological distress, and much higher levels of deprivation in terms of items not included in the basic index, than those on low incomes but not reporting enforced basic deprivation. The key message about the importance of distinguishing between these groups was therefore reinforced. We also looked at the items not in the basic index and at how the clustering of items may differ across societies, affecting which types are best used as indicators of generalized deprivation.

The data available to us on deprivation, labour market histories, and attitudes were also useful in assessing whether the concept of an 'underclass' can be fruitfully applied in societies such as Ireland facing sustained high unemployment. Following Gallie (1994), we took labour market marginality, extreme deprivation, and a distinctive sub-culture as the crucial elements constituting an underclass. In applying the concept here we first identified a marginalized working class in terms of labour market experience, then assessed whether their levels of deprivation were significantly higher than the manual working class, and finally examined whether the levels of fatalism found among that group were consistent with the effects that Wilson hypothesized labour force marginalization and social isolation to have on attitudes and behaviour. Those identified on the basis of labour force histories as marginalized were found to have much higher levels of deprivation than the non-marginalized working class, even where the latter were currently unemployed. Measuring poverty in terms of our combined income and basic deprivation criteria, poverty rates for the marginalized working class were similarly much higher than for the non-marginalized working class. Simply distinguishing those who are marginalized in that sense therefore serves to focus attention both on their particular needs, and on the processes at work in producing labour market detachment as the crucial point for intervention.

Calling this group an underclass, however, most often carries with it the connotation of what are loosely called sub-cultural effects. The distinctive underclass sub-cultural characteristics identified by Wilson are seen to arise from the combination of labour market detachment and social isolation, that isolation being a result of spatial segregation and concentration. We therefore focused attention on those who are marginalized in labour force terms and living in rented public housing in large urban centres, who could most plausibly be hypothesized to face such social isolation. These were found to make up a relatively small proportion of the marginalized, so the explanatory focus of the underclass concept is on a relatively small sub-set. In any case, the analysis failed to show a significantly higher level of fatalism for the marginalized in these urban public housing estates than elsewhere, having controlled for other relevant personal and household characteristics. In the absence of evidence for such patterns of causation, the underclass framework is in our view redundant, and it is sufficient to refer to the *extent* of marginalization and deprivation.

10.3   The Implications

The results set out in this volume have serious implications for the way poverty is conceptualized and measured, and throw a good deal of light on current debates in the literature. We have sought to clarify the concepts involved and to set out clearly the sense in which we ourselves have used them. Deprivation we take to mean *inability* to obtain the types of diet, clothing, housing, household facilities and environmental, educational, working, and social conditions generally regarded as acceptable in the community in question. In deciding what constitutes 'generally acceptable', we have taken *views* in the society about what constitutes necessities as the touchstone, rather than what most people have or do. Poverty, defined in terms of inability to participate owing to lack of resources, is taken to occur when people lack such items or are unable to participate in society because they do not have the financial resources to do so. Poverty refers to enforced and generalized deprivation, rather than either to multiple deprivation attributable to factors other than lack of resources, or to deprivation that is enforced but only in an isolated area of life. This is not the only way in which poverty has been or could be defined, but it is in our view the most logical and consistent interpretation of Townsend's widely accepted definition.

   We have seen that this definition of poverty is usually applied through income poverty lines, and the evidence we have presented supports the contention that income alone is not a reliable indicator of enforced generalized deprivation. To have consistency between concept and measure, one is in effect faced with the choice of rethinking the concept, or coming up with better ways of identifying those experiencing enforced generalized deprivation. In developing further our approach to using both resources and deprivation indicators, much can undoubtedly be done to improve the measures of each element. Our results have shown the importance of financial resources going beyond current weekly or annual income in influencing living patterns, and it may be possible to broaden the measure of income to take other financial resources into account. However, we have

also demonstrated that measuring those on low current incomes and reporting little or no financial savings, though more effective in identifying those
experiencing deprivation than an income cut-off alone, was not an adequate
substitute for income together with direct indicators of deprivation.

In measuring deprivation, the set of indicators available to us was limited
in coverage, and a good deal of thought needs to be given to developing the
range and type of indicators employed. However, there is a danger that the
object of the exercise will be lost sight off in attempting to encompass
various aspects of living conditions. We have emphasized that the aim, in
the context of poverty measurement, is not to capture in a multidimensional
manner the level of adequacy or participation in each and every aspect of
life: it is rather to identify those who are experiencing generalized deprivation. Some of the deprivation indicators employed in other studies appear unsuitable to us for that purpose, and there is a good deal of confusion
about what is to be achieved by distinguishing different life-style or deprivation dimensions. There is also a risk that, in trying to identify items or
activities that most people would do without only if they had to, a prescriptive element can creep in. Further, even conditions that would be seen by
most people as inherently painful or unpleasant may be traded off against
other goals. Rather than any specific item or activity, it is those items that
can be demonstrated to be usually associated with other 'bads', and thus
serve as reliable indicators of a more generalized state of deprivation, that
are of primary interest. It also seems more productive to see factors that
can cause deprivation and poverty—such as unemployment or racial
discrimination—as processes rather than to use them as deprivation
indicators *per se*.

As Sen's much discussed capability approach to assessing living standards
highlights, it is freedom or ability to achieve rather than simply outcomes
that we fundamentally care about; however, that approach has not been
particularly helpful in advancing ways of improving empirical measurement. Sen sees poverty as the failure of basic capabilities to reach certain
minimally acceptable standards. While our conceptual framework is clearly
somewhat different from his, non-monetary indicators of deprivation such
as those included in our basic deprivation index can be seen as direct, if
crude, measures of success or failure in achieving particular concrete aspects of the broader functionings entailed, while our use of both income and
deprivation goes some way towards incorporating opportunity sets rather
than simply achieved states in the poverty measure. The capability approach also emphasizes that a poverty analysis concentrating only on incomes can be quite remote from the main motivation with our concern with
poverty (viz. the limitation of the *lives* that some people are forced to live),
and may fail to provide empirical guidance regarding the genesis and prevalence of deprivation. Our poverty measure includes direct measures of the
limited lives that people are actually leading, and our findings regarding the

extent of poverty and the processes generating it do differ from those produced by a focus on income poverty lines alone. However, the challenge for advocates of the capability approach is to show whether distinguishing different 'functionings' makes any easier the selection of indicators of success or failure to achieve participation in society, and how that approach can be implemented empirically. The capability approach also stresses that the conversion of income into capabilities may vary a great deal not only across communities but also across individuals. Apart from disability, however, our results do not suggest that such interpersonal variation is so pronounced as to pose a major problem.

'Social exclusion' has replaced poverty in official EU terminology, partly because it can be directly related to concerns about the impact of the move towards closer economic integration within the Union. Substantive claims have been made for the advantages of a conceptualization in terms of social exclusion, which is presented as relating to dynamics and processes, to multidimensional disadvantage, and to inadequate social participation, whereas poverty is presented as static and descriptive, unidimensional, and narrowly financial. Our own analysis illustrates that this contrast is based to a significant degree on a caricature of the concept of poverty. There is nothing in the way poverty is generally conceptualized that necessarily has a static or descriptive connotation, as recent US emphasis on poverty dynamics demonstrates, and many studies of poverty from Rowntree on have taken the description of those identified as poor as the starting-point for an analysis of processes. The criticism that poverty is unidimensional, 'just about money', whereas social exclusion relates to multidimensional disadvantage, is valid more for the way poverty is often measured than for the way it is conceptualized. Poverty is centrally about lack of financial resources, but Townsend's definition makes clear that the importance of inadequate resources is that it manifests itself in an inability to participate across a wide spectrum of activities and possessions. These need to be taken directly into account in measuring poverty, for the reasons we have set out, but that is a criticism of conventional measures rather than the concept itself. In emphasizing detachment from societal values, social exclusion has close links with the underclass debate. However, the precise relevance of this notion to issues relating to the creation and transmission of poverty has yet to be demonstrated. Where there are in fact substantive differences between the concepts, in our view what 'poverty' loses in terms of breadth may for many purposes be offset by the fact that it is less diffuse and more in tune with popular notions of social goals. Moving from poverty to social exclusion may help to sensitize researchers and policy-makers to dynamics, processes, and multiple disadvantage, but at a cost.

We have taken the Townsend-type definition of poverty to involve 'inability to participate' rather than simply low income, but some may see this as unduly restrictive: one response would clearly be to frame a broader definition. Much has been made in the recent literature of the distinction between notions of poverty arising out of concern with living standards and those based on minimum rights to resources necessary to permit full participation in the life of society. We have seen that a substantial proportion of those below a minimum income line are likely not to be experiencing basic deprivation: one would have to ask whether such people are necessarily being deprived of an entitlement, regardless of other circumstances; and even if they are, does it help to call them 'poor'? Some (though only a few) of those on low incomes are avoiding deprivation because they have very substantial assets: how are they to be regarded? The right to income support from the state, which is one indicator of prevailing conceptions of social rights, has itself always been conditional. We need to know *how* some of those on low incomes are avoiding basic deprivation before we can properly assess their situation, and see how others would regard it. Some are avoiding deprivation only by recourse to expedients which would be widely regarded as unacceptable, and our results focus attention on the need to distinguish circumstances in which low income is generally regarded as unacceptable from those in which it is not.

We have also addressed what can be learnt from our approach and findings about how anti-poverty strategies should be designed. Townsend's use of deprivation indicators brought a new dimension to studies of the adequacy of social security support rates, and he placed a great deal of emphasis on the gap between those rates and the income threshold below which he argued deprivation 'escalated disproportionately'. Indeed, one of the reasons why identifying a threshold was so important to his argument was precisely because it allowed that comparison. Without accepting that such a threshold can be identified, deprivation indicators have considerable potential for assessing the adequacy of social security rates. We have shown how such indicators can reveal the extent of deprivation being experienced by those relying on different schemes, giving some indication of the relative effectiveness of these schemes in providing the support required to avoid deprivation. However, the nature of the income–deprivation relationship which we have found means that even an income band or range below which most people are severely deprived cannot easily be identified. Deprivation indicators thus do not provide a basis for easy identification of the 'adequate' level of support, even if that is conceived as a range rather than a single threshold. This reflects the findings of our analysis of the relationship between deprivation, income, and broader resources that current income is only one—though a key—determinant of deprivation, and that how households arrived at that income greatly influences its impact on living standards. Rather than simply showing how much more difficult this makes it to identify a current income level or range that is adequate to avoid basic deprivation, this highlights the need for a dynamic perspective in assessing adequacy and framing policy. This involves taking into account the facts that resources and needs may vary for households at similar current income levels, that the point at which intervention takes place is crucial, and that social security can be seen only in the broader context of other policies.

The changing profile of those in poverty over the past twenty years—notably the fact that far more of the poor are now actually or potentially in the labour force—has major implications for the role of social security and its relationship with other policies, and for the design of social security systems. Increases in the levels of social security coverage and support have been central to the improvement in the relative position of the elderly, although its continuance cannot be taken for granted, as growing numbers depending on pensions put pressure on the levels of support provided. While one cannot conclude that poverty among the elderly has been 'solved' by social security, the predominance of other types of household among the poor means that poverty is now much less amenable to a strategy relying primarily on social security. The dominant role of unemployment in producing poverty means that labour market policy moves centre-stage.

Much attention has been focused on the need for social security and other policies to be more 'job-friendly', though the extent to which current systems in fact act as a disincentive to taking up employment or to job creation by employers remains hotly contested. However, a central message from our results was the importance of the processes whereby resources are accumulated or eroded over time, in particular the way in which long-term or repeated experience of unemployment leaves those affected much less able to avoid deprivation than others on a similar income level, because they often have no other resources on which to draw. It is not simply unemployment, but the marginalization or exclusion from the labour force that sustained unemployment produces, which is critical in producing deprivation; a policy response that concentrates on being job-friendly and maximizing job creation will not help those who need it most. Our results demonstrated just how much failure to obtain some second-level educational qualification increased the risk of poverty, of current and long-term unemployment, of lengthy unemployment experience over one's career, and of low pay when employed. Owing to changes in the occupational structure, the consequences of educational failure have become more serious over time, with an ever sharper polarization between those who leave school early without any qualification and their more successful peers.

General training schemes tend to help those most able to take advantage of them, rather than those most in need, and even with second-chance education and targeted training, those currently marginalized in labour force terms find it very difficult to compete effectively for available jobs. A common response internationally has been programmes providing an incentive for employers to increase employment levels and/or to hire the long-term unemployed, though employers' reluctance to hire the long-term unemployed appears difficult to overcome. In assessing the potential of such measures, it needs to be emphasized that sizeable employment subsidies aimed at the long-term unemployed, which brought about a more equitable sharing of the burden of unemployment, could have a substantial impact on deprivation even if they did not have much impact on overall numbers in employment. Direct employment of the long-term unemployed by public authorities for a time, at something approaching market wage rates, could also have a role in assisting the reintegration of those who appear unlikely to obtain employment otherwise. Such options will probably cost substantially more than simply continuing to provide income support, but assessments of costs and benefits should take fully into account the impact that such targeted programmes could have on current living standards and long-term prospects of those most exposed to deprivation. By reintegrating the marginalized, they could also make wage bargaining more sensitive to the level of unemployment.

Our findings on the extent and nature of poverty and of labour market marginalization also have implications for the role of area-based strategies, which have featured prominently in the evolution of anti-poverty policy at EU level. Purely local action can generally be expected to have little impact on unemployment in an area, and in any case, while unemployment and poverty rates are indeed very high in certain areas or types of area, most of the unemployed and most poor households are not to be found in these areas. This we have found to be the case even when focusing on the sub-set of the poor or unemployed who are marginalized in labour market terms and experiencing basic deprivation. Those living in 'black spot' areas are indeed particularly likely to be experiencing deprivation and face especially severe problems for a variety of reasons, but policies to meet their particular needs will affect only a minority of the unemployed or the poor. This is relevant not only to policy but also to perceptions of the extent and nature of poverty: the poor are not simply to be identified with those living in particularly disadvantaged urban public authority housing estates, and poverty is a good deal more prevalent than concentration on such areas would suggest.

As well as affecting the role of social security versus other policy responses, the changing nature of poverty has major implications for the design of social security systems and how they interact with taxation. There has been a resurgence of interest in radical restructuring of the way income support is provided by the State, including basic income schemes which break the links between labour market status and entitlement to income support. Assessing the costs and benefits of such schemes poses a variety of complex methodological problems and must take the specific setting in which they would operate into account. However, it is clear that means-testing is by no means a *sine qua non* for effective targeting, and that reducing rather than increasing the role of means-testing is the best way to improve incentives and reduce dependency. Improved benefits for children are a particularly effective way to improve incentives; they can be seen by proponents of a basic income as a step in that direction, but have an independent justification in their own right.

10.4   Future Directions?

Many questions are raised but not fully resolved by our analysis, and they are prime candidates for further research. We have seen that a substantial number of households are not on low incomes but do report enforced basic deprivation: although our findings point to the importance of long-term factors, we need to know more about how this comes about. The relationship between housing/durables, current income, and broader resources, and its implications both for assessing the position of households experiencing housing deprivation and for policy, need to be examined further. Analysis of the satisfaction of educational or health needs, which are largely organized outside the market in many countries, would complement the study of exclusion from goods and services for which access is governed through the market, on which we have concentrated attention. Indicators of deprivation at the level of the individual also have considerable potential for the analysis of differences in living standards within the household. Some of our basic deprivation indicators do apply to the position of the individual rather than the household, and we have confirmed that using the responses of the spouse rather than the household head in those cases makes little difference to our results. We have not however explored differences between spouses on the other items, or variation between individual adults in different families within a household, each of which would be valuable research projects in their own right.

Moving from a point in time to the analysis of changes in poverty over time would raise a further host of questions about the way in which the deprivation and income criteria would reflect changes in the general standard of living. Income thresholds moving in line with average incomes could be applied together with a set of deprivation indicators which changed to reflect perceptions of what constituted necessities—but precisely how are the latter best established? Similarly, comparisons across countries at a point in time could employ the same combined income–deprivation approach, using relative income lines and views in each country about what items constitute necessities. This would however have to take into account the fact that institutional and other differences could mean that, even if views about necessities were identical, the same items might not be appropriate as indicators of generalized deprivation in different countries. Establishing whether this was in fact the case would require analysis of the way items relate to each other in different countries, along the lines of the factor analysis described here. The data that will be provided by the panel study being carried out for Eurostat throughout EU member states, which includes both income and a set of indicators of life-styles similar to that we have employed in this study, will open up new possibilities for such cross-country comparisons on a harmonized data-base.

The approach set out in this volume has focused on how to incorporate multidimensional measures of disadvantage into poverty measurement, and the results direct one firmly towards a dynamic analysis of processes, particularly in the labour market. Pursuing this research agenda will itself bring research on poverty closer to mainstream economics' analysis of the labour market and the sociological analysis of class and social mobility. We conclude by reiterating our belief in the value of non-monetary indicators of living standards for the study of poverty. This is not because they offer a way to identify 'the poor' on which everyone can agree. Rather, they are most valuable as a tool in following Atkinson's (1985) 'intermediate path' of seeking partial orderings even when unanimity cannot be achieved. Atkinson (1987) has also noted how the impact of poverty studies is reduced by the reliance of researchers on volumes of statistics in presenting their results. Using non-monetary indicators together with income allows one to tap into popular conceptions of what poverty means and to reforge the links between the results of research and the underlying attitudes and values on which that research relies for its justification.

APPENDIX 1

The Data

A1.1 Introduction

This appendix provides a detailed description of the survey data on which this study has been based. The data were obtained from a specially designed large-scale household survey carried out throughout the Republic of Ireland in 1987 by the Economic and Social Research Institute. The appendix describes first the survey itself, then the information obtained, and finally the validation of the data by reference to external sources.

A1.2 The Survey

The survey was designed to provide a national sample from the population resident in private households. Those living in institutions such as hospitals, hotels, and prisons thus did not form part of the target population. (Private households contain about 97 per cent of all persons in the country.) The sampling frame for the survey was the official Register of Electors, which is revised annually. The sampling was performed using the RANSAM program developed at the ESRI (see B. J. Whelan 1979), which implements a multi-stage random sample incorporating both stratification and clustering, and gives each individual on the Register an equal probability of being selected. The usefulness of the Register as sampling frame has been confirmed by Keogh and Whelan, though it may under-represent young single persons and newly formed households.

The target sample for the survey comprised 5,850 households, selected as 225 clusters of 26 each. Within clusters, respondents were selected on a systematic basis, giving an implicit geographic stratification. The survey was carried out by the Institute's own Survey Unit and panel of experienced interviewers. After exclusion of addresses that turned out to be institutions and of persons who could not be contacted—mostly because they had moved and could not be traced or had died—a total effective sample of 5,165 households remained. A sample of 3,294 households was achieved, representing an effective response rate of 64 per cent. This is comparable with other such surveys covering the sensitive area of incomes, such as the Household Budget Surveys carried out by the Irish Central Statistics Office or the Family Expenditure Surveys in Britain. The refusal rate was 24 per cent, 9 per cent were never available when the interviewer called despite repeated visits, 2 per cent were too ill or senile to take part, and 1 per cent completed part of the interview but were not included in the analysis owing to missing information in crucial areas.

Post-sample correction through reweighting of the sample was employed to take into account the fact that use of the Register of Electors as sampling frame meant that households had a probability of selection proportional to the number of electors they contained, and to adjust for biases that may be introduced by non-random non-response. The sample for analysis was reweighted to accord with information from the Labour Force Survey in terms of the cross-tabulation of households by four characteristics: the number of adults in the household, urban/rural location, and the age and occupational group of the household head. The reweighted sample of households thus corresponds with what the much larger Labour Force Survey shows to be the number of households in each of the cells produced by this cross-tabulation.

A1.3 The Information Obtained

The survey obtained a very wide range of information on household and individual characteristics, participation in the labour force, income from different sources, lifestyle, assets and debts, attitudes, and background. Here we describe only the information employed in the present study.

The age, sex, and marital status of each person in the household, and the relationships between these individuals, were obtained. The location of the household—whether in open country, a village, a town of specified sizes, or a city—was noted.

The current income of each individual and household from different sources was covered in great detail in the questionnaire. The way in which income data were collected corresponds closely with the British Family Expenditure Survey, except that particular attention was paid to the measurement of income from farming, involving a separate detailed questionnaire. As described in Chapter 3 above, for most income sources respondents were asked about the amount received in the previous week (or month), but for the types of income that are particularly likely to fluctuate over the year or be received intermittently—namely income from self-employment (including farming) and rent, interest, and dividends—a twelve-month reference period was used. Specific questions covered the following income sources:

- earnings from employment, with deductions at source for income tax, social insurance contributions, pension contributions, and trade union dues;
- profit from self-employment;
- retirement pension;
- regular allowance from someone outside the household;
- sick pay from employer;
- trade union strike pay;
- rent;
- interest and dividends;
- social security cash transfers, itemized by scheme;
- any other occasional or regular income;
- any income tax or social insurance contributions paid directly to Revenue Commissioners/Department of Social Welfare (rather than deducted at source).

A separate detailed questionnaire was administered to households engaged in farming, to allow income from farming to be estimated. This covered stock numbers by type, stock sold during the year, milk and crops sold, expenditure on production by type (e.g. fertilizer, feed, seed), and information from farm accounts, if any, on gross output, costs, and net output. For those without farm accounts, farms were cross-classified by size, soil type, and activity type, and information from external sources on average output and costs for such farms was used to estimate those elements of output and costs on which information could not be collected directly. The concept of farm income used is gross output plus grants less total direct and overhead costs, representing the total return to the labour, management and capital input in the farm in a similar way to net profit for other self-employed.

Information was also obtained in the survey on savings and other assets. Respondents were asked about the level of savings and investments in the form of bank or building society deposits, Post Office deposits, and Saving Certificates, gilts and equities, and various types of unit-linked and other investment funds. In addition, the market value of the house was sought for owner-occupiers, together with detailed information on their mortgage if any. This allows the outstanding debt on the mortgage to be calculated, so that the net value of the household's saving in the form of housing can be estimated by subtracting this from the value of the house. Nolan (1991b) contains a detailed description and analysis of the assets data obtained, including a comparison with external totals for each type.

Chapter 4 has already described the set of twenty indicators of possessions and life-style, about which respondents were asked:

1. whether they have the item in question;
2. whether they are doing without it because of lack of money;
3. whether they regarded the item as a necessity, i.e. something everyone should be able to have and no one should have to do without.

For several other indicators, respondents were simply asked whether they did or did not have the item or take part in the activity in question. The items covered household durables, heating, food, clothes, running into arrears, and social activities and hobbies.

The survey sought detailed information about the current labour force status of each adult member. In addition, those currently at work were asked how long they had been in their job and about any time spent unemployed during the previous twelve months. Those currently away from work were asked how long they had been away, and how long they had spent in work during the period. On this basis, a picture of unemployment/employment experiences during the previous year could be constructed. All respondents were also asked about the number of weeks in the previous year spent in receipt of the various social welfare schemes. As far as lifetime labour market experiences are concerned, adults were also asked when they left full-time education, and how many years were subsequently spent in employment, unemployed, ill/disabled, in home duties, retired, or in a return to full-time education or training.

The information obtained also allows both the current social class of the individual and household—the latter generally being based on that of the household head—and the class from which they originally came to be identified. For adults in the sample, detailed information was sought on their current (or if not now working, previous) occupation, which was then coded according to the three-digit occupational categorization used by the Irish Central Statistics Office. Based on this information, various social class scales, including the CASMIN schema developed by Erikson and Goldthorpe (1992), can be applied. As far as social class background is concerned, adults were asked who was the main breadwinner in their family while they were growing up, and what that person's principal occupation then was. Coding these responses in the same way, the social class of origin can be derived for whichever class schema is to be employed.

Detailed information was also obtained in the survey about the educational level reached by respondents, and by their parents. The categories employed were: none beyond primary, primary certificate, some second-level, intermediate second-level certificate, certificate on completing second-level, post-secondary certificate/diploma, university primary degree or equivalent, and university higher degree or equivalent.

As far as health status is concerned, adults in the sample were asked whether they had a 'major illness, physical disability or infirmity that has troubled you for at least the past year or that is likely to go on troubling you in the future?' Adults were also asked a version of the General Health Questionnaire to measure levels of psychological distress. Twelve items were employed, and respondents were asked whether they had recently been feeling that way more/the same/less than usual/much less than usual, or not at all/no more than usual/rather more than usual/much more than usual:

1. been feeling unhappy and depressed;
2. felt capable of making decisions about things;
3. felt you couldn't overcome your difficulties;
4. been feeling reasonably happy all things considered;
5. been able to face up to your problems;
6. been thinking of yourself as a worthless person;
7. felt able to enjoy your day-to-day activities;
8. lost much sleep over worry;
9. felt that you are playing a useful part in things;
10. felt constantly under strain;
11. been able to concentrate on what you are doing;
12. been losing confidence in yourself.

Designed to measure levels of fatalism, respondents were asked if they strongly agree/agree/disagree/strongly disagree with the statements:

- I can do just about anything I set my mind to.
- I have little control over the things that happen to me.
- What happens to me in the future depends on me.
- I often feel helpless in dealing with the problems of life.
- Sometimes I feel I am being pushed around in life.
- There is a lot I can do to change my life if I want to.
- There is really no way I can solve some of the problems I have.

Respondents were asked whether, if they were to get into financial difficulty, they thought relatives (outside the household) would help out, with prompted responses being 'yes, definitely', 'yes, probably', 'probably not', and 'definitely not'.

Respondents were asked, with reference to the household's total weekly income, whether the household able to make ends meet:

- with great difficulty?
- with some difficulty?
- with a little difficulty?

- fairly easily?
- easily?
- very easily?

Respondents were also asked: when they were growing up, 'How would you say your family was able to manage financially, compared to other families at that time? Was it able to make ends meet?' with the same response categories.

A1.4   Validation

A range of validation checks against external information provide the basis for confidence in the overall representativeness of the reweighted sample in terms of such crucial variables as age and sex distribution of the population, numbers in receipt of different social security schemes, labour force status, occupation and industry of employees, and the shape of the distribution of household income. We briefly describe the areas where such validation has been carried out and provide references to the detailed studies setting out the results: in this context, by 'sample' we mean the reweighted sample.

The demographic composition of the sample has been compared with that shown by the Census of Population, and the two accord closely (see Callan, Nolan, *et al.* 1989: 44–5). Where there are differences the sample slightly under-represents the elderly, which is largely explained by the fact that the sample refers only to those in private households while the Census refers to the entire population, and a relatively high proportion of the elderly are in institutions.

Comparison with administrative statistics on the numbers in receipt of social welfare payments of different types shows a close correspondance between the grossed-up sample and the population totals, except for some of the illness/disability-related schemes which are somewhat under-represented in the sample (Callan, Nolan, *et al.* 1989: 45–6; Callan 1991: 31–2). Unsurprisingly, schemes paying only very small numbers in the population—such as the Family Income Supplement, which then had only about 7,000 recipients—were not well represented in the sample. Overall, the total number of social security recipients estimated by the survey is 93 per cent of the relevant administrative total, and a similar figure applies to expenditure on social security transfers.

The distribution of income among tax units in the survey has been compared with statistics published by the Revenue Commissioners (Callan 1991: 40–54). The distribution of tax units over income ranges and over marginal tax rates were found to be very close to those suggested by Revenue Commissioners' data. As a result, the tax–benefit model constructed by Callan on the basis of this sample performs well in predicting tax payments. The sample also has the correct percentage of persons with entitlement to full free health care from the state, which is means-tested, and the correct percentage of persons with private health insurance, which is purchased for the most part by those on higher income (Nolan 1991*c*).

Focusing on employees, the sample has been shown to represent the population well in terms of age/sex composition, although having slightly too low a proportion aged under 25 (Nolan 1993: 13). The breakdown of employees by broad occupation and industry categories in the sample corresponds quite well with that shown by the Labour Force Survey (Nolan 1993: 14–15). The average earnings reported by employees in the sample in industry are similar to those in the Central Statistics Office's Quarterly Industrial Inquiry (Nolan 1993: 16–17).

The data obtained in the survey on financial assets have been assessed and compared with external totals where available in Nolan (1991*b*) and Honohan and Nolan (1993). As would be expected, there is a very sizeable under-representation of these assets, consistent with experience elsewhere in trying to measure wealth through general household surveys. About 40 per cent of total household deposits appear to be captured in the survey, though there is some uncertainty about the external total with which the survey figure is to be compared; and the proportion for shares and gilts (not employed in the present study) is even lower. The discrepancies are no larger than those experienced by comparable UK and US surveys such as the Oxford Savings Surveys from the 1950s and surveys carried out by the Federal Reserve Board in the 1980s. The experience of the Federal Reserve Board is particularly instructive: because such a high proportion of assets are held by those right at the top of the distribution, only when a general survey was augmented by a special non-random sample of high-income households (with the sampling frame coming from tax records) have they been able to identify a much higher proportion of household assets. The particular difficulties in securing participation by very wealthy households leads to under-representation of these households in surveys, as has been well documented in the UK and the USA. US studies comparing survey responses with bank records also suggest that, among households that do participate, failure to report any holding is a more important source of error than understatement of the amount held by those reporting some holding (see Ferber 1965; Avery *et al.* 1988)

APPENDIX 2

Lack Versus Enforced Lack of Items

Chapters 4 and 5 contain a discussion of lack versus self-reported enforced lack of twenty life-style items, and their relationships with income. The data presented in the text tables refer to self-reported enforced lack of the items. The corresponding figures for simple lack of the items—whether considered by the respondent to be by choice or because they could not afford it—may also be of interest, and are given in this appendix. Table A2.1 corresponds to Table 4.5, A2.2 to Table 4.7, and A2.3 to Table 5.1. The text discussion also refers to the mean incomes of those having each item, those reporting enforced lack, and those reporting that they are doing without by choice: the detailed figures underlying this discussion are given in Table A2.4.

Table A2.1   Correlation between lack of items and income

Item	Correlation between lack and:	
	Income	Equivalent income
Refrigerator	−0.11	−0.08
Washing machine	−0.20	−0.11
Telephone	−0.23	−0.25
Car	−0.22	−0.20
Colour TV	−0.18	−0.14
A week's annual holiday away from home	−0.20	−0.26
A dry damp-free dwelling	−0.07	−0.09
Heating for the living rooms when it is cold	−0.06	−0.06
Central heating in the house	−0.21	−0.21
An indoor toilet in the dwelling	−0.11	−0.08
Bath or shower	−0.13	−0.09
A meal with meat, chicken, or fish every second day	−0.14	−0.14
A warm, waterproof overcoat	−0.09	−0.10
Two pairs of strong shoes	−0.10	−0.13
To be able to save	−0.19	−0.25
A daily newspaper	−0.22	−0.22
A roast meat joint or equivalent once a week	−0.17	−0.13
A hobby or leisure activity	−0.13	−0.17
New, not secondhand, clothes	−0.10	−0.12
Presents for friends or family once a year	−0.17	−0.18

Table A2.2 Scores on 24-item lack index by household equivalent income

Equivalent Income decile[a]	Mean score on index	% with score of 10 or higher	% with score of 5 or less
Bottom	8.1	34.8	30.7
2	8.1	36.0	31.0
3	8.1	29.8	27.5
4	6.6	20.6	42.9
5	5.8	15.9	52.7
6	5.0	11.9	65.4
7	3.8	4.8	75.3
8	3.9	7.6	72.5
9	2.7	3.2	87.3
Top	2.1	1.7	92.3

[a] Equivalence scale 1 for household head, 0.66 for each other adult, 0.33 for each child.

Table A2.3 Scores on basic, housing, and secondary lack indices, by household equivalent income

Equivalent income decile[a]	Basic		Housing		Secondary	
	Mean score on index	% scoring >0	Mean score on index	% scoring >0	Mean score on index	% scoring >0
Bottom	1.5	56.8	0.6	35.0	3.6	90.2
2	1.7	60.3	0.7	39.0	3.9	95.5
3	1.2	54.0	0.8	45.7	3.4	92.3
4	0.8	42.1	0.7	38.0	3.0	87.8
5	0.5	25.4	0.5	28.5	2.6	80.2
6	0.7	28.0	0.4	21.7	2.5	75.6
7	0.4	22.1	0.2	16.8	1.8	76.6
8	0.3	18.5	0.3	19.1	1.6	65.2
9	0.2	12.3	0.2	12.6	1.2	56.9
Top	0.1	10.5	0.1	5.7	0.7	38.9
All	0.8	32.8	0.5	26.1	2.4	75.8

[a] Equivalence scale 1 for household head, 0.66 for each other adult, 0.33 for each child.

Table A2.4   Mean equivalent income by possession/unenforced lack/enforced lack of items

Item	Mean equivalent income (£ per week)		
	Have	Unenforced lack	Enforced lack
Refrigerator	86.19	73.70	53.58
Washing machine	88.33	79.24	62.84
Telephone	102.32	73.66	62.62
Car	97.26	64.79	63.90
Colour TV	89.28	75.04	60.16
A week's annual holiday away from home	114.06	82.49	67.64
A dry damp-free dwelling	87.17	100.60	61.66
Heating for the living rooms when it is cold	85.75	81.51	53.72
Central heating in the house	99.45	74.64	63.47
An indoor toilet in the dewlling	86.58	90.41	59.01
Bath or shower	86.96	78.17	61.72
A meal with meat, chicken, or fish every second day	88.68	81.51	52.85
A warm, waterproof overcoat	87.93	83.35	56.65
Two pairs of strong shoes	89.43	82.41	54.44
To be able to save	107.47	70.21	68.87
A daily newspapaer	99.15	71.73	61.31
A roast meat joint or equivalent once a week	90.54	83.00	54.39
A hobby or leisure activity	93.79	71.05	60.30
New, not secondhand, clothes	88.29	72.30	51.10
Presents for friends or family once a year	93.08	67.44	52.99

REFERENCES

Abel-Smith, B. and Townsend, P. (1965) *The Poor and the Poorest*. London: Bell.
Allardt, E. (1993) 'Having, Loving, Being: An Alternative to the Swedish Model of Welfare Research', in M. Nussbaum and A. Sen (eds.), *The Quality of Life*. Oxford: Clarendon Press.
Anand, S. (1977) 'Aspects of Poverty in Malaysia', *Review of Income and Wealth*, 23 (1): 1–16.
——(1983) *Inequality and Poverty in Malaysia*. Oxford: Oxford University Press.
Aponte, R. (1990) 'Definitions of the Underclass: A Critical Analysis', in H. J. Gans (ed.), *Sociology in America*. London: Sage.
Atkinson, A. B. (1983) *The Economics of Inequality*. 2nd edn. Oxford: Oxford University Press.
——(1985a) *How Should We Measure Poverty?* ESRC Programme on Taxation, Incentives and the Distribution of Income, Discussion Paper No. 82.
——(1985b) *On the Measurement of Poverty*, ESRC Programme on Taxation, Incentives and the Distribution of Income, Working Paper 90, London School of Economics.
——(1987) 'On the Measurement of Poverty', *Econometrica*, 55 (4): 749–64.
——(1989) *Poverty and Social Security*. Hemel Hempstead: Harvester Wheatsheaf.
——(1990) *A National Minimum? A History of Ambiguity in the Determination of Benefit Scales in Britain*, ST/ICERD Welfare State Programme Discussion Paper No. 47, London School of Economics.
——(1992) *The Western Experience of Social Safety Nets*. ST/ICERD Welfare State Programme, Discussion Paper No. 80.
——(1993a) *Beveridge, the National Minimum, and its Future in a European Context*. ST/ICERD Welfare State Programme, Discussion Paper No. 85.
——(1993b) *The Institution of an Official Poverty Line and Economic Policy*. ST/ICERD Welfare State Programme, Discussion Paper No. 98.
——(1995) *Public Economics in Action: The Basic Income/Flat Tax Proposal*. Oxford: Clarendon Press.
——and Micklewright, J. (1983) 'On the Reliability of Income Data in the Family Expenditure Survey', *Journal of the Royal Statistical Society*, Series A, 146 (I): 33–61.
——, Gomulka, J., and Sutherland, H. (1988) 'Grossing Up FES Data for Tax-Benefit Models', in A. B. Atkinson and H. Sutherland (eds.), *Tax-Benefit Models*. London: STICERD London School of Economics.
Avery, R., Eliahausen, G. E., and Kennickell, A. B. (1988) 'Measuring Wealth with Survey Data: An Evaluation of the 1983 Survey of Consumer Finances', *Review of Income and Wealth*, 34 (4): 339–70.
Bandura, A. (1982) 'Self-Efficacy Mechanisms in Human Ageing', *American Psychologist*, 37: 122–47.

Bane, M. J. and Ellwood, D. (1986) 'Slipping Into and Out of Poverty: The Dynamics of Spells', *Journal of Human Resources*, 21 (1): 1–23.

Banks, J. and Johnson, P. (1993) *Children and Household Living Standards*. London: Institute for Fiscal Studies.

Beckerman, W. (1979) 'The Impact of Income Maintenance Payments on Poverty in Britain', *Economic Journal*, 89: 261–79.

Berghman, J. (1994) *The Measurement and Analysis of Social Exclusion in Europe: Two Paradoxes for Researchers*, paper presented to the Seminar on the Measurement and Analysis of Social Exclusion, Commission of the European Communities/Department of Social Security, Centre for Research in European Social and Employment Policy, University of Bath.

——and Cantillon, B. (1993) *The European Face of Social Security*. Aldershot: Avebury.

Blackorby, C. and Donaldson, D. (1980) 'Ethical Indices for the Measurement of Poverty', *Econometrica*, 48: 1053–60.

Blackwell, J. (1991) 'The Labour Market Impacts of Income-Support and Child-Care Programmes: A Cross-Country Review', in *Evaluating Labour Market and Social Programmes: The State of a Complex Art*. Paris: OECD.

Bradbury, B. (1989) 'Family Size Equivalence Scales and Survey Evaluations of Income and Well-Being', *Journal of Social Policy*, 18 (3): 383–409.

Bradshaw, J. (ed.) (1993) *Budget Standards for the United Kingdom*. Aldershot: Avebury.

——and Morgan, J. (1987) *Budgeting on Benefit*, Family Policy Studies Centre, Occasional Paper No. 5, York: University of York.

Breen, R. (1984) *Education and the Labour Market: Work and Unemployment among Recent Cohorts of Irish School Leavers*, General Research Series Paper 119. Dublin: Economic and Social Research Institute.

——and Whelan, C. T. (1992) 'Explaining the Irish Pattern of Social Fluidity: The Role of the Political', in J. H. Goldthorpe and C. T. Whelan (eds.), *The Development of Industrial Society in Ireland*, Proceedings of the British Academy, 79. Oxford: Oxford University Press.

————(1993) 'From Ascription to Achievement? Origins, Education and Entry to the Labour Force in the Republic of Ireland During the Twentieth Century', *Acta Sociologica*, 36 (1): 3–17.

——, Hannan, D. F., Rottman, D., and Whelan, C. T. (1990) *Understanding Contemporary Ireland: State, Class, and Development in the Republic of Ireland*. London: Macmillan.

——, Hannan, D. F., and O'Leary, R. (1995) 'Returns to Education: Taking Account of Employers' Perceptions and Use of Educational Credentials', *European Sociological Review*, 11 (1): 59–74.

Brown, M. and Madge, N. (1982) *Despite the Welfare State*. London: Heinemann Educational Books.

Browning, M. (1992) 'Children and Household Economic Behaviour', *Journal of Economic Literature*, 30 (3): 1434–75.

Buck, N. (1992) 'Labour Market Inactivity and Polarization: A Household Perspective on the Idea of an Underclass', in D. J. Smith (ed.), *Understanding the Underclass*. London: Policy Studies Institute.

Buhman, B., Rainwater, L., Schmaus, G., and Smeeding, T. (1988) 'Equivalence

Scales, Well-being, Inequality and Poverty: Sensitivity Estimates across Ten Countries using the Luxembourg Income Study Database', *Review of Income and Wealth*, 33 (2): 115–42.

Bureau of the Census (1989) *Transitions in Income and Poverty Status: 1984–1985*, Current Population Reports, Household Economic Studies, Series P-70 No. 15-RD-1. Washington DC: US Government Printing Office.

Callan, T. (1991) *Income Tax and Welfare Reform: Microsimulation Modelling and Analysis*, General Research Series No. 154. Dublin: Economic and Social Research Institute.

——and Nolan, B. (1989) 'Evaluating Social Welfare Expenditures: How Well Does the System Perform in Reducing Poverty?' *Economic and Social Review*, 20 (4): 329–52.

——— (1991) 'Concepts of Poverty and the Poverty Line: A Critical Survey of Approaches to Measuring Poverty', *Journal of Economic Surveys*, 5 (3): 243–62.

——— (forthcoming) 'Income Inequality and Poverty in Ireland in the 1970s and 1980s', in P. Gottschalk, B. Gustafsson, and E. Palmer (eds.), *The Distribution of Economic Well-being in the 1980s: an International Perspective*. Cambridge: Cambridge University Press.

———, and Whelan, B. J., Hannan, D. F. with Creighton, S. (1989) *Poverty, Income and Welfare in Ireland*, General Research Series No. 146. Dublin: Economic and Social Research Institute.

——————(1993) 'Resources, Deprivation and the Measurement of Poverty', *Journal of Social Policy*, 22 (2): 141–72.

——, O'Donoghue, C., and O'Neill, C. (1994) *Analysis of Basic Income Schemes for Ireland*, Policy Research Series Paper No. 21. Dublin: Economic and Social Research Institute.

Carmines, E. C. and Zeller, R. A. (1979) *Reliability and Validity Assessment*. London: Sage.

Carney, C., FitzGerald, E., Kiely, G., and Quinn, P. (1994) *The Cost of a Child*. Dublin: Combat Poverty Agency.

Castel, R. (1990) *Les situations-limite du processus de marginalisation: de la vulnerabilité à la désaffiliation*, paper presented at the European Commission Conference on Poverty, Marginalization and Social Exclusion, Alghero, April.

Clark, S., Hemming, R., and Ulph, D. (1981) 'On Indices for the Measurement of Poverty', *Economic Journal*, 91: 515–26.

Coates, K. and Silburn, R. (1970) *Poverty: The Forgotten Englishmen*. Harmondsworth: Penguin.

Commins, P. (1993) *Combatting Exclusion in Ireland 1990–1994: A Midway Report*. Dublin: Combat Poverty Agency/Poverty 3.

Commission of the European Communities (1981) *Final Report from the Commission to the Council on the First Programme of Pilot Schemes and Studies to Combat Poverty*, COM(81) 769. Brussels: Commission of the European Communities.

——(1991) *Final Report on the Second European Poverty Programme*, COM(91) 29. Luxembourg: Office for Official Publications of the European Communities.

——(1993) *Medium-Term Action Programme to Combat Social Exclusion and Promote Solidarity, and Report on the Implementation of the Community Programme for the Social and Economic Integration of the Least Privileged Groups*

(1989–1994). COM(93) 435. Luxembourg: Office for Official Publications of the European Communities.

Commission on Social Welfare (1986) *Report of the Commission on Social Welfare*. Dublin: Stationery Office.

Conniffe, D. (1992) 'The Non-Constancy of Equivalence Scales', *Review of Income and Wealth*, 38 (4): 429–44.

——and Keogh, G. (1988) *Equivalence Scales and Costs of Children*, General Research Series Paper No. 142. Dublin: Economic and Social Research Institute.

Council and Commission of the European Communities (1992) *Treaty on European Union*. Luxembourg: Office for Official Publications of the European Communities.

Crompton, R. (1993) *Class and Stratification: An Introduction to Current Debates*. Cambridge: Polity Press.

Danziger, S., Haveman, R., and Plotnick, R. (1986) 'Anti-Poverty Policy: Effects on the Poor and the Nonpoor', in S. Danziger and D. Weinberg (eds.), *Fighting Poverty: What Works and What Doesn't*. Cambridge, Mass.: Harvard University Press.

Dasgupta, P. (1993) *An Inquiry into Well-Being and Destitution*. Oxford: Clarendon Press.

Davies, M. (1994) *Household Incomes and Living Standards*, paper presented to the 23rd General Conference of the International Association for Research in Income and Wealth, St Andrew's, New Brunswick.

Dean, H. (1991) 'In Search of the Underclass', in P. Brown and R. Scase (eds.), *Poor Work: Disadvantage and the Division of Labour*. Milton Keynes: Open University Press.

Deleeck, H., Van den Bosch, K., and De Lathouwer, L. (eds.) (1992) *Poverty and the Adequacy of Social Security in Europe*. Aldershot: Avebury.

Department of Social Security (1988a) *Low Income Families 1985*. London: DSS.

——(1988b) *Low Income Statistics: Report of a Technical Review*. London: DSS.

——(1988c) *Households below Average Income: A Statistical Analysis 1981–85*. London: HMSO.

——(1991) *Households below Average Income: Stocktaking Report of a Working Group*. London: DSS.

——(1992) *Households Below Average Income: A Statistical Analysis 1979–1988/89*. London: HMSO.

——(1994) *Households Below Average Income: A Statistical Analysis 1979–1991/92*. London: HMSO.

Desai, M. (1986) 'Drawing the Line: On Defining the Poverty Threshold', in P. Golding (ed.), *Excluding the Poor*. London: Child Poverty Action Group.

——and Shah, A. (1988) 'An Econometric Approach to the Measurement of Poverty', *Oxford Economic Papers*, 40 (3): 505–22.

Dilnot, A. (1992) 'Social Security and Labour Market Policy', in E. McLaughlin (ed.), *Understanding Unemployment*. London: Routledge.

Donnison, D. (1988) 'Defining and Measuring Poverty: A Reply to Stein Ringen', *Journal of Social Policy*, 17 (3): 367–74.

Dubnoff, S. (1985) 'How Much Income Is Enough? Measuring Public Judgements', *Public Opinion Quarterly*, 49: 285–99.

——, Vaughan, D., and Lancaster, C. (1981) 'Income Satisfaction Measures in Equivalence Scale Applications', *American Statistical Association Proceedings*.

Duncan, G. J. and Hoffman, S. D. (1991) 'Teenage Underclass Behaviour and Subsequent Poverty: Have The Rules Changed?' in C. Jencks and P. E. Peterson (eds.), *The Urban Underclass*. Washington: Brookings Institution.

——, Coe, R., and Hill, M. (1984) 'The Dynamics of Poverty', in G. Duncan (ed.), *Years of Poverty, Years of Plenty*. Ann Arbor: Institute for Social Research, University of Michigan.

Elwood, D. T. (1989) 'The Origins of Dependency: Choices, Confidence or Culture', *Focus*, 12 (1): 6–13.

Erikson, R. (1984) 'Social Class of Men, Women and Families', *Sociology*, 18 (4): 500–14.

——(1993) 'Descriptions of Inequality: The Swedish Approach to Welfare Research', in M. Nussbaum and A. Sen (eds.), *The Quality of Life*. Oxford: Clarendon Press.

——and Aberg, R. (eds.) (1987) *Welfare in Transition: Living Conditions in Sweden 1968–1981*. Oxford: Clarendon Press.

——and Goldthorpe, J. H. (1992) *The Constant Flux: A Study of Class Mobility in Industrial Societies*. Oxford: Oxford University Press.

Erikson, R., Hansen, E. J., Ringen, S., and Uusitaalo, H. (eds.) (1993) *The Scandinavian Model: Welfare States and Welfare Research*. New York: Sharpe.

Fainstein, N. (1993) 'Race, Class and Segregation: Discourses about African Americans', *International Journal of Urban and Regional Research*, 17 (3): 384–403.

Ferber, R. (1965) 'The Reliability of Consumer Surveys of Financial Holdings: Time Deposits', *Journal of the American Statistical Association*, 60: 148–63.

Foster, J. E. (1984) 'On Economic Poverty: A Survey of Aggregate Measures', *Advances in Econometrics*, 3: 215–51.

——and Shorrocks, A. F. (1988a) 'Poverty Orderings', *Econometrica*, 56: 173–7.

————(1988b) 'Poverty Orderings and Welfare Dominance', *Social Choice and Welfare*, 5 (2/3): 179–98.

————(1991) 'Subgroup Consistent Poverty Indices', *Econometrica*, 59: 687–709.

——, Greer, J., and Thorbecke, E. (1984) 'A Class of Decomposable Poverty Measures', *Econometrica*, 52: 761–6.

Frayman, H., Mack, J., Lansley, S., Gordon, D., and Hills, J. (1991) *Breadline Britain 1990s: The Findings of the Television Series*. London: London Weekend Television.

Gallie, D. (1994) 'Are the Unemployed an Underclass? Some Evidence from the Social Change and Economic Life Initiative', *Sociology*, 28 (3): 737–57.

Gans, H. J. (1990) 'Deconstructing the Underclass: The Term's Danger as a Planning Concept', *Journal of the American Planning Association*, 56: 271–7.

Glendinning, C. and Millar, J. (1987) *Women and Poverty in Britain*. Brighton: Wheatsheaf.

Goedhart, T., Halberstadt, V., Kapteyn, A., and Van Praag, B. (1977) 'The Poverty Line: Concept and Measurement', *Journal of Human Resources*, 12: 503–20.

Goldberg, D. P. (1972) *The Detection of Psychiatric Illness by Questionnaire*. Oxford: Oxford University Press.

Goldthorpe, J.H. and Marshall, G. (1992) 'The Promising Future of Class Analysis: A Response to Recent Critiques', *Sociology*, 26 (8): 381–400.

——and Whelan, C. T. (eds.) (1992), *The Development of Industrial Society in Ireland*, Proceedings of the British Academy, 79. Oxford: Oxford University Press.

Goodman, A. and Webb, S. (1994) *For Richer, For Poorer: The Changing Distribution of Income in the United Kingdom, 1961–1991*, Commentary No. 42. London: Insitute for Fiscal Studies.

Gordon, D., Pantazis, C. with Townsend, P., Bramley, G., Bradshaw, J., Holmes, H., and Hallerod, B. (1995) *Breadline Britain in the 1990s: A Report to the Joseph Rowntree Foundation*. Bristol: Department of Social Policy and Planning, University of Bristol.

Hagenaars, A. (1986) *The Perception of Poverty*. Amsterdam: North-Holland.

——and Van Praag, B. (1985) 'A Synthesis of Poverty Line Definitions', *Review of Income and Wealth*, 31 (2): 139–54.

——, de Vos, K., and Zaidi, M. A. (1994) *Patterns of Poverty in Europe*, paper presented to Seminar on the Measurement and Analysis of Social Exclusion, Commission of the European Communities/Department of Social Security. Bath: Centre for Research in European Social and Employment Policy.

Hallerod, B. (1995) 'The Truly Poor: Direct and Indirect Measurement of Consensual Poverty in Sweden', *European Journal of Social Policy*, 5 (2): 111–29.

——, Bradshaw, J., and Holmes, H. (1995) 'Adapting the Consensual Definition of Poverty', in D. Gordon, C. Pantazis, with P. Townsend, G. Bramley, J. Bradshaw, H. Holmes, and B. Hallerod (eds.), *Breadline Britain in the 1990s: A Report to the Joseph Rowntree Foundation*. Bristol: Department of Social Policy and Planning, University of Bristol.

Hannan, D. F. and Commins, P. (1992) 'The Significance of Small Scale Landholders in Ireland's Socio-Economic Transformation', in J. H. Goldthorpe and C. T. Whelan (eds.), *The Development of Industrial Society in Ireland*, Proceedings of the British Academy, 79. Oxford: Oxford University Press.

Hardiman N. and Whelan, C. T. (1994) 'Politics and Democratic Values', in C. T. Whelan (ed.), *Values and Social Change in Ireland*. Dublin: Gill & Macmillan.

Healy, S. and Reynolds, B. (1992) 'Participation: A Values Perspective', in B. Reynolds and S. Healy (eds.), *Power, Participation and Exclusion*. Dublin: CMRS.

Heath, A. (1992) 'The Attitudes of the Underclass', in D. Smith (ed.), *Understanding the Underclass*. London: Policy Studies Institute.

Hernstein, R. J. and Murray, C. (1994) *The Bell Curve: Intelligence and Class Structure in American Life*. New York: Free Press.

Hill, M. (1981) 'Some Dynamic Aspects of Poverty', in M. Hill, D. H. Hill, and J. N. Morgan (eds.), *Five Thousand American Families: Patterns in Economic Progress*, Vol. 9. Ann Arbor: Institute for Social Research, University of Michigan.

Honohan, P. and Nolan, B. (1993) *The Financial Assets of Households in Ireland*, General Research Series Paper No. 162. Dublin: Economic and Social Research Institute.

House of Commons Social Services Committee (1990) *Fourth Report: Low Income Statistics*. London: HMSO.

Hughes, M. A. (1989) 'Mispeaking the Truth to Power: A Geographical Perspective on the Underclass Fallacy', *Economic Geography*, 65 (3): 187–207.

Hutton, S. (1991) 'Measuring Living Standards using Existing National Data Sets', *Journal of Social Policy*, 20: 237–57.

Institute of Social Studies Advisory Service (ISSAS) (1990) *Poverty in Figures: Europe in the Early 1980s*. Luxembourg: Eurostat.

International Labour Office (1976) *Employment, Growth and Basic Needs: A One-World Problem*, Report of the Director-General to the World Employment Conference. Geneva: ILO.

Jencks, C. (1991) 'Is the American Underclass Growing?' in C. Jencks and P. E. Petersen (eds.), *The Urban Underclass*. Washington: Brookings Institution.

Jenkins, S. P. (1991) 'Poverty Measurement and the Within-Household Distribution: Agenda for Action', *Journal of Social Policy*, 20 (4): 457–83.

Johnson, P. and Webb, S. (1989) 'Counting People with Low Incomes: The Impact of Recent Changes in Official Statistics', *Fiscal Studies*, 10 (4): 66–82.

——(1990) *Poverty in Official Statistics: Two Reports*, Commentary No. 24. London: Institute for Fiscal Studies.

——(1991) *UK Poverty Statistics: A Comparative Study*. Commentary No. 27. London: Institute for Fiscal Studies.

Jones, A. and O'Donnell, O. (1995) 'Equivalence Scales and the Costs of Disability', *Journal of Public Economics*, 56 (2): 273–90.

Jordan, B. and Redley, M. (1994) 'Polarisation, Underclass and the Welfare State', *Work, Employment and Society*, 8 (2): 153–76.

Kane, T. J. (1987) 'Giving Back Control: Long-Term Poverty and Motivation', *Social Service Review*, 61 (3): 405–19.

Kapteyn, A., van de Geer, S. and van de Stadt, H. (1985) 'The Impact of Changes in Income and Family Composition on Subjective Measures of Well-Being', in M. David and T. Smeeding (eds.), *Horizontal Equity, Uncertainty and Economic Well-Being*. Chicago: University of Chicago Press.

——, Kooreman, P., and Willemsee, R. (1988) 'Some Methodological Issues in the Implementation of Subjective Poverty Definitions', *Journal of Human Resources*, 23 (2): 222–42.

Katz, M. B. (1993) 'Reframing the "Underclass Debate"', in M. B. Katz (ed.), *The 'Underclass': Views from History*. Princeton: Princeton University Press.

Kelvin, P. and Jarrett, J. E. (1985) *Unemployment: Its Social Psychological Effects*, Cambridge: Cambridge University Press.

Lampman, R. (1971) *Ends and Means of Reducing Income Poverty*. New York: Basic Books.

Lister, R. (1991) *The Exclusive Society: Citizenship and the Poor*. London: Child Poverty Action Group.

Mack, J. and Lansley, S. (1985) *Poor Britain*. London: Allen & Unwin.

Macnicol, J. (1987) 'In Pursuit of the Underclass', *Journal of Social Policy*, 16 (3): 293–318.

Mansfield, M. (1986) 'The Political Arithmetic of Poverty', *Social Policy and Administration*, 20 (1): 47–57.

Marks, C. (1991) 'The Urban Underclass', in W. R. Scott and J. Blake (eds.), *Annual Review of Sociology*, 17: 445–66.

Marshall, G., Roberts, R., Burgoyne, C., and Routh, D. (forthcoming) *Social Class and Underclass in Britain and the United States*. Oxford: Nuffield College.

Marshall, T. H. (1950) *Citizenship and Social Class*. Cambridge: Cambridge University Press.

Mayer, S. (1993) 'Living Conditions among the Poor in Four Rich Countries', *Journal of Population Economics*, 6: 261–86.

——and Jencks, C. (1988) 'Poverty and the Distribution of Material Hardship', *Journal of Human Resources*, 24 (1): 88–114.

————(1993) 'Recent Trends in Economic Inequality in the United States: Income vs. Expenditure vs. Material Well-being', in D. Popadimitrou and E. Wolff (eds.), *Poverty and Prosperity in America at the Close of the Twentieth Century*. New York: St Martin Press.

McClements, L. D. (1977) 'Equivalence Scales for Children', *Journal of Public Economics*, 8: 191–210.

McGregor, P. P. L. and Borooah, V. K. (1992) 'Is Low Income or Low Expenditure a Better Indicator of Whether or Not a Household is Poor? Some Results From the 1985 Family Expenditure Survey', *Journal of Social Policy*, 21 (1): 53–70.

Mirowsky, J. and Ross, C. (1990) 'The Consolation Prize Theory of Alienation', *American Journal of Sociology*, 95 (6): 1505–35.

Moffit, R. (1992) 'Incentive Effects of the US Welfare System: a Review', *Journal of Economic Literature*, 30 (1): 1–61.

Moon, M. (1977) *The Measurement of Economic Welfare: Its Application to the Aged Poor*. New York: Academic Press.

Morris, L. D. (1993) 'Is There a British Underclass?' *International Journal of Urban and Regional Research*, 17 (3): 404–12.

——(1994) *Dangerous Classes: The Underclass and Social Citizenship*. London: Routledge.

——and Irwin, S. (1992) 'Employment Histories and the Concept of the Underclass', *Sociology*, 28 (3): 401–21.

Moynihan, D. (1965) *The Negro Family*. Washington: Department of Labor.

Muffels, R. (1993) 'Deprivation Standards and Style of Living Indices', in J. Berghman and B. Cantillon (eds.), *The European Face of Social Security*. Aldershot: Avebury.

——and Vrien, M. (1991) 'The Comparison of Definitions of Consumption Deprivation and Income Deprivation', mimeo, Tilburg University.

Murray, C. A. (1984) *Losing Ground: American Social Policy, 1950–1980*. New York: Basic Books.

——(1986) 'No Welfare Isn't Really the Problem', *Public Interest*, 84 (Summer): 3–11.

——(1990) *The Emerging British Underclass*. London: Institute of Economic Affairs.

Muthen, B. (1988) *Liscomp* (Computer Program) 2nd edn. Chicago: Scientific Software.

NESF (1994) *Ending Long-Term Unemployment*, Report No. 4. Dublin: National Economic and Social Forum.

Nolan, B. (1989) 'An Evaluation of the New Low Income Statistics', *Fiscal Studies*, 10 (4): 53–66.

——(1991a) *Recent EC Commission Statistics on Trends in Poverty*, Project on

Income Distribution, Poverty and Usage of State Services Working Paper 22. Dublin: Economic and Social Research Institute.

——(1991*b*) *The Wealth of Irish Households: What Can We Learn from Survey Data?* Dublin: Combat Poverty Agency.

——(1991*c*) *The Utilisation and Financing of Health Services in Ireland*, General Research Series Paper No. 155. Dublin: Economic and Social Research Institue.

——(1993) *Low Pay in Ireland*. General Research Series Paper No. 159. Dublin: Economic and Social Research Institute.

——and Callan, T. (1989) 'Measuring Trends in Poverty over Time: Some Robust Results for Ireland 1980–1987', *Economic and Social Review*, 20 (4): 309–28.

————(1990) 'Cross-National Poverty Comparisons using Relative Poverty Lines: An Application and Some Lessons', *Research on Economic Inequality*, 3: 277–309.

————(eds.) (1994) *Poverty and Policy in Ireland*. Dublin: Gill & Macmillan.

——and Farrell, B. (1990) *Child Poverty in Ireland*. Dublin: Combat Poverty Agency.

——, Whelan, C. T., and Williams, J. (1994) 'Spatial Aspects of Poverty and Disadvantage', in B. Nolan and T. Callan (eds.), *Poverty and Policy in Ireland*. Dublin: Gill & Macmillan.

Nussbaum, M. and Sen, A. (eds.) (1993) *The Quality of Life*. Oxford: Clarendon Press.

O'Cinneide, S. (1992) *Social Exclusion in Ireland, 1991–1992: The Second Annual Report for Ireland for the EC Observatory on National Policies to Combat Social Exclusion*. Maynooth: St Patrick's College.

O'Connell, P. J. and Rottman, D. B. (1992) 'The Irish Welfare State in Comparative Perspective', in J. H. Goldthorpe and C. T. Whelan (eds.), *The Development of Industrial Society in Ireland*, Proceedings of the British Academy, 79. Oxford: Oxford University Press.

——and Sexton, J. J. (1994) 'Labour Market Developments in Ireland 1973–1993', in S. Cantillon, J. Curtis, and J. Fitz Gerald (eds.), *Economic Perspectives for the Medium Term*. Dublin: Economic and Social Research Institute.

OECD (1976) *Public Expenditure on Income Maintenance Programmes*. Paris: OECD.

O'Higgins, M. and Jenkins, S. P. (1990) 'Poverty in the EC: Estimates for 1975, 1980 and 1985', in R. Teekens and B. Van Praag (eds.), *Analysing Poverty in the European Community*. Luxembourg: Eurostat.

Organisation for Economic Cooperation and Development (OECD) (1991) *Evaluating Labour Market and Social Programmes: The State of a Complex Art*. Paris: OECD.

Orshansky, M. (1965) 'Counting the Poor: Another Look at the Poverty Profile', *Social Security Bulletin*, 28 (Jan.): 3–29.

——(1988) 'Commentary: The Poverty Measure', *Social Security Bulletin*, 51 (Oct.): 1–4.

Pahl, J. (1983) 'The Allocation of Money and the Structuring of Inequality within Marriage', *Sociological Review*, 31: 235–62.

——(1989) *Money and Marriage*. London: Macmillan.

Pahl, J. (1991) 'Money and Power in Marriage', in P. Abbott and L. Wallace (eds.), *Gender, Power, and Sexuality*. London: Macmillan.

Pahl, R. E. (1989) 'Is the Emperor Naked? Some Comments on the Adequacy of Sociological Theory on Urban and Regional Research', *International Journal of Urban and Regional Research*, 13: 709–20.

Palmer, J. L., Smeeding, T., and Torrey, B. B. (eds.) (1988) *The Vulnerable*. Washington: Urban Institute Press.

Pearlin, L., Menaghan, E., Lieberman, M., and Mullan, J. T. (1981) 'The Stress Process', *Journal of Health and Social Behaviour*, 22: 337–51.

Peterson, P. E. (1991) 'The Urban Underclass and the Poverty Paradox', in C. Jencks and P. E. Petersen (eds.), *The Urban Underclass*. Washington: Brookings Institution.

Piachaud, D. (1979) *The Cost of a Child*, Poverty Pamphlet 43. London: Child Poverty Action Group.

——(1981) 'Peter Townsend and the Holy Grail', *New Society*, 10 Sept.: 419–21.

——(1987) 'Problems in the Definition and Measurement of Poverty', *Journal of Social Policy*, 16 (2): 147–64.

Plant, R. (1988) *Citizenship, Rights and Socialism*. London: Fabian Society.

Prosser, W. (1991) 'The Underclass: Assessing What We Have Learned', *Focus*, 13 (2): 1–18.

Raftery, A. and Hout, H. (1993) 'Maximally Maintained Inequality: Expansion, Reform and Opportunity in Irish Education 1921–1975', *Sociology of Education*, 66 (1): 44–62.

Rainwater, L. (1974) *What Money Buys: Inequality and the Social Meaning of Income*. New York: Basic Books.

——(1990) *Poverty and Equivalence as Social Constructions*, Working Paper 55, Luxembourg Income Study. Luxembourg: CEPS.

Rao, V. V. (1981) 'Measurement of Deprivation and Poverty based on the Proportion Spent on Food', *World Development*, 9 (4): 337–53.

Rein, M. (1969) 'Problems in the Definition and Measurement of Poverty', in L. Ferman and J. Kornbluth (eds.), *Poverty in America*. Ann Arbor: University of Michigan.

Ricketts, E. R. and Sawhill, I. V. (1988) 'Defining and Measuring the Underclass', *Journal of Policy Analysis and Management*, 7 (2): 316–25.

Ringen, S. (1987) *The Possibility of Politics*. Oxford: Clarendon Press.

——(1988) 'Direct and Indirect Measures of Poverty', *Journal of Social Policy*, 17: 351–66.

Room, G. (1994) *Understanding Social Exclusion: Lessons from Transnational Research Studies*, paper presented to Conference on Transnational Studies on Poverty, Policy Studies Institute, London, November.

——(ed. in collaboration with others) (1992) *National Policies to Combat Social Exclusion: First Annual Report of the European Community Observatory*, Directorate General V, Commission of the European Communities. Bath: Centre for Research in European Social and Employment Policy.

——(ed. in collaboration with others) (1994) *Observatory on National Policies to Combat Social Exclusion: Second Annual Report*, Directorate General V, Commission of the European Communities Bath: Centre for Research in European Social and Employment Policy.

Robbins, D. (1991) 'Marginalization and Social Exclusion', in G. Room (ed.), *Research Problematics*, Poverty 3/Directorate General for Employment, Industrial Relations and Social Affairs. Brussels: Commission of the European Communities.

Rottman, D. (1994a) 'Allocating Money within Households: Better Off Poorer?' in B. Nolan and T. Callan (eds.), *Poverty and Policy in Ireland*. Dublin: Gill and Macmillan.

——(1994b) *Income Distribution within Irish Households: Allocating Resources within Irish Families*. Dublin: Combat Poverty Agency.

Ruggles, P. (1990) *Drawing the Line: Alternative Poverty Measures and their Implications for Public Policy*. Washington: Urban Institute Press.

——and Williams, R. (1989) 'Longitudinal Measures of Poverty: Accounting for Income and Assets over Time', *Review of Income and Wealth*, 35 (3): 225–44.

Runciman, G. (1990) 'How Many Classes Are There in Contemporary British Society?' *Sociology*, 24 (3): 377–96.

Sawhill, I. V. (1988) 'Poverty in the US: Why Is It So Persistent?' *Journal of Economic Literature*, 26: 1037–119.

Sen, A. (1976) 'Poverty: An Ordinal Approach to Measurement', *Econometrica*, 44: 219–31.

——(1979) 'Issues in the Measurement of Poverty', *Scandinavian Journal of Economics*, 81: 285–307.

——(1980) 'Equality of What', in S. M. McMurrin (ed.), *Tanner Lectures on Human Values*, i. Cambridge University Press.

——(1983) 'Poor, Relatively Speaking', *Oxford Economic Papers*, 35 (2): 153–69.

——(1985) 'A Sociological Approach to the Measurement of Poverty: A Reply to Peter Townsend', *Oxford Economic Papers*, 37: 669–76.

——(1987) *On Ethics and Economics*. Oxford: Basil Blackwell.

——(1992) *Inequality Reexamined*. Oxford: Clarendon Press.

——(1993) 'Capability and Well-Being', in M. Nussbaum and A. Sen (eds.), *The Quality of Life*. Oxford: Clarendon Press.

Sexton, J. J. and O'Connell, P. (1993) *Evaluation of Operational Programme to Combat Long-Term Unemployment Among Adults in Ireland: Objective 3 of the Community Support Framework*. Dublin: Economic and Social Research Institute.

Shorrocks, A. F. (1978) 'Income Inequality and Income Mobility', *Journal of Economic Theory*, 19 (2): 376–93.

Smeeding, T. (1982) 'An Anti-Poverty Effect of In-Kind Transfers: A "Good Thing" Gone Too Far?' *Policy Studies Journal*, 10: 499–522.

——, Rainwater, L., and O'Higgins, M. (1988) *Poverty, Inequality and the Distribution of Income in an International Context: Initial Research from the Luxembourg Income Study (LIS)*. Brighton: Wheatsheaf.

Smith, D. J. (1992) 'Defining the Underclass', in D. J. Smith (ed.), *Understanding the Underclass*. London: Policy Studies Institute.

Stewart, F. (1985) *Planning to Meet Basic Needs*. London: Macmillan.

Streeten, P., Burki, J., Ul Haq, M., Hicks, N., and Stewart, F. (1981) *First Things First: Meeting Basic Needs in Developing Countries*. Oxford: Oxford University Press.

Sullivan, M. (1989) 'Absent Fathers in the Inner City', *Annals*, January: 48–58.

Thon, D. (1979) 'On Measuring Poverty', *Review of Income and Wealth*, 25: 429–40.

Tobin, J. (1969) 'Raising the Incomes of the Poor', in K. Gordon (ed.), *Agenda for the Nation*. Washington: Brookings Institution.

Townsend, P. (1970) *The Concept of Poverty*. London: Heinemann.

——(1979) *Poverty in the United Kingdom*. Harmondsworth: Penguin.

——(1985) 'A Sociological Approach to the Measurement of Poverty: A Rejoinder to Professor Sen', *Oxford Economic Papers*, 37: 659–68.

——(1988) 'Deprivation', *Journal of Social Policy*, 16 (2): 125–46.

——and Gordon, D. (1989) 'Memorandum submitted to Social Services Committee of the House of Commons', in *Minimum Income: Memoranda Laid before the Committee*, Session 1988–89. London: HMSO.

Ultee, W., Dessens, J., and Jansen, W. (1988) 'Why Does Unemployment Come in Couples? An Analysis of (Un)employment and (Non)Employment Homogamy Tables for Canada, The Netherlands and the United States in the 1980s', *European Sociological Review*, 4 (2): 111–22.

Van Praag, B., Hagenaars, A., and Van Weeren, J. (1982) 'Poverty in Europe', *Review of Income and Wealth*, 28: 345–59.

Veit-Wilson, J. (1987) 'Consensual Approaches to Poverty Lines and Social Security', *Journal of Social Policy*, 16 (2): 183–211.

——(1989) 'Memorandum submitted to Social Services Committee of the House of Commons', in *Minimum Income: Memoranda Laid before the Committee*, Session 1988–89. London: HMSO.

——(1994) *Dignity not Poverty: a Minimum Income Standard for the UK*, Commission on Social Justice Issue Paper 6. London: Institute for Public Policy Research.

Walker, R. (1987) 'Consensual Approaches to the Definition of Poverty: Towards an Alternative Methodology', *Journal of Social Policy*, 16 (2): 213–26.

Weisbrod, B. and Hansen, W. (1968) 'An Income–Net Worth Approach to Measuring Economic Welfare', *American Economic Review*, 58: 1315–29.

Wheaton, B. (1983) 'Stress, Personal Coping Resources and Psychiatric Symptoms: An Investigation of Interactive Models', *Journal of Health and Social Behaviour*, 24: 208–29.

Whelan, B. J. (1979) 'RANSAM: A Random Sample Design for Ireland', *Economic and Social Review*, 10 (2): 169–74.

——(1993) 'Non-monetary Indicators of Poverty', in J. Berghman and B. Cantillon (eds.), *The European Face of Social Security*. Aldershot: Avebury.

Whelan, C. T. (1992a) 'The Role of Income, Life-Style Deprivation and Financial Strain in Mediating the Impact of Unemployment on Psychological Distress: Evidence from the Republic of Ireland', *Journal of Occupational and Organisational Psychology*, 65: 331–44.

——(1992b) 'The Impact of Realistic and Illusory Conrol on Psychological Distress: A Test of the Model of Instrumental Realism', *Economic and Social Review*, 23 (4): 439–54.

——(1994) 'Social Class, Unemployment and Psychological Distress', *European Sociological Review*, 10 (1): 49–62.

——(1969) 'Marginalization, Deprivation and Fatalism in the Republic of Ireland: Class and Underclass Perspectives', *European Sociological Review*, 12 (1).

——, Hannan, D. F., and Creighton, S. (1991) *Unemployment, Poverty and Psychological Distress*, General Research Series Paper 150. Dublin: Economic and Social Research Institute.

——, Breen, R., and Whelan, B. J. (1992) 'Industrialisation, Class Formation and Social Mobility in Ireland', in J. H. Goldthorpe and C. T. Whelan (eds.), *The Development of Industrial Society in Ireland*, Proceedings of the British Academy, 79. Oxford: Oxford University Press.

Whelan, K. (1994) 'The Persistence of Unemployment: An Exploration of the Irish Experience', mimeo, Department of Economics, Massachusetts Institute of Technology.

Whiteford, P. (1985) *A Family's Needs: Equivalence Scales, Poverty and Social Security*, Research Paper No. 27. Canberra: Department of Social Security.

Williams, J. (1994) *Spatial Variations in Deprivation Surrogates*. Dublin: Combat Poverty Agency.

——and Whelan, B. J. (1993) *Short-Term Poverty Dynamics in Ireland*. Dublin: Combat Poverty Agency.

Wilson, W. J. (1978) *The Declining Significance of Race*. Chicago: Chicago University Press.

——(1987) *The Truly Disadvantaged: The Inner City, the Underclass and Public Policy*. Chicago: University of Chicago Press.

——(1991) 'Studying Inner City Social Dislocations', *American Sociological Review*, 56 (1): 1–14.

Wolfson, M. C. and Evans, J. M. (1990) *Statistics Canada's Low Income Cut-Offs Methodological Concerns and Possibilities: A Discussion Paper*. Ottawa: Statistics Canada.

Ysander, B.-C. (1993) 'Robert Erikson: Descriptions of Inequality', in M. Nussbaum and A. Sen (eds.), *The Quality of Life*. Oxford: Clarendon Press.

Zelditch, M., Jr (1993) 'Levels in the Logic of Macro-Historical Exploration', in J. Huber (ed.), *Macro–Micro Linkages in Sociology*. London: Sage.

INDEX